Applied Ethics
in a World
Church

Applied Ethics in a World Church

THE PADUA CONFERENCE

EDITED BY
LINDA HOGAN

ORBIS BOOKS

Maryknoll, New York 10545

Copyright © 2008 by Linda Hogan.

Published by Orbis Books, Maryknoll, New York 10545-0308.

All rights reserved.

No part of this publication may be reproduced or transmitted in any form or by any means, electronic or mechanical, including photocopying, recording, or any information storage or retrieval system, without prior permission in writing from the publisher.

Queries regarding rights and permissions should be addressed to
Orbis Books, P.O. Box 308, Maryknoll, NY 10545-0308.

Manufactured in the United States of America.

Library of Congress Cataloging-in-Publication Data

Applied ethics in a world church : the Padua conference / Linda Hogan, editor.
     p.   cm.
   Proceedings of a conference held July 8–11, 2006 in Padua, Italy.
   ISBN-13: 978-1-57075-759-4
   1. Christian ethics – Catholic authors – Congresses. 2. Applied ethics –
Congresses. I. Hogan, Linda, 1964–
BJ1249.A67 2008
241′.042 – dc22

                                                              2008001443

*To the church, university, and people of Padua,
especially Renzo Pegoraro and the Fondazione Lanza*

Contents

Part Seven
CHALLENGES TO METHOD
IN MORAL THEOLOGY

Contributors

Philippe Bordeyne is a priest of the diocese of Nanterre and a professor of moral theology at the Institut Catholique in Paris, France.

John Chathanatt, S.J., teaches theology and ethics and is the principal of Vidyajyoti College of Theology in Delhi, India. He is an executive member of the Justice and Peace Commission of the Archdiocese of Delhi and a member of the Justice, Peace, and Development Commission of the Catholic Bishops Conference of India.

Paul Chummar, C.M.I., born in India, is a senior lecturer in theological ethics at the Catholic University of Eastern Africa, Nairobi, Kenya.

Johan De Tavernier, a professor of theology and ethics, is a co-holder of the Boerenbond Chair in Agriculture and Society and coordinator of the Centre for Science, Technology, and Ethics at the Katholieke Universiteit Leuven, Belgium.

Jorge José Ferrer is an associate professor of humanities at the University of Puerto Rico in Mayagüez, Puerto Rico.

Catherine Fino, a Salesian religious, teaches moral theology and ethics at the Institut Catholique in Paris, France.

Aristide Fumagalli, a priest of the diocese of Milan, is a professor of moral theology at the Seminario Arcivescovile di Venegono in Milan, Italy.

Karl Golser is president of the Institute for Justice, Peace, and Integrity of the Creation, Bressanone, and a member of the Faculty in Computer Science at the Free University of Bolzano-Bozen, Bolzano, Italy.

Christine E. Gudorf is a professor of Christian ethics at Florida International University, Miami, Florida, USA, and a past president of the Society of Christian Ethics.

Michael J. Hartwig serves as the in-house scholar at the illume organization in Boston (*www.travelillume.com*). He is an adjunct professor at Emmanuel College in Boston, Massachusetts, and Charter Oak College in Connecticut, USA.

Kenneth R. Himes, O.F.M., is chair and a professor of theology at Boston College, Chestnut Hill, Massachusetts, USA.

Teresia Hinga, originally from Kenya, is an associate professor of religious studies at Santa Clara University, Santa Clara, California, USA.

Gustavo Irrazábal, a priest of the archdiocese of Buenos Aires, is a professor of moral theology at the Facultad de Teología of the Pontificia Universidad Católica Argentina, Buenos Aires, Argentina.

Pushpa Joseph, F.M.M., teaches in the Department of Christian Studies at the University of Madras, India, where she is a post-doctoral fellow.

José Roque Junges, S.J., is a Brazilian priest who is a professor of moral theology at the Centro de Estudos Superiores da Companhia de Jesus, Belo Horizonte/MG, Brazil, and of bioethics at the Universidade do Vale do Rio dos Sinos/UNISINOS, São Leopoldo/RS, Brazil.

Emmanuel Katongole, a Catholic priest from Uganda, is an associate research professor of theology and world Christianity, and co-director of the Center for Reconciliation at Duke Divinity School, Duke University, Durham, North Carolina, USA.

Michael G. Lawler is a professor emeritus of Catholic theology and the director of the Center for Marriage and Family at Creighton University, Omaha, Nebraska, USA.

Bertrand Lebouché, O.P., M.D., is completing his doctorate at Laval University in Quebec, Canada. He works as a physician in the AIDS unit in the university hospital Hôtel-Dieu in Lyons, France.

Alejandro C. Llorente, a Catholic priest, is a professor at the Facultad de Teología of the Pontificia Universidad Católica Argentina, Buenos Aires, Argentina.

Simone Morandini is the coordinator of research in ethics, philosophy, and theology for the Fondazione Lanza, in Padua, Italy, and an advisor to the Italian Bishops Conference.

Agbonkhianmeghe E. Orobator, S.J., a Catholic priest from Nigeria, is rector and lecturer at Hekima College, Jesuit School of Theology, and the Institute of Peace Studies and International Relations, Nairobi, Kenya.

Gillian Paterson is an independent consultant and writer on development issues, specializing in HIV and AIDS. She is currently completing a doctorate at Heythrop College, London, England, on the theological implications of AIDS-related stigma.

Stephen J. Pope is a professor of social ethics in the Department of Theology at Boston College in Chestnut Hill, Massachusetts, USA.

Todd A. Salzman is a faculty associate at the Center for Health Policy and Ethics and an associate professor in the Department of Theology at Creighton University, Omaha, Nebraska, USA.

Aquiline Tarimo, S.J., a Catholic priest from Tanzania, is an associate professor of Christian social ethics at Hekima College, Jesuit School of Theology, Catholic University of Eastern Africa, Nairobi, Kenya, and an adjunct associate professor at Santa Clara University, California, USA.

Marie-Jo Thiel is a university professor in the Faculté de Théologie Catholique at the Université Marc Bloch in Strasbourg, France, and director of the Centre Européen d'Enseignement et de Recherche en Ethique (CEERE), also in Strasbourg.

Johan Verstraeten is a professor of moral theology in the Department of Theological Ethics at the Katholieke Universiteit, Leuven, Belgium.

Kenneth M. Weare, a Catholic moral theologian, teaches social ethics at the University of San Francisco and serves as pastor at St. Rita's Church in Fairfax, California, USA.

Darlene Fozard Weaver is director of the Theology Institute and an associate professor of theology and religious studies at Villanova University, Villanova, Pennsylvania, USA.

William Werpehowski is a professor of theology and religious studies at Villanova University. He is also the director of Villanova's Center for Peace and Justice Education, Villanova, Pennsylvania, USA.

Humberto Miguel Yáñez, S.J., teaches moral theology at the Universidad del Salvador (área San Miguel) and is the director of the Centro de Investigación y Acción Social (CIAS-Bs.As.) for the archbishop of Corrientes, Argentina-Hipólito.

Abbreviations

CA	*Centesimus annus*, encyclical, John Paul II, 1987
CCC	*Catechism of the Catholic Church*, 1994
CCE	Congregation for Catholic Education
CDF	Congregation for the Doctrine of the Faith
CRP	*Considerations Regarding Proposals to Give Legal Recognition to Unions between Homosexual Persons*, Congregation for the Doctrine of the Faith, 2003
CSDC	*Compendium of the Social Doctrine of the Church*, Pontifical Council for Justice and Peace, 2004
DCE	*Deus caritas est*, encyclical, Pope Benedict XVI, 2005
DV	*Donum vitae*, Instruction on Respect for Human Life in Its Origin and on the Dignity of Procreation: Replies to Certain Questions of the Day, Congregation for the Doctrine of the Faith, 1987
EGHL	*Educational Guidance in Human Love: Outlines for Sex Education*, Congregation for Catholic Education, 1983
FC	*Familiaris consortio* apostolic exhortation, John Paul II, 1981
HV	*Humanae vitae*, encyclical, Paul VI , 1968
JW	*Justice in the World*, World Synod of Catholic Bishops, 1971
MM	*Mater et Magistra*, encyclical, John XXIII, 1961
PP	*Populorum progressio*, encyclical, Paul VI, 1967
SRS	*Sollicitudo rei socialis*, encyclical, John Paul II, 1987
VS	*Veritatis splendor*, encyclical, John Paul II, 1993

Introduction

Cross-cultural Conversations

Applied Ethics in a World Church

LINDA HOGAN

In June 2006 over four hundred Catholic moral theologians from all over the world gathered in Padua, Italy, to take part in the first international, cross-cultural conversation on theological ethics. The program's structure reflected the planning committee's desire to bring together the manifold conversations that together embody the diversity of the Catholic moral tradition. Thus, we heard theologians from Africa, Asia, Latin America, Europe, and North America reflect on the key moral challenges and the church's responses on their respective continents.

The issues with which the participants engaged reflected those concerns that frame the contexts in which millions worldwide live and work, namely, the effects of chronic poverty, deep-seated structural inequalities, violence, and environmental destruction. Not only were the ethical challenges parsed and analyzed, but the discussions also focused on the role of the church's moral tradition, both as a voice of protest and of prophetic insight. During the conference theologians from the five continents also debated the enduring theological concerns of conscience and the Magisterium, of method, and of religious pluralism.[1] Here again the creativity of the tradition was in evidence, with theological insight profoundly shaped by the reality of the church's "situatedness" in different global contexts.

In this collection our focus is on the field of applied ethics. From the 120 papers from around the world originally presented at this conference, all focused on issues of critical global social, political, and economic concern, we present 30 that represent the key challenges that lie ahead.

Globalization as the Context

It is evident through this collection that globalization is the context in which Catholic ethicists engage the challenges of social and political life. Yet, although the language of globalization is prominent, the manner in which the essayists interpret and experience this phenomenon is complex. Indeed,

1

what these essays indicate is that the contemporary experience of the reality of globalization is a paradoxical one: although we live in ever closer relationships with one another, we are ever more attentive to our differences.

The essays herein illustrate that globalization through trade, technology, and tourism has created an interdependence that impacts us all, so that neither geographical remoteness nor cultural isolationism can disrupt its homogenizing trajectory. Yet far from being a relentless driver of integration, globalization, the evidence throughout this collection also suggests, sets in train a number of contradictory processes, including a trajectory of fragmentation, seen in the forces of nationalism, identity politics, and religious fundamentalism.

Moreover, although globalization has made available to many an experience of personal and social life that is not only novel but exhilarating, it also has its shadow side of emmiseration and violence. This shadow side and the dominant responses to it are well captured by Zigmunt Bauman in his essay entitled "On Glocalization: Globalization for Some, Localization for Others."[2] Bauman explains the dynamic inherent in globalization thus: "Globalization reinforces already existing patterns of domination, while glocalization indicates trends to dispersal and conflict on neo-traditional grounds. The privileged walk, or fly, away: the others take revenge upon each other."[3] This scenario in which the economic, cultural, and political forces of globalization create contradictory processes of integration and fragmentation, both within and between communities, is familiar to the essayists in this collection, and is at the heart of the challenge that it poses for Christians. There is no doubt that this peculiar interplay of global and local has transformed the manner in which ethical questions concerned with human relationships, whether intimate or political, are raised, pursued, and resolved.

Moreover, in this collection it is clear that this complicated dynamic impacts too on the discursive tradition that is Catholicism. Thus the themes with which we are concerned here — namely, economic and cultural globalization, environment, gender, war and peace, HIV/AIDS, bioethics, and sexuality — are explored by Catholic ethicists from a variety of cultural, political, and economic contexts. The global perspectives that are evident enable us, as church, to appreciate the difficult and highly differentiated conditions in which we seek to affirm the dignity and worth of every human being. Indeed, the Catholic moral tradition is evoked, developed, reaffirmed, and challenged as these authors dialogue to and from the local and global contexts within which the faith is lived today.

Poverty and Environmental Destruction

In the first section, entitled "Globalization, Justice, and Environment," the ever increasing economic disparity between North and South as well as the shameful impoverishment of the African continent are addressed by authors from a range of economic contexts. Authors from developed and developing countries are acutely aware of the negative effects of globalization, namely, chronic poverty, increasing inequality between and within states, and environmental destruction. While the countries of the South are affected disproportionately by these problems, difficulties are also emerging in advanced economies so that although wealth is increasing, inequality is also growing, with minority groups and migrants experiencing new levels of poverty, threat, and social exclusion.[4] In this collection Humberto Miguel Yáñez and Alejandro Llorente from Argentina, John Chathanatt from India, and Aquiline Tarimo from Kenya each provide searing analyses of the impact that unregulated and unfairly regulated trade has on the lives of the poor. The immorality of this impoverishment and marginalization is clearly articulated as is its challenge to all those who seek to live according to gospel values. In each case the language of social justice, the option for the poor, and liberation is evoked in order to convey the conviction that there is a fundamental incompatibility between neo-liberal economics and the values espoused in the gospels.

Kenneth M. Weare from the United States and Johan Verstraeten from Belgium are also troubled by this scandal of global poverty and inequality, and especially by the extent to which some commentators believe that (neo)-liberal economics can be regarded as consistent with the norms of Catholic social thought. As suggested by his title "A Ringing Endorsement of Capitalism? The Influence of the Neo-liberal Agenda on Official Catholic Social Teaching," Verstraeten is deeply concerned with what he regards as the tradition's ambivalence on the matter of neo-liberal economics. Although he acknowledges that *Centesimus annus* (1991) and the *Compendium of the Social Doctrine of the Church* (2004) offer only a very conditional approval of capitalism, he believes that the neo-liberal agenda has gained influence and is particularly evident in its radical rejection of the social-assistance state and in what he regards as the subordination of justice to a discourse of love and solidarity. Weare is also critical of free trade policies and discusses an initiative, developed by the Hemispheric Social Alliance (HSA), whose purpose is to build an alternative model of development in the face of the currently proposed international trade agreements. In his informative and persuasive discussion of this model, Weare makes a case for its adoption, claiming that it is consistent with Catholic teaching since it aims to achieve just and sustainable development for all.

Also in this section Karl Golser and Simone Morandini take up the issue of sustainable development by focusing on the urgent matter of the environment. Both of these essays take as their starting point the *Compendium of the Social Doctrine of the Church* (2004), and provide analyses that contribute to our understanding of how the tradition is evolving, while also discussing the substantive issue of environmental ethics. Each author draws attention to the duties of stewardship of the earth and in particular how this prodigious gift for us and for succeeding generations must be safeguarded.

Gender Justice

A concern for ethical forms of globalization, based upon respect for human dignity, social justice, and ecological sustainability also feature prominently in the discussions of Sr. Pushpa Joseph and Teresia Hinga. Both are acutely aware of economic and environmental problems as they reflect on the manner in which many women in the developing world seek to develop their capabilities and live just and fruitful lives. Both work within a feminist framework: Joseph as she explores the struggles of the women of the tribal communities of Chhattisgarh to manage the sustainability of their natural ecosystems; and Hinga as she discusses the feminization of poverty in Africa. Both Joseph and Hinga are concerned with how gender impacts on vulnerability to poverty. Each draws on the feminist theological scholarship that, over the past four decades, has transformed the manner in which questions of social justice, especially as they relate to women, have been conceptualized and resolved.

In "Gendered Identity Formation and Moral Theology," Christine Gudorf, who has been at the forefront in Catholic theological ethics, particularly pushing the boundaries of our understanding of gendered relations, challenges our understanding even further. In a provocative essay that discusses a host of recent scientific studies relating to the sexual basis of the ability to read the emotions of others, Gudorf raises questions that she herself terms "uncomfortable." In brief, Gudorf interprets scientific evidence to suggest that females have a significant advantage in interpreting what actions "love your neighbor" or "do no harm" require in specific situations, because they are better able than most males to read the feelings of others; she suggests that male-types seem disadvantaged in their ability to recognize and therefore respond to suffering in others. Following the logic of this data, Gudorf raises a host of challenging questions about moral formation and concludes that research demands that we give serious attention to the possibility that the persistence of different models for the exercise of moral development among humans is related to the complex and varied nature of what she calls the "hardwiring" of humans.

HIV/AIDS

The prominence in this collection of essays focused on the ethical challenges associated with the HIV/AIDS pandemic signals just how devastating its impact has been, particularly though not exclusively in sub-Saharan Africa. What each of the essays by theologians from Uganda, Kenya, Nigeria,

France, and Britain share is a recognition that poverty, deprivation, and the denial of human rights all figure in one's vulnerability to HIV/AIDS and that the pandemic is deeply destructive of the protective social fabric of societies. Emmanuel Katongole, Agbonkhianmeghe Orobator, and Paul Chummar are each concerned with developing new paradigms that take seriously the complex synergy of deprivation and disenfranchisement that is at the heart of the progress of this pandemic. Katongole argues that what HIV/AIDS has exposed is not only the urgent need for treatment of the sick bodies of Africans, but the need for healing the divide between Africa and the rest of the world. He also argues that the creation of "caring/receiving/supporting communities across the East-West/North-South divides have the potential not only to call the dominant culture into question, but also to embody new communions that transcend our usual tribal, national, regional, or class enclaves."

Bertrand Lebouché's analysis complements that of Katongole, particularly in terms of the way in which it challenges the church to rediscover its prophetic role and to become a space where individuals who have been marginalized and silenced by HIV/AIDS can reconstruct themselves as subjects. He maintains that the church can be a place wherein solidarities can be established, and "where human persons may recognize one another." Both Orobator and Chummar take the church a considerable way on the journey toward rediscovering a prophetic role and articulating a new theological discourse. Both draw on the rich heritage of African cultural and religious traditions and combine their insights with normative Christian values. In this way, as Orobator explains, the horizon of Catholic sexual ethics expands and a broader framework for a new ethical discourse on HIV/AIDS prevention is created.

War and Peace

Much of the poverty experienced globally is exacerbated by civil conflict and war. Two essays in this collection, both written by North Americans, are concerned with the phenomenon of war and in particular with the Christian tradition of just war. William Werpehowski's "A Tale of Two Presumptions: The Development of Roman Catholic Just War Theory" defends the just war tradition, understanding it as one that proceeds from the presumption in favor of peace and against war. He suggests that nonviolence and just war are complementary strategies, both of which can serve the common good, but recognizes that there are situations in which the presumption in favor of peace has to cede to the decision to go to war. He is particularly concerned to illustrate how humanitarian interventions, focused on protecting the vulnerable against lethal attack, can indeed be justified within the just war tradition.

The essay of Kenneth Himes is also concerned with the contemporary international political order, specifically with the emerging threat of "horizontal" nuclear proliferation and its destabilizing effects. Himes considers the manner in which international power relations are shifting and asks the reader to consider whether the notion of military intervention as a counter-proliferation strategy might be acceptable within the just war framework. Since the idea that a nation may mount an armed intervention to destroy another nation's nuclear capability is gaining momentum, Himes asks whether this should be regarded as an inappropriate expansion of the traditional *casus belli,* or simply an application of traditional norms to a new situation.

Questions about the nature of the Christian response to political violence, about the appropriateness of recourse to any form of violence, about the adequacy of nonviolence as a strategy, and about the acceptability of using violence to address humanitarian crises will continue to dominate the field of political ethics for many years to come. However there is little doubt that a complex synergy of violence and poverty is at the heart of the current instability of the international order and that this instability is unlikely to be addressed appropriately until issues of social justice (within and between states) are firmly on the agenda.

Bioethics and Social Justice

Issues of social justice are also central to many of the discussions that cluster around bioethical questions. Throughout this section, in the essays of Jorge José Ferrer (Puerto Rico), José Roque Junges (Brazil), Darlene Fozard Weaver (USA), Marie-Jo Thiel and Catherine Fino (France), it becomes clear that the field of bioethics has undergone a major transformation, not only by the inclusion of voices from the South, but also by theologians from the North who refuse to construe the ethical issues as concerned first and foremost with individual decision-making. For many decades, a great deal of bioethical literature left the broader social context untouched. More recently, however, theologians have come to recognize that individual bioethical decisions are never made in a vacuum and can never be separated from social ethics. Thus a number of theological bioethicists, especially those from Latin America, have begun to insist that the social context is vital and to argue that important cultural norms and economic patterns shape how the dynamic of "individual dignity in-relation-to the common good" is played out. This interplay is demonstrated in the essays of Jorge José Ferrer and José Roque Junges, as well as in Darlene Fozard Weaver's essay on embryo adoption, which argues for a more comprehensive analysis of the practice that considers its social and political dimensions.

The forces of economic globalization also significantly impact this field, as Ferrer's essay makes clear. Indeed, globalization now shapes the institutional contexts in which the social practices and norms of bioethics are made and in which individual bioethical decisions are pursued. Inevitably therefore questions of distributive justice and of global solidarity have emerged as new items on the agenda of bioethics. Although Marie-Jo Thiel and Catherine Fino have different concerns, their essays also convey the significance of the social and communitarian dimensions of bioethical decisions: Thiel in the context of decisions about the continuation of nutrition and hydration to patients who are terminally ill, and Fino in her fascinating discussion of hospital care as a praxis of charity. What all five essays illustrate is that individual bioethical decisions can never be separated from social ethics since there exist important cultural norms and assumptions that shape how the dynamic of individual dignity and the common good is played out.

Sexuality and Marriage

Among the many urgent issues that are raised by Catholic theologians world-wide are questions relating to sexuality and marriage. Interestingly, however, the essays in this collection that are immediately concerned both with marriage and with same-sex relationships come from North Americans and Europeans. Undoubtedly theologians from the South are also concerned with these questions; however, for them these questions are contextualized within the urgent tasks of addressing structural injustices that create vulnerability, either to HIV infection or to gender inequality.

In the essays that address sexual issues directly, both Philippe Bordeyne's "The Fragility of Marriage: Concerning Methodology in Christian Ethics" and Aristide Fumagalli's " 'What God Has Joined Together': The Specifically Christian Quality of Conjugal Love" are concerned with the ways in which the durability of Christian marriage has apparently been undermined. Fumagalli suggests that "the relationship of love is no longer crystallized in the premodern form of the patriarchal family or in the modern form of bour-geois marriage." Thus "not only does it seem fragile and unstable, as we see in the consistent growth in the number of separations and divorces and in the diffusion of cohabitation either prior to marriage or as an alternative to marriage, it also appears to be shapeless and changeable."

Bordeyne shares this analysis of the disintegration of the traditional patterns of marriage and family. These two creative and insightful theologians also share a determination not to resort to a mode of condemnation, but rather to seek resources both within the tradition and within pastoral practice to make sense of and to address this contemporary phenomenon. Thus Fumagalli suggests that Christians should not be concerned primarily with the durability or dissolution of an institution (and, as he points out, marriage is one of the most ancient and universal examples of an institution), but rather with the extent to which an institution such as marriage is "in harmony with that love that is revealed in Christ and that he himself envis-ages as the criterion of every human relationship." His conclusion then is that the norm of Christian love, namely, "that love which has its identity in the manner in which Christ loved," rather than the norm of durability, ought to function as the decisive criterion for the evaluation of the quality of contemporary relationships of love.

Bordeyne addresses the ethical challenge of durability by looking toward Christian practices within marriage. When Bordeyne examines this context, which he claims gives access to the way people try to shape their own lives in a responsible way, he finds new practices that prove families to be subject to fragility and inventiveness at the same time. In a provocative and compelling analysis, Bordeyne sheds new light on today's pluralism as the major *locus theologicus* for ethics and argues that pastoral life is the concrete, historical space of interactivity between the living faith and today's cultures. He suggests that by referring to pastoral life theologians can avoid building too rigid an opposition between faith and ethics and between individual faith and community faith. Pastoral life thereby "embodies the creativity of faith when exposed to diverse and emerging cultural trends."

The essays of Michael J. Hartwig and of Michael G. Lawler and Todd A. Salzman are equally concerned with the gap between Catholic sexual ethics and current practice. Hartwig recommends using information from the personal and social sciences to try to understand the nature of the concerns of those seeking to live just and integrated sexual lives. Hartwig's probing analysis opens up a space in which questions about human nature and human flourishing are asked anew. In particular Hartwig asks how Catholic sexual ethics should integrate the evidence from the social sciences that gay men and women who have accepted their sexual orientation can integrate their orientation into a rich and flourishing life that includes life-long and intimate committed relationships. Lawler and Salzman evoke the tradition's categories of "truly human" and of "complementarity" to press the case. They argue that homosexual couples can engage in sexual acts that are natural and reasonable and therefore moral. Moreover, in their development of the tradition they propose an alternative, more expansive set of foundational principles for an authentic moral sexual act, arguing for a holistic rather than a truncated understanding of complementarity.

Method in Moral Theology

It is somewhat artificial to include a section entitled "Challenges to Method in Moral Theology," since each of the essays in the collection contributes to the discourse about method. For example, both Golser and Morandini contextualize their respective discussions about environmental ethics in relation to the methodological developments evident in the *Compendium of the Social Doctrine of the Church*, while Orobator and Chummar recommend methodological changes as part of their focus on HIV/AIDS. In this section, however, the discussion is more explicitly methodological, as, for example, with Gustavo Irrazábal's consideration of whether dialogue is possible between the two dominant methodological approaches within Catholic moral theology today, namely, proportionalism and the ethic of virtue. Irrazábal pursues this question in the context where he claims the confrontation began, namely, with the debate over *Humanae vitae* in 1968. He argues that both methodological approaches have their roots in the church's moral tradition and that each perspective has its merits. He also questions whether it is necessary to think of this as an either-or confrontation and proposes instead that the apparent confrontation could be seen primarily as a reciprocal stimulus enabling each side to move forward from within, based on its own premises.

A double set of divergences is at issue for Stephen J. Pope in his analysis of Benedict XVI's *Deus Caritas Est*. Pope claims that the encyclical's persuasiveness is compromised by its treatment of two sets of key theological and moral terms, namely, agape and eros, and love and justice. Pope's argument is subtle and convincing and it conveys the practical significance of such methodological concerns. Ultimately Pope suggests that *Deus Caritas Est* would have been more effective had more careful distinctions been made and the tendency to separate agape from both eros and justice been avoided.

The collection ends, appropriately, with a sophisticated discussion by Johan De Tavernier of the complex relationship between tolerance, pluralism, and religious truth. De Tavernier asks if there is "a theological justification for tolerance," and he answers it in the affirmative by articulating the conviction that Christians are not the owners but rather the servants of truth. Viewed this way, he suggests, one can scarcely maintain a fanatical defense of one's own convictions. Clearly De Tavernier's position is not a relativist one. Rather, drawing on the moral theology of Franz Böckle, he suggests that it is possible to reconcile tolerance with truth once we understand tolerance, not in terms of taking a stand on the truth question, but instead in terms of underwriting an independent faith-rooted relationship with our fellow human beings.

Conclusion

It is clear that the complex economic and cultural contexts in which we find ourselves today have had a significant impact on the discursive traditions of Catholicism, and especially on its ethical discourse. Moreover, this impact is seen in terms of the nature of the practical issues with which moral theology is concerned, but also in the way in which the idiom of moral theology itself is changing. Throughout this collection this changing idiom is evident in the increasingly interdisciplinary character of moral theology, as well as in the manner in which it proceeds from local cultural contexts, inductively, in dialogue with the classic articulations of the tradition. There is no doubt that the Catholic moral tradition is experiencing a period of great creativity

worldwide. The voices of scholars of color, scholars from the South, indigenous scholars, and women scholars are increasingly visible in the debates
about the ability of Catholicism's moral categories to address the urgent
issues of the day. This present volume presents just a handful of the many
varied and challenging voices that are interpreting the gospel today.

This collection seeks to be a catalyst for a further international exchange
of ideas among Catholic theological ethicists by challenging ethicists to dialogue from and beyond their local culture and to interconnect within a world
church not dominated solely by a northern paradigm. In so doing, the essays
in this collection demonstrate the creativity, dynamism, and diversity of the
Catholic moral tradition as it proceeds from local cultures, opens itself to
cross-cultural conversations, and progresses in a spirit of mercy and care.

Finally, the task of choosing 30 essays from among the 120 excellent
submissions was a difficult one. I was greatly assisted by the expert advice
of my colleagues on the planning committee: Soosai Arokiasamy (India),
Bénézet Bujo (Congo, Switzerland), Margaret Farley (USA), José Roque
Junges (Brazil), José Rojas (Philippines), Paul Schotsmans (Belgium), Renzo
Pegoraro (Italy), and Hans Wennink (Netherlands), as well as by Julie Clague
(UK), Marianne Heimbach-Steins (Germany), Maureen Junker-Kenny (Ire-
land), Kevin Kelly (UK), and Tony Mifsud (Chile), who assisted in a further
review process. Sincere gratitude is also due to Toni Ross, who has been
an invaluable colleague throughout, to Lúcás Chan, and to Dylan Lehrke,
who, with his customary good will, has helped with many aspects of the
process. Hans Wennink and Peter Merkx have been constant and generous
supporters of the entire project. I appreciate too the enthusiasm with which
Susan Perry at Orbis Books took up this project, and I am grateful to our
translators, Brian McNeil and Margaret Wilde, both of whom dealt with
the texts with care and attention. The last word of gratitude, however, must
go to my friend Jim Keenan, whose original vision animated the conference
and whose commitment to an inclusive theology helped bring it to fruition.

Notes

1. These papers have been published in James F. Keenan, ed., *Catholic Theological Ethics in the World Church* (New York: Continuum, 2007).

2. Zigmunt Bauman, "On Glocalization: Globalization for Some, Localization
for Others," in *Thesis Eleven* 54 (1998): 37–49.

3. Ibid., 37.

4. See Tadeusz Budinski and Dariusz Dobrzanski, eds., *Eastern Europe and the
Challenges of Globalization* (Washington: Council for Research in Values and Philosophy, 2005), and Marianne Heimbach-Steins's contribution to "The European
Continental Panel," in *Catholic Theological Ethics in the World Church*, ed. Keenan,
101–7.

PART ONE

GLOBALIZATION, JUSTICE, AND ENVIRONMENT

Opting for the Poor
in the Face of Growing Poverty

HUMBERTO MIGUEL YÁÑEZ

This is not the time to retell the well-known story of the "option for the poor": how it began in the theology of liberation and was gradually incorporated into the Magisterium, first at the regional and then the universal level. This critical process, as encouraging as it seems, also has its ambiguities. The main one is that as the term gained acceptance in the universal hierarchy it lost some of its "historic bite," as Gustavo Gutiérrez has said. We also know that its acceptance was accompanied by a careful purification of what was thought to be its "ideological roots." It is also true that after accepting it, both the universal and the regional Magisterium began to abandon its use. What is most telling is the complete absence of the concept in the first encyclical of Pope Benedict XVI. Finally, although so much has been written on the subject, it doesn't seem to have led to a reduction in poverty. On the contrary, despite the valid efforts that have been made in this sense, the topic still cries out for serious reflection and articulation, at least from the standpoint of Christian theology and ethics.

In my view, both the theology of liberation and the Magisterium have developed the option for the poor as an extraneous model. The goal of "freeing the poor" (Enrique Dussel), no matter how scriptural it is, needs to be internalized, engraved on the heart, and responsibly incorporated. The fact that it is presented as an extraneous model has detracted from its specific practical significance except in certain ecclesial sectors, such as the base Christian communities and many personal testimonies, as well as in religious communities that sought to instill it at the popular level.

I would like to share my experience in Argentina, a country best known until recently for its lack of poverty, or at least of misery, although that impression may have been exaggerated or partial, since there were always poor people. Regardless, poverty has grown at a dizzying pace since the mid-twentieth century — spectacularly so since the late 1990s.

My reflection stems from the drama suffered by our society as it saw itself trampled and mutilated in a long process.[1] Our problem is related to the new world economic order implanted in our country "in the Argentine way"; that is, the economic and political crisis is ours, but in a context of global crisis. The historical peak of our crisis came in 2002, when poverty in Argentina stood at 57.5 percent and deep poverty at 27.5 percent[2] due to a long, deeply underlying process of injury to the people. The economic dimension also affected the cultural and moral dimension of our society, especially at its most peripheral and marginal levels. Not only was there a quantitative growth in poverty, but also in the forms of poverty: the elderly with meager or nonexistent pensions,[3] homelessness,[4] children abandoned or on the street, etc. So we are not speaking abstractly, but of real and specific poverty.

What does this situation mean for us, as Argentines and as Christians? First, we must understand poverty not only in terms of statistics, which are necessary but only give us a quantitative picture. We must enter into the existential, personal, and community significance of poverty, of misery, of marginalization, and of exclusion.

We Argentines must learn that *development is acceptable only if it is ethical*, that is, if it is understood and planned on the basis of justice,[5] which means that any policy of growth must focus primarily on the least privileged.

Poverty Affects Us All

Our nation has become impoverished; we have all become impoverished. Poverty emerged in a specific time and occupies a specific space; its emergence, structuring, and shape are part of our history, but one that has yet to be written in our country. In the face of the recent economic growth (we have been growing by an average of almost 9 percent for the past four years), we are in danger of forgetting the tragic history of poverty, and thus repeating in the future the same mistakes of the past — or others that will lead to the same or even worse consequences.

Poverty, as a situation of injustice, is also *a situation of violence*. The poor themselves, many of them young people with a history of deprivation and aggression, are growing up in this institutionalized violence and will return to society what they have received from it; poverty has brought crime and violence.[6] In addition, economic benefits are not equally distributed; one sector of the population is excluded, without future horizons, reduced to the most extreme misery.

Poverty, in its diverse manifestations (structural, contextual, inertial; rural or urban),[7] produces *a new kind of human being* whose basic characteristic is the deprivation of the fundamental necessities for a dignified life. This occurs "within individuals, in their motivations, in the degree to which their values are internalized."[8] We still feel the effects of the crisis in the *structural poverty*, which is mainly seen on the outskirts of the large cities where it remains the reality in which many Argentines are born, grow, develop, and die. Thus, poverty is our reality, in contrast with the opulence that has emerged at the same time. *But structural poverty is a fairly recent phenomenon in our country,* where it should not exist in view of the country's natural and human resources. It is therefore obvious, or perhaps not, that *poverty is a human creation* and thus subject to ethical judgment.

Poverty Generates a Culture

If culture is the way a human group expresses meaning,[9] here it refers to the group of marginalized and excluded people who develop a new way of expressing their fundamental experiences.[10] For them, it is the self-affirmation of the identity of a relatively closed, endogenous group. To the extent that the group is marginalized, it develops ways of life that are also expressed culturally. The group harbors those left exposed by their lack of employment and creates links of solidarity based on a common identity, often rooted in rebellion and resentment. Thus, the culture of deep poverty takes on violent and tragic connotations. Life loses its value, but the people are determined to give some meaning to an existence too absurd to accept. In the midst of perverse behavior there are reactions of solidarity, albeit a closed solidarity, often like that of the mafia: an intense but contextual solidarity.[11]

At the extreme levels of poverty there is a loss of the cultural values that form the common value base of our people, provoking a detachment that is not only economic but also cultural, the result of the extreme privation they have suffered. Thus new value criteria, values and countervalues, emerge from the new culture of the poor.

Unemployment leads to a *crisis and reformulation of social roles:* the emergence of dysfunctional, depressed, devaluated males, and female heads of household who suffer from overwork and lack of understanding in a stressful and lonely situation. This leads to new kinds of gender relationships in the adult world, and between parents and children. The family nucleus is resented, interpersonal relations become unstable, neglect and a lack of discipline for children and adolescents increase. In this sense, *cultural poverty in turn generates more poverty:*[12] weaker links, declining motivation, shrinking horizons.

Poverty and Cultural Identity

Thus poverty affects cultural identity: who we are and what it means to be Argentine.

First, poverty changes our national identity by fragmenting it. We must remember that the gap between rich and poor has grown uncontrollably. In the mid-twentieth century, 40 percent of the Gross Internal Product (Gross Domestic Product) was distributed among wage earners; today it is only 20 percent, and even that distribution is increasingly unequal. In terms of income distribution between the richest and poorest tenths of the population, in Argentina the difference increased from a ratio of 8:1 to 37:1 during the crises of 2001–2002.

Second, life in the big cities causes rootlessness and identity crisis in citizens. Migration due to poverty produces a tear in the original social fabric and the creation of a new fabric, with new cultural characteristics that bring about a new subjectivity tending toward massification.

Third, the creation of a powerful and often beneficent state has led many sectors of society to demand a share of power. This has led to group entitlements in our country, caused by the integration of diverse social sectors in the exercise of public power: first the radicalism of Irigoyen on behalf of the immigrant-descended middle class, then the justicialism of Perón for the predominantly Creole and *mestizo* working class. The rise of these new social actors was assisted by a process of polarization. In a *caudillo*[13] *culture* such as ours, in some parts of the interior of our country people have become accustomed to not speaking out, to rallying around the *caudillo*, to taking orders from the political vanguard.[14] An exception is the recent action of Msgr. Joaquín Piña in the Province of Misiones, which showed the ability of a people subjected to the servitude of political clientelism to react.[15]

There has also been a reaction against the invasion of the market culture, a closing off to outside influences, which leads many subcultures to isolate themselves from global culture or the globalization process — holding up traditional cultural forms and stereotypes more than cultural values as a means of self-defense.

Poverty has resulted in school-drop-outs, illiteracy, less access to higher education, and a deterioration in public education itself, especially in the provinces where maintaining discipline of children and adolescents has taken priority over providing them a quality education. At the same time, private education offers first-world levels of education for the minority who can afford it. This creates a paradox: that in a country with our high level of unemployment, corporations cannot fill their need for technicians and skilled labor. And this is one of the things that prevents us from overcoming poverty: one sector of the population cannot move forward economically for *structural* reasons. That is, no matter how much they want to join the work force, the conditions for doing so are not present: skill training and access, that is, information about the kind of workers the market needs, especially among youth.

Poverty Challenges the Legitimacy of Systems

Poverty challenges the legitimacy of the systems around which civilization coalesces. When this legitimacy is damaged, the bonds that cause these systems to function break. Economic life, democracy, and society itself become perversions of themselves.

Of the Economic System

The market and its laws need to be regulated by a political power with real social meaning. Political parties and trade unions must work for market regulation with a high degree of technical expertise so that the cure will not be worse than the disease; that is, so that regulation does not strangle the market but humanizes it and places it at the service of society (especially of the poorest) rather than against it.

Of the Political System

The highest levels of poverty have come in times of democracy, betraying its basic principles: freedom, equality, and participation. It is a task of the state to create the conditions to make citizenship a reality for everyone. In our capitalist society, the have-nots are unable to exercise their rights; that is, they are excluded from real citizenship.

Of the Constitution of Society

As poverty has increased, so has wealth, and the gap between rich and poor has grown. Misery and exclusion have gone hand in hand with opulence and the creation of wealthy enclaves. The social fabric has come apart in this society that moves at two speeds. The poor are not really citizens. Society must recognize them as citizens, by giving them full access to basic goods, allowing them to exercise not only their first-order but also their second- and third-order rights.

Ethical Challenges

At the beginning of this essay, I criticized the presentation of the option for the poor as an extraneous model. The question this raises is: why should I get involved in the struggle to eradicate poverty?

The first step in a commitment to eradicate structural poverty in our society is to take it on ourselves; that requires us to understand it, both quantitatively and qualitatively. Thus the ethical task must include *the basic imperative of challenging reality* (Xavier Zubiri). The reality is that poverty is growing spectacularly in both quantity and quality; that is, it affects human beings in their constitution and their dignity. For this reason, poverty is the principal ethical problem of a society: eradicating it is the fundamental imperative of all ethics, and it should be the principal goal of state policy. There is no justification for the existence of poverty in a country like ours. We must learn from the past and establish laws to protect the most vulnerable: the retirees who have so often been victimized by the state; the children born in poverty-stricken homes who need at least good food, health care, and education; the women who bear impossible burdens with their husbands absent and children to raise. The "hard core" of poverty is the great challenge to any society, not only to mitigate but to eliminate it from a country as rich as ours in both raw materials and social capital.

This suggests that liberation must be reframed and reformulated, on the basis of solidarity.[16] We urgently need an ethic that recognizes the linkages for the mending of the social fabric, which would enable us to reconstitute our society as a unity in plurality. Unity can be built only on the recognition of *asymmetry*. This means that responsibility must be lived out as "co-responsibility." We need to rebuild community linkages on the basis of social justice.[17]

The principle of preference for the poor provides an "epistemological break,"[18] an understanding given us by the experience of the poor, in this case not only the marginalized but even more the excluded. They have the last word on the legitimacy of systems.[19] Therefore, recognition is the true form of understanding; that is, confronting truth as a totality, not indirectly or in part, and certainly not as a process imposed by the center on the margins.

Thus, the theological ethics of liberation understands the option for the poor as the *forma moralitatis,* a bias consciously present in all ethical reflection.[20] The option for the poor becomes the practical application of the search for universal interests. This is the only possible basis for integration and true communion. It is what makes human beings truly human.

But it is also necessary to rebuild a culture of work, of professional responsibility, of honesty and of effort, which are fundamental values for a society seeking to overcome the endemic vices that have contributed to the deplorable present situation: the law of minimum effort and even of deception, pretense, apathy, and idleness. We need to overcome clientelism, *caudillismo,* corruption, and other ways of compromising with a hopeless situation by leaving social responsibility to others.[21]

The church has a prophetic mission to denounce poverty as the fruit of structural, social, and individual sin.

The individual conscience in turn is called to an awareness of the poor that leads to commitment to their cause in order to fulfill the calling of community that faces every human being who seeks human fulfillment. The way to meet this challenge is through effective solidarity,[22] through discernment as a way of seeking God's will in history.[23] Solidarity considers the dignity of the poor in asymmetric relationships, and rather than suppressing that dignity seeks to promote it by involving the poor as protagonists on the way to their own social and personal liberation. But that cannot be done without building "communities of solidarity,"[24] which can bring together those who live in marginality or exclusion and integrate them into the social fabric. Such integration must be done not only from the top down but also from the bottom up, in a movement of reciprocal recognition and progressive integration.

—*English translation by Margaret D. Wilde*

Notes

1. S. Ciancaglini, "La miseria planificada," in *Argentina: Un país desperdiciado* (Buenos Aires: Paradigma Libros, 2003), 149–53.

2. H. M. Yáñez, "Ante la irrupción de la pobreza, el despertar de las conciencias," in *Suena la campana de palo: Ensayos de escucha a los pobres, Revista Proyecto* 15, no. 44 (Buenos Aires: Centro de Estudios Salesianos, 2003), 82.

3. The government of Néstor Kirchner recently established a pension for all those who have reached retirement age without making social security payments. It is a minimal amount, which is very helpful to those who have no stable income, but it is not enough to live in dignity.

4. D. Fares, "La vulnerabilidad de las personas en la calle," in *De la solidaridad a la justicia: VII Jornada de Reflexión Etico-Teológica,* ed. H. M. Yáñez (Buenos Aires: Facultades de Filosofía y Teología, Universidad del Salvador, 2004).

5. D. García Delgado and M. G. Molina, "Etica y desarrollo: El conflicto de las interpretaciones," in *Suena la campana de palo,* ed. Yáñez, 33–83.

6. "According to official statistics, in 2002 in metropolitan Buenos Aires the level of violence — already the highest in Argentina — increased by 50 percent from the previous year" (D. P. Gorgal, "Buenos Aires y La Ciudad de Dios," *Valores en la Sociedad Industrial* 21, no. 56 [2003]: 39).

7. N. Redondo, "Pobreza urbana en Argentina desde un enfoque multidisciplinar hacia una praxis interdisciplinaria. Informe final: IV. Pobreza y reproducción social a fines de la convertibilidad," 10. Available at *www.uca.edu.ar/esp/sec-universidad/docs-investigacion/pdsa/2002/or-sociologica/docs/03-car-din-sit-pob-arg.pdf.*

8. Editorial, *Valores en la Sociedad Industrial* 21, 56 (2003): 4.

9. T. Mifsud, "El imperativo ético de una cultura de la solidaridad," in *La solidaridad como excelencia: VI Jornada de Reflexión Etico-Teológica,* ed. H. M. Yáñez (Buenos Aires: Facultades de Filosofía y Teología, Universidad del Salvador, 2003), 97.

10. A. R. Ameigeiras, "Religiosidad popular: Transformaciones socio-culturales y perspectivas de análisis a comienzos del siglo XXI," *CIAS* 51, 519 (2002): 607–8.

11. J. Cela, "La cultura de la pobreza," *Vida Nueva* 2267 (2001): 27.

12. Ibid., 29.

13. A *caudillo* is a political-military leader, a "strongman." Often used pejoratively, the term can also refer to charismatic populist leaders.

14. H. M. Yáñez, "El desafío ético de una cultura de solidaridad," *Nuevas Propuestas: Revista de la Universidad Católica de Santiago del Estero* 34 (December 2003): 12.

15. Msgr. Joaquín Piña, S.J., bishop emeritus of the diocese of Puerto Iguazú in the Province of Misiones, headed an opposition slate in the election of a Constituent Assembly in the province, called by the ruling party to amend the provincial constitution and permit the indefinite re-election of the governor.

16. H. M. Yáñez, "Jalones para fundamentar una etica de la solidaridad esperante," *Stromata* 56, nos. 1/2 (2000): 1–26.

17. A. Cortina, "Del intercambio infinito al reconocimiento compasivo," *Stromata* 62, nos. 1/2 (2006): 71–84; H. M. Yáñez, "Del reconocimiento a la comunión: La responsabilidad ampliada: Comentario a la conferencia de Adela Cortina," *Stromata* 62, 85–91.

18. J. C. Scannone, "Cuestiones actuales de epistemología teológica: Aportes de la teología de liberación," *Stromata* 46 (1990): 334.

19. A. González, "Fundamentos filosóficos de una 'Civilización de la Pobreza,' " *Estudios Centroamericanos (ECA)* 583 (May 1997): 417–23. The author cites Ignacio Ellacuría's affirmation that the poor question the legitimacy of the Western lifestyle.

20. M. Vidal, "La preferencia por el pobre, criterio de moral," *Studia Moralia* 20, no. 2 (1982): 279–304.

21. A. Gilotti, "Los vicios cívicos del cristiano en la sociedad Argentina," in *El Cristiano ante la Responsabilidad Ciudadana: VIII Jornada de Reflexión Etico-Teológica,* ed. H. M. Yáñez (Buenos Aires: Facultades de Filosofía y Teología, Universidad del Salvador, 2005).

22. H. M. Yáñez, "Ahora urge educar la solidaridad," *CIAS* 52, no. 526 (2003): 431–44.

23. T. Mifsud, *Moral de discernimiento,* vol. 1: *Moral fundamental: Libres para amar* (Santiago, Chile: San Pablo, 2002), 396–404.

24. 34th General Congregation of the Company of Jesus, *Decreto 3, Nuestra misión y la justicia,* no. 10; see also J. Alvarez de los Mozos, *Comunidades de solidaridad* (Bilbao: Mensajero, 2002).

2

An Ethical Analysis of Globalization from an Indian Perspective

JOHN CHATHANATT

Is globalization a threat or an opportunity for the poor in India? One can assume that the phenomenon of globalization is here to stay. This phenomenon has both positive and negative results. For a developing country like India it has wide repercussions.

India became a parliamentary democracy fifty-seven years ago, and the country has made significant progress in certain sectors with its option for democracy.[1] Globalization too has aided India's achievements in some way. It has brought new opportunities to India, including greater access to more markets and technology transfer, and thus it holds the promise of improved productivity and higher living standards.

At the same time, it has brought new challenges, like the growing inequality across and within nations, the volatility in financial markets, and serious environmental deterioration. Nor should one attribute all the injustices that plague Indian society to globalization. Not everything that happens under the umbrella of globalization should be branded as a pernicious neo-imperialist plot of international trade. Not every byte in this "globalization file" is corrupt, nor is this "virus" of globalization totally destructive.[2] At the same time, one ought to emphasize that the globe is beautiful even today, but globalization, as it manifests itself to the poor in India, seems to be ugly.

An attempt is made in the following pages to look at the effects of globalization on the lives of the poor in India. A thesis could be proposed that for a developing country like India, the fringe benefits of globalization are but a tiny ripple effect, and in the long run the impact as far as the poor of India are concerned will be life-negating. It is time to take stock of the various ramifications of globalization from the vantage point of a religious ethical analysis and from the "viewing point" of the economically poor, the politically marginalized, and the socially outcast. A few pertinent questions related to the topic will be raised without our pretending to answer them. The attempt here is to analyze the concept and processes of globalization and to look critically at its impact, especially on the poor and the marginal in a developing country like ours. A few general ethical guidelines and possible general directions for action will be proposed.

The Indian Experience

With the introduction of the New Economic Policy (NEP) in June 1991, India openly entered the phase of what is called economic liberalism, throwing overboard the cherished and constitutionally supported social policies of the earlier decades. This does not suggest that the globalization process is totally new.[3] Deeply ingrained in the very nature of capitalism, it cannot be considered a completely new phenomenon. What is perhaps new is that today's global integration is qualitatively different on account of the scale, intensity, and rapidity of the processes involved. Today's communication revolution has brought the world very close and has given a new orientation to globalization.

Some people argue that globalization has helped the Indian economy and that it cannot be blamed for any economic destabilization or instability.[4] This author begs to differ. Let me start with a few concrete experiences:

1. Recently the Indian prime minister had to dash to Vidharbha, a district in the State of Maharastra, where a number of farmers had committed suicide. This is by no means the first time that this has happened. From the year 2000, over nineteen hundred farmers have committed suicide in Andhra Pradesh alone.[5]

2. The poor people in Plachimada in Kerala are still struggling to ensure that their drinking water is safe after being polluted by a Coca-Cola bottling plant. They are still struggling in spite of a favorable local *panchayat* governing body. In 2000 Coke started its biggest Indian plant in the water-rich Plachimada. Daily it used 3.5 million liters of ground water. In two years the water level went down and started polluting drinking and agricultural water resources.[6]

3. On July 25, 2005, in a Honda factory in Gurgaon, Haryana, thousands of workers were dismissed and eventually work was suspended because of attempts by workers to maintain decent working conditions.[7]

In all these cases the capital investment is interested only in maximizing profit to ensure very high salaries for the multinational managers, of course at the expense of very low wages for the workers. Is the latter's welfare a concern of the former?

An Attempt at Description

"Undergoing globalization" is often associated with "becoming modern," where "modern" is understood in terms of adopting Western cultural practices and technologies. Thus it is more than an economic phenomenon and also has cultural and environmental impacts. The heart of globalization is concerned with money-making, and the driving force is profit maximization through the fast flow of capital, without any concern for social effects.

Definitions of globalization vary depending upon who is defining it. The three "catch words" are liberalization, privatization, and deregulation. The priorities and strategies of globalization could be summed up as follows:

1. pursuing economic growth as the top priority over all other social goods;

2. freeing up the mobility of capital;

3. increasing privatization;

4. reducing government regulation of economic activity;

5. producing for export rather than for domestic markets; and

6. seeking short-term profitability at the expense of long-term social well-being and environmental sustainability.

One could describe this phenomenon as a process by which capital, goods, services, technologies, and sometimes labor cross national borders and acquire a transnational character, accompanied by a flow of related tastes, ideas, values, and even cultures across boundaries, thus reshaping local political institutions, social relationships, and cultural patterns, hoping to lead to a single global system and global unity. All this is undertaken for the sole purpose of profit maximization.

The question to ask, therefore, is just what we are becoming in this emerging context? One thinks the way one lives. We are all at the mercy of conditions, actions, and choices made far away by persons we neither know nor understand, and who may have no concern for our collective welfare. Moreover, globalization can become an opportune moment for some of the Indian businessmen and bureaucrats to exploit their own people, as is already happening. Thus we may ask, isn't this phenomenon, then, manifesting a subtle form of recolonization?

The blessings of a few are adversely affecting a large section of the people in India. A vast majority of the world's poor are excluded from many of the benefits of globalization. An important negative aspect of globalization is that a great majority of developing countries remain removed from the very process. After six decades of independence a new ideology is emerging in India (or was it already there?) that the existence of the poor has to be taken for granted, that they will always be there and they are dispensable. The destitution of the many does not seem to trouble the consciences of the planners and politicians who decide the destiny of the nation. Their marginalization and displacement are considered as the unavoidable social cost of development. The recent displacement of slum dwellers in the cities of Delhi and Mumbai, without adequate alternative arrangements being put in place, bears witness to this. Instead of removing poverty, it is the poor who are being removed. The little social space they occupy at present is also being stolen from them in the name of privatization and of urbanization.

One should not forget that there are fringe benefits, even for the poor. There are people like Gail Omvedt and Kancha Ilaiah, who advocate what they call "realism" in our approach to globalization. One could propose, along with Bryan Hehir, Julian Filochowski (a former director of CAFOD), and a host of others that we should work for globalization, with globalization, and against globalization. And I may add, that given the present pattern of the workings of globalization, we will have to do quite a lot of work against it in the Indian context.

Today's globalization, which privileges capital, is extremely skewed. Poverty and inequality are there for everyone to see. Utter destitution persists in pockets of the world even though human conditions have improved more in the past century than in the rest of history. Global wealth and capital, technological advancements, and global communications have never been greater. But, unfortunately, the distribution of these global gains is extraordinarily unequal. The *World Development Report 2000/2001* points out that the average income in the richest twenty countries is thirty-seven times the average in the poorest twenty — a gap that has doubled in the past forty years.[8] According to Angus Maddison's estimates, although western Europe and its colonies in North America and Oceania had already pulled ahead of other regions by 1820, the gap between western Europe and the world's poorest region (sub-Saharan Africa) was only three to one.[9] By the 1990s however, the gap between the richest region and the poorest rose to around twenty to one.[10]

The massive poverty of India could be explained by the subservient nature of its economy, subservient both to the dominant economies of the industrialized nations and to the already wealthy baskets of the rich elites in India itself. This subtle form of imperialism, neo-colonialism, and interior colonization is reinforced by the designs of international institutions (including the IMF, the World Bank, and GATT), socio-cultural mechanisms (like the caste system), and more importantly by internal structural factors that allow a tiny minority of the rich elite to control the vast majority, and this is perpetuated by economic and political devices.

Increasing debt burdens are weighing India down like other poor, indebted countries. Many think otherwise. In the last decade India's debt service payment alone amounted to close to the entire debt. Let us look at some figures. According to the World Bank the developing countries collectively borrowed $1.935 trillion and repaid $2.237 trillion between 1972 and 1992. Despite these payments, today they owe $1.7 trillion to northern governments (the United States, the U.K., Germany, Japan, and so on), commercial banks (such as Citibank or Barclay's Bank), and multilateral institutions (the World Bank, the IMF, and regional development banks).

In an address at Harvard in 2000 Secretary General of the United Nations Kofi Annan pointed out: "Today globalization is losing its luster in parts of the world. Globalization is seen by a growing number of people not as a friend of prosperity, but as its enemy; not as a vehicle for development but as an ever-tightening vice increasing the demands on states to find safety-nets while limiting their ability to do so."[11] And in an address to the Holy See's Advisory Committee on Science a few years ago, Pope John Paul II cautioned that globalization must not be a new version of colonialism.[12]

India clearly lags behind in being a country that affirms equality and equal opportunity for everyone. In order to take full advantage of globalization one requires a huge amount of capital and access to the latest technology. On both counts India lags behind. A number of countries have a clear lead over India. Among them are China, a large part of East and Far East Asia, and some countries in Eastern Europe.[13]

As Amartya Sen and many others have pointed out, India, as a geographical, politico-cultural entity, has been interacting with the outside world throughout its history and still continues to do so. It has had to adapt, to assimilate, and to contribute. Today we need a change of priorities. Gandhiji's concerns point the way and challenge us to let his soul-searching and probing give us direction as we seek to give an ethical orientation to globalization.[14]

An Ethical Inquiry

Human consciousness has come to accept that certain values ought to have a bearing on economic life. The values that ought to inform economic activity include the recognition that:

1. every person is sacred and should be treated with dignity and equality;
2. every economic system or economic decision must be judged in the light of whether it protects or undermines the dignity of the human person;
3. all people have a right to participate in the economic life of society as equals;
4. all members of society have a special obligation toward the poor and the marginalized;
5. the objective of economic institutions is the common good; and
6. there can be no common good without social justice.

Experience of Dignity and Relationality through Solidarity and Fellow-Feeling

After analyzing the cultural and structural factors responsible for the continued poverty in India, where a tiny minority of the rich control and exploit masses of the poor, George Soares-Prabhu, a well-known scripture scholar, concluded: "The root cause of India's massive poverty is therefore injustice. India's underdevelopment (and this is true for the rest of the developing countries too) is a historical and a dialectical process."[15] Such analysis is definitely challenging. We need to understand better our inter-relatedness, especially today in a world of globalized economies. As a relational, corporate, and communitarian being, a person is made for friendship, community, public life, and the achievement of self-realization in interaction with others. We need the guidance of the norm of at least basic justice in all our interactions. This justice calls for the establishment of a basis of material well-being on which all can stand. This is the duty of the whole society, and it is a particular obligation of those with greater resources. This implies that one must examine one's way of living in the light of the needs of the poor. The way a society or a polity responds to the needs of the broken and the marginalized ones through public policies is the litmus test of the presence or absence of justice in that society. It is also the litmus test of democracy itself. The deprivation and powerlessness of one section of a society wounds the whole society.

It is in this respect that the basic principles laid down by Gandhi become central.[16] Moreover, these principles are also evident in Christian ethics, especially in Catholic social ethics, where the notion of solidarity is essential.[17] In fact we need a globalization of solidarity. As a Christian believer I hear the words of the prophet Ezekiel: "From all your idols I will cleanse you. A new heart I will give you and a new spirit I will put within you. I will remove from your body a heart of stone and give you a heart of flesh. I will put my spirit within you. . . . You shall be my people and I will be your God" (Ezek. 36:25–28).

One ought to reject the liberal, individualistic, asocial representation of the human person and instead embrace his or her fundamental socio-relational character. We are creatures who require community in order to become what God has intended us to be. Thus interdependence is the condition within which the dignity and sacredness of the human person is either honored or abused.

Conclusion

Key insights from Catholic social teaching include the recognition that:

1. the rediscovery of the social, relational, corporate, and communitarian dimensions of the human person brought a newness in our understanding of justice (*as fidelity to the demands of a relationship*). Thus this trio of faith-justice-love is essential for a new social order (*a social order founded on faith/truth, built on justice, and cemented by love*);

2. working for development without challenging structural injustices is not sufficient;

3. an integrated and holistic liberation requires both liberation from unjust structures combined with the formation of relationships and the creation of communities;

4. in a divided world, charity, based on pity or sympathy, is not enough;

5. in a divided world, a commitment to integral liberation and to the promotion of justice and human rights is effective only through an option for the marginalized. The rights of the poor and marginalized become the criterion for action, decision, priority, and policy. Hence our approach is structural, political, and always one of solidarity.[18]

What brings about transformation in a society and people? The following proposals could be made:

1. It is important to build a social movement correctly rather than just to have "correct" analysis or a correct set of demands.

2. Organizing opposition to the negative effects of corporately sponsored phenomena like globalization must be built from the bottom up.

3. Incorporating various constituencies the world over and garnishing support from whatever quarter it emerges in the campaign against the global "race to the bottom" is a correct approach.

4. Basing the movements principally on grassroots organizations, unions, and independent institutions and coalitions, rather than just on politicians and governments seems to be the right approach. If possible, a partnership approach, though difficult, needs to be developed.

Interdependent solidarity ought to be the basis and foundation of globalization. If globalization cannot be stopped, it can be controlled. It can be shaped and directed.[19]

The apparently uncontrolled process of contemporary globalization creates a variety of problems. If one serves only the aims of the economy, the result is poverty for many. The economic system today, especially when kept at a distance from ethical analysis, does not appear to be concerned for homeless people or for those who are impoverished. Neither does it seem to be concerned to limit environmental degradation. It produces refugees (and then perhaps founds organizations to take care of them!). The economy alone cannot be the determinant of human relationships. How can one speak of solidarity, mutuality, and cooperation as the main characteristics of modern progress, when cutthroat competition and the impersonality of the market are projected as values?

The answer to the negative effects of the globalization of the economy is the creation of a common front against them and the adoption of a new paradigm that will demystify the dominant economic ideology.[20] It is not prudent to leave life to the mercy of the economically powerful with their technocratic decisions and pursuits.

The church is beckoning us: "Action on behalf of justice and participation in the transformation of the world fully appear to us as a constitutive dimension of the preaching of the Gospel, or, in other words, of the Church's mission for the redemption of the human race and its liberation from every oppressive situation."[21] What is our response?

In conclusion, it could be said that globalization without marginalization is possible. Globalization of solidarity is possible. We can still hope for a world order that is based on truth, built on justice, and cemented by love — and all this achieved in freedom.

Notes

1. An awakening among the historically marginalized — *dalits,* tribals, and women — is taking place, giving hope to a people's power for a new India. In the public and civic life various liberal and democratic values have been accepted. The integrity of the higher judicial system is commendable indeed. Despite the innumerable scams and corrupt practices, a ray of hope through a call to accountability and transparency is manifested in the life of the nation. The Election Commission is working hard to improve the electoral process to pave the way for better democratic governance. On the economic front too growth is clearly seen. Definitely the country has progressed in various ways from what it was at the time of independence.

2. See John Chathanatt, "Globalization Virus: An Ethical Scanning," in *Third Millennium* 3 (2000): 3, 6–23.

3. I am not here entering into a discussion of the historical nuances of the growth of "cosmopolitanism," the trade of the precolonial and colonial periods, the rise of capitalism, and the intense globalization that was taking place from the early nineteenth century.

4. In *India's Globalization: Evaluating the Economic Consequences* (Washington, D.C.: East-West Center, 2006), Baldev Raj Nayar argues that globalization has helped the Indian economy and cannot be blamed for any economic destabilization or instability. He further argues that globalization has helped the Indian economy record a 6 percent to 7 percent growth rate. In a similar vein, a recent issue of *Time* magazine (June 26, 2006) lauds India's progress and notes that India is the world's second fastest-growing economy. Just to put the record straight, the economic indicators of the last five years do not place India in second place. Besides, economic growth by itself is not an indication of the distribution of wealth, especially to the lowest strata of the economy.

5. Farmers are particularly vulnerable to changes in the market. Many farmers are under severe pressure because of their debt. The interest exceeds the original loan in many cases and the interest due in the six districts of Maharastra alone is around Rs 712 *crore* ($170 million). The prime minister developed a package for the benefit of the farmers, who under the weight of the debt burden were at risk of ending their lives. Because of the seriousness of the most recent problem he appointed an expert group to look into the problem of rural indebtedness in its totality.

6. For more detailed description of many more cases of the exploitation of the poor in India, see Arokiadoss Peter, "Encountering Globalization: The Experience of the Marginalized," a paper presented at the Annual Meeting of the Association of Moral Theologians of India in December 2005.

7. In Honda's Gurgaon factory three thousand workers are employed. Of these only seventeen hundred are permanent workers. The remaining thirteen hundred are temporary workers, and they can be fired at any moment with or without reason. When one worker was attacked by one of the officers, four workers objected. They were summarily dismissed. When fifty workers protested, they too were dismissed. Afterward another one thousand workers were dismissed amid the strong protest of the remaining workers. The company decided to suspend work from July 27. All the workers gathered to protest against this injustice. It was at that time the Haryana police let loose its brutal force against the agitating workers, on the pretext that the workers manhandled police personnel. Gradually a settlement was reached, and the company agreed to take back all the workers. But before being readmitted, all the workers were asked to sign a humiliating declaration. It contained various promises similar to the following, devastating the workers hard-earned rights and dignity: "I will work hard to achieve the production target fixed by the company. I will not associate with any Labour Union activities. I will not ask for pay raise for one year. . . . " The next day Honda dismissed two hundred contract workers and charged sixty-three prominent workers with attempted murder. Charges of premeditated murder and theft were also registered against four union leaders. See Rakhi Sehgal, "Gurgaon, July 25: Police Brutality Not an Aberration," *Economic and Political Weekly*, August 27, 2005, 3796–97; Nagaraj Adve, "Living to Fight Another Day: The Attack on Honda's Workers," *Economic and Political Weekly*, September 10, 2005, 40415–18; and the Tamil monthly *Puthia Jananayagam* (New Democracy), November 2005, 14–16. These details are taken from the essay of Arokiadoss Peter, "Encountering Globalization," 7.

8. The World Bank, *World Development Report 2000/2001: Attacking Poverty* (New York: Oxford University Press, 2001), 3.

9. See Jeffrey Sachs, "Notes on a New Sociology of Economic Development," in *Culture Matters: How Values Shape Human Progress,* ed. Lawrence E. Harrison and Samuel P. Huntington (New York: Basic Books, 2001), 29–30. Sachs is referring to data of Angus Maddison, *Monitoring the World Economy, 1820–1992* (Paris: OECD, Development Center, 1995).

10. All the same, history should not be forgotten. In the fifteenth and sixteenth centuries about 77 percent of the wealth of the world was in Asia. India's share was over 60 percent. Of the calculated total world GNP of $155 billion, $120 billion was the share of Asia (see Andre Gunder Frank, "India and World Economy — 1400–1750," in *Economic and Political Weekly,* July 27, 1996, 50–64). However, in 2004 India's share was 1.69 percent and in 2000 it was 1.51 percent. What has happened? Today the income of the richest 1 percent in our world is equal to the combined income of the poorest 57 percent, and the gap is getting wider. India belongs to that 57 percent. See Julian Filochowski, "A Theology of Protest in a Globalized World," Valedictory Speech at the 25th Conference of the National Justice and Peace Network, July 11, 2003, London; *www.caritas-europa.org/code/en/speeches.asp?pk_id_speeches=27.*

11. As quoted by Bryan Hehir, "Making Globalisation Work for the World's Poor," fifteenth CAFOD Pope Paul VI Memorial Lecture (London, November 16, 2001), 2; *www.catholicireland.net/pages/index.php?nd=193+art=737.*

12. Ibid.

13. A few indicators show how much India and other developing countries lag behind. Over the past decade foreign direct investment (FDI) flows into India have averaged around 0.5 percent of GDP against 5 percent for China and 5.5 percent for Brazil. FDI inflows into China now exceed US$50 billion annually. It is only US$4 billion in the case of India. Consider global trade: India's share of world merchandise exports increased from 0.05 percent to 0.07 percent over the past twenty years. Over the same period China's share has tripled to almost 4 percent. India's share of global trade is similar to that of the Philippines, an economy six times smaller, according to IMF estimates. India undertrades by 70 to 80 percent, given its size, proximity to markets, and labor cost advantages. According to the UNDP Report (*Human Development Report 2000* [Delhi: Oxford University Press, 2000], 82) the forty-eight least-developed countries attracted less that $3 billion in 1998, a mere 0.4 percent of the total. The combined wealth of the top 200 billionaires hit $1.135 billion in 1999, up from 1.042 billion in 1998. Just compare this with the combined incomes of $146 billion for the 582 million people in all the least-developed countries.

It is interesting to note the remark made last year by Bimal Jalan, governor of the Reserve Bank of India. Despite all the talk, we are nowhere close to being globalized in terms of any commonly used indicator of globalization. In fact, he said, we are among the least globalized among the major countries — however we look at it.

14. Once Rabindranath Tagore asked Gandhiji: "Gandhiji, are you so unromantic? When in the early dawn the morning sun rises, does it not fill your heart with joy to see its reddish glow? When the birds sing does not your heart thrill with its divine music? When the rose opens its petals and blooms in the garden does its sight not bring cheer to your heart?"

The Mahatma replied: "Gurudeve, I am not so dumb or insensitive as not to be moved by the beauty of the rose or the morning rays of the sun or the divine music of the birds. But what can I do? My one desire, my one anxiety, my one ambition is, when shall I see the red tint of the rose on the cheeks of hungry naked millions of my people? When shall I hear the sweet and melodious song of the birds in the place of their agonizing sighs? When will such music come out of their soul and when will that day come when the light of the morning sun will illumine the heart of the common man in India? When will I see its luster and brightness on his face?"

Gandhiji's priorities are very clear.

15. George Soares-Prabhu, "Jesus and Social Justice" (Mumbai: Basic Community Library Service, n.d.), 1.

16. "I will give you a talisman," Gandhi says. "Whenever you are in doubt, or when the self becomes too much with you, apply the following test. Recall the face of the poorest and weakest man you have seen, and ask yourself if the step you contemplate is going to be of any use to him. Will he gain anything by it? Will it restore to him control over his own life and destiny? In other words, will it lead to *Swaraj* for the hungry and spiritually starving millions?"

17. In *Sollicitudo rei socialis,* John Paul II summarizes a reflection on the social challenges facing contemporary societies by emphasizing the fact of interdependence and singling out solidarity as a moral response: "It is above all a question of interdependence, sensed as a system determining relationships in the contemporary world, in its economic, cultural, political, and religious elements, and accepted as a moral category. When interdependence becomes recognized in this way, the correct response

as a moral and social attitude, as a virtue, is solidarity" (*SRS* no. 38). If globaliza-tion is concerned about our interdependence going beyond time and space, then, definitely, solidarity is the virtue to be emulated. Here the pope is rejecting global-ization as a value-neutral category or as something inevitable. Our interdependence and relationality must be recognized as a "moral category" that makes moral de-mands upon us. Our interdependence has an essential moral character calling us to embrace the virtue of solidarity. We don't have to learn to live with globalization; globalization has to learn to live with us.

18. What *Gaudium et spes* points out is very appropriate: "It is the task of the Church to stand as the sign and safeguard of the transcendent dignity of the human person. The Church will be judged by its fidelity to this task." It is not a purely secular task, it is not a purely moral task; it is a religious mandate for the church. If globalization has a dynamic that threatens human dignity then that part of it needs to be addressed by the church. Besides, the principles of common good, social justice, solidarity, subsidiarity, and preferential option for the marginalized ought to be taken seriously in our deliberation and action.

19. It can be directed to what John Paul II calls a "civilization of love"; it can be directed to a global common good and to the unity of the whole human family, where human dignity is assured and economic, social, and political rights are respected for each and every one in the world.

20. The world just cannot survive if it accepts the options imposed by today's globalization, namely, a tiny minority of the powerful imposing their will on the weak, a system where only the powerful have rights.

21. *Justice in the World,* no. 6, Synod of Bishops Second General Assembly, November 30, 1971.

3

Globalization and
African Economic Reforms

AQUILINE TARIMO

African poverty, which could be interpreted as a deprivation of capabilities and a lack of basic freedoms, is largely perpetuated by ill-founded development theories and policies, by erroneous assumptions, and by misguided economic reforms. Almost all African countries are engaged in some kind of economic reform program with funding from outside the continent. Most of these programs, however, seem to be artificial, ineffective, and problematic. Instead of reducing poverty, on the contrary, they have become ingredients designed to maintain the status quo. Thus it becomes necessary to evaluate the effectiveness of the proposed economic reform programs with the aim of establishing approaches that can address poverty from its root causes. My analysis links the loss of local survival mechanisms with the decay of social institutions, itself the result of the imposition of economic reform programs and of economic globalization. In search of lasting economic recovery, this investigation proposes a localization of economic reforms aimed at reviving the spirit of survival, thereby challenging the mentality of excessive dependency.

The Decline of Economic Development

Africa faces challenges that militate against its economic development. This claim is justified by the many reports from the World Bank and from the United Nations Development Program. These reports reveal that the proportion of people living below the poverty line is gradually increasing. The decline of living standards puts African countries under severe pressure and results in social conditions that undermine moral standards by producing an endless wave of internal strife as people fight for insufficient resources. It is a situation that discourages people, especially the youth, who see no hope for their future as they seek security in new religious movements and drugs. At the national level, the economic crisis is evident in foreign debt, unemployment, illiteracy, the spread of diseases, civil wars, an increase of slums, and so forth. The decline in economic development is partly caused by the ineffective participation of the majority of the people in economic activities. In addition, the political environment often generates conditions that make valuable economic programs impossible to implement.

Although Africa is endowed with abundant resources, its people continue to suffer from abject poverty. The primary reason is that Africa's economic infrastructure and human resources are underdeveloped and often controlled by people from other continents.

Economic Globalization and Marginalization

The dynamics of economic globalization have brought into being transnational financial institutions whose power exceeds that of nation-states and whose policies frequently result in massive violations of human rights. For instance, the imposed structural adjustment programs have created unbearable burdens of unemployment, a decline of local initiative, and the destruction of social programs that defend the welfare of the poor. The effects of such programs include increased dependence on child labor, low wages, and environmental destruction. They also lead to local disempowerment vis-à-vis the production of locally consumed goods. It is true that Africa cannot escape economic globalization since it is a part of the changing world. Nevertheless, it is wise to acknowledge that Africa is more of a victim and object of charity than a determining participant in the global trade system. Under this framework, economic globalization is progressively opening up African resources toward mechanisms of wealth transfer designed to enrich rich countries. Through the multinational companies, wealth is transferred at an electronic speed across the world. The phenomenon is reinforced by increased mobility of capital and skilled labor to those areas where big profits are assured. This accounts for job losses, migration of skilled workers, and exploitation of the poor. The economic mechanisms of globalization are designed to enrich the rich at the expense of the poor. The underpinning ideology of this phenomenon discriminates against Africa despite its ability to supply much of the raw materials required for international industrial activities.

It is evident that the processes of economic globalization have failed to produce the anticipated benefits heralded by its proponents and instead have created massive deprivation and inequality. The situation has already relegated Africa to a consumer of goods manufactured from outside rather than a producer of such goods. With such outcomes, the existing framework of economic globalization does not seem to have a liberating effect on Africa because it results in wealth transfer from the periphery to the center rather than leading to the empowerment of the poor. The expected economic convergence for the benefit of all is not happening. Instead, there is a perpetuation of the periphery-center paradigm through which Africa is being further marginalized. This is evident in the continent's inability to break into new markets at the international level. It is apparent that globalization, in its current manifestation, cannot build a global community sustained by the virtues of solidarity and the common good. As such, the Christian maxim of the love of neighbor raises a serious challenge for economic globalization.

The Loss of Survival Mechanisms

Before colonization African traditional societies were able to meet their economic needs without depending on help from outside. In those days, Africa had prosperous civilizations like Songhai, Kanem-Bornu, Baganda, Monomotapa, and many others. Indeed the dependence on external forces to develop Africa is rather a recent phenomenon. In simple terms, this dependence emerged from an excessive love of free things, from an alienation from the local context of life, and from a paternalism instituted by former colonial powers. Because of the lack of self-innovation and self-confidence, the situation has ultimately resulted in the loss of survival mechanisms among the present generation of Africans.

In recent years, the continent of Africa has been affected by changes in the global economy and in the geopolitical configuration. The impact of these changes has been intensified with economic reform programs imposed by international financial institutions and donors. This situation is accompanied by the disintegration of basic institutions and by local corruption, mismanagement, and inept leadership. In an attempt to address this situation I suggest that we begin by exploring the causes of the problem, namely, its unfavorable political conditions and its vulnerability to the international trade systems.

The decline in African economic development has often been explained in terms of a lack of entrepreneurial skills, incompetent management, shifting of market policies, a decrease of investment, low prices for agricultural products, and corruption. However external interference has also contributed to this decline. This can take the form of sponsorship of dictatorial regimes, the support of armed conflicts, and a looting of natural resources. Thus populations have suffered to such an extent that the average African family is poorer today than it was four decades ago.

If we look at economic development during the first decade after independence, we notice that Africa enjoyed significant economic growth. In the second decade, on the contrary, Africa's economic growth started to slow down. In the third decade, it turned into a deep crisis characterized by declining agricultural and industrial production, deteriorating terms of trade, and a rising debt burden. There is little agreement, however, as to why this happened. Most often critics focus either on external or internal causes in isolation, whereas the fact is that they coexist and reinforce each other in reproducing a persistent crisis of underdevelopment. For example, the decline in agricultural production was accompanied by Africa's vulnerability vis-à-vis the world's trade systems and overdependence on foreign aid. Thus as economic conditions have deteriorated, so too have political conditions, and the two have reinforced each other to create an environment that militates against economic development.

Moreover there is a decline in the role of the state in providing social services. Instead the effort to reform the state structure consists in encouraging multinational companies to invest in Africa as a means of creating an enabling environment for the market and the private sector to thrive. In addition, this has led to a revival within ethnic communities and religious networks whose aim is to consolidate private interests and to advance sectarian interests. At its starkest, one could say that Africa is now regarded as a provider of raw materials and of cheap human labor, as a market for substandard goods, as a dumping ground for industrial waste, and as a laboratory for medical research on human subjects. The former colonizing powers are present under the cover of international cooperation and investment in order to use corrupt leaders as tools of exploitation by proxy. Thus local leaders often become instruments of oppression in exchange for bribes. Various forms of manipulation flourish because African politics is focused primarily on fulfilling immediate needs.

African economies are vulnerable to external forces and interests because donations, loans, and investments are strategically organized to support the economic and political agenda of the lender at the expense of the recipient. Thus the power of the donor overrides local initiatives and interests. The structural adjustment programs, in particular, make Africa vulnerable to foreign interests by demanding that governments be accountable to international financial institutions and to donors instead of to the local population. External paternalism of this kind ultimately inhibits the population from making radical decisions that could benefit the people. In the end the situation results in the loss of survival mechanisms.

Imposition of Economic Reform Programs

Reform programs proposed to address the African economic crisis include structural adjustment programs that comprise the liberalization of domestic markets, the privatization of state-owned firms, financial deregulation, debt cancellation, and foreign aid. Under the influence of these programs, African governments prepare annual budgets on the basis of promises. The expectation that governments should prepare development strategies based upon their own domestic capacity has almost disappeared. Instead of investing in projects that could enhance economic growth, governments concentrate on allocating money for consumption. This is evident when the priority in allocating public funds is given to non-productive sectors. National models of economic planning and governance are limited because the policy-making

mechanisms on which they are based do not consider the economic contributions of grassroots communities. There is no clear vision demonstrating
how grassroots structures of wealth production relate to the national planning. Most national strategies concentrate on the allocation of public funds
to the salaries of civil servants and non-productive activities. As a result they
lack the ability to create self-sustaining structures.

Reform policies are planned outside and imposed on the local economic
infrastructure without concern for their long-term effects. Many leaders,
professionals, and entrepreneurs whose activities are controlled from outside become agents of external forces. The institutionalization of dependence
relations is a principal mechanism of domination. Dependence limits choices
available to the poor, and the alternatives set by external forces of domination become the only available option. Excessive control from outside leads
to the breakdown of the domestic ability and willingness to do anything
that could bring about radical change. It is true that external control inhibits
local initiative. However a significant degree of blame must also be directed
toward African leaders. In particular there is a problem with national resources being used for expenditures that do not benefit the majority. Public
funds are often diverted to non-productive activities, including sustaining
the luxurious lifestyles of some political leaders who are unsympathetic to
the people they rule.

It seems that programs devised by international financial institutions are
the only available initiative for economic reform. In reality, local initiatives
intended to promote economic recovery do not exist. Many leaders seem
to believe that the power to stabilize the continent's fragile economy lies
with external actors. Under the influence of this thinking, reform programs
devised from outside ignore local capacities, bypass social needs, neglect initiatives for sustainable development emerging from grassroots communities,
and accentuate internal fragmentation. This approach limits the capacity of
the local leadership by externalizing decision-making processes. There is a
belief that poor countries can improve their economies only if they follow
the development models operating in rich countries. We forget that economic development is a socio-cultural process by which people rediscover
themselves and life conditions to realize higher levels of growth in accordance with their own choices and values. It is something that people must
do for themselves, although the help of others can facilitate it.

If people are the end of development, they are also necessarily its agents
and its means. By following the framework of this argument one could
conclude that the international financial institutions and donor agencies
are mistaken in seeking to dictate reform programs without considering
local involvement. The international agencies and consultancies that advise African leadership assume that African traditions are primitive. The
arrogance of donors is not constructive because the money poured into the

continent without considering local contexts of life, value systems, responsible leadership, and good governance may not bring forth the expected economic recovery.

The focus on implementing the conditions devised by international financial institutions is stifling local initiative and creativity. Leaders and scholars alike are all caught up in the framework of intellectual and material dependency. Proposed development strategies tend to follow whatever comes from outside, even when it is irrelevant to Africa. The mechanism of foreign aid propagates unrealistic expectations by encouraging leaders to leave everything to the mercy of donors. Many leaders see the task of promoting economic progress as a responsibility of foreign investors and donors.

Localization of Economic Reforms

In searching for lasting solutions to poverty it is not enough to concentrate on the role of international financial institutions, on aid, or on markets. It is also imperative that development strategies be localized in order to engage the capacity of the people concerned. Development strategies have a possibility of becoming reality when they are geared to build permanent economic infrastructures rather than when they remain focused on disaster relief or temporary solutions. Local development strategies enable people to think creatively in order to involve the majority of the population in the activity of wealth production. The economic challenge facing contemporary Africa requires new ways of thinking so that the inherited models of wealth production and distribution can be transformed. Such effort must go together with the mobilization of domestic savings for investment and with the diversification of the economic base. In order to halt the growing rate of poverty, people must be made aware that the forces that can transform the continent will emerge from themselves. People are therefore called to ignore ideologies that play down the value of self-reliance. If we want to reform African economies we have to depend on ourselves without isolating ourselves from global interaction, collaboration, and mutual enrichment. Donors alone, no matter how rich, powerful, and generous they may be, cannot overcome the African plight. It is self-evident that nobody can develop a foreign country on behalf of the dwellers in that country.

The empowerment of people at the grassroots level is essential for wealth production. This is because the dynamics of development strategies are closely influenced by the public's willingness to transform the economic dimension in a way that is accountable to its public. In extending further the realization of this ideal, the expansion of state responsibilities provides the opportunities essential for local communities to be involved in production. Initiatives of this sort require knowledge-building activities accompanied by the strengthening of linkages between economic strategies and grassroots organizations. Popular involvement is crucial for economic survival because we have to build upon what people know and are able to do. A creative involvement of this sort requires accountability in the management of public resources, the institutionalization of democratic ideals, and the development of stable institutions of governance. Economic development strategies are best realized through the promotion of wealth production, thereby attracting investment from different sources.

Conclusion

The promotion of economic development is not merely a matter of increasing foreign investment and aid. It also requires effective management, a transformation of the value system, and responsible leadership. Economic growth depends on the relationship between various factors. Proposed economic strategies must be able to make people the agents, the means, and the end of development. This makes development an experience of participation and self-realization. Such initiative requires strategic planning founded upon educational training geared toward self-transformation. Participation builds self-confidence among the people concerned because it encourages them to take the initiative. The process builds local capacities by making leadership, self-reliance, and self-esteem integral parts of moral formation. Such awareness would also be supported by education that is aimed at promoting a transformation in the value systems and in the structures of participation.

4

Globalization and Free Trade Agreements

Ethical Analysis and Alternatives

KENNETH M. WEARE

In their visionary and prophetic pastoral letter *Economic Justice for All,* the U.S. Catholic bishops offer a far-reaching moral perspective on the global economy. They teach that "every economic decision and institution must be judged in light of whether it protects or undermines the dignity of the human person."[1]

In proposing such a Christian ethical criterion for economic life, the bishops rely upon the Second Vatican Council's seminal document *Gaudium et spes,* and Pope John XXIII's encyclical *Mater et Magistra.*[2] They affirm: "The dignity of the human person, realized in community with others, is the criterion against which all aspects of economic life must be measured."

Articulated in a more direct and unequivocal way, the bishops, at the very beginning of their pastoral letter, state emphatically: "Every perspective on economic life that is human, moral, and Christian must be shaped by three questions: What does the economy do *for* people? What does the economy do *to* people? And how do people *participate* in it?"

In the two decades since its 1986 promulgation, the moral insight and wisdom of the Catholic bishop's economic analysis and ethical evaluation have not been well heeded by the market players in either political or economic circles. Contrary to Catholic teaching, from the Americas to Asia and around the world, the gap between rich and poor has escalated steadily; women and children are exploited; rainforests continue to disappear; fish stocks are depleted; natural resources are ravaged; environmental pollution continues to increase; poverty remains unabated; and the dignity of God's people is defamed on every side by neo-liberalism's economic flagellation.

This global face of poverty is perhaps best documented in the annual United Nations *Human Development Report.*[3] Also, John Iceland's recently updated text, *Poverty in America,* provides a candid survey of the historical characteristics and current statistics of this nation's increasing poverty.[4]

39

Constituent to global poverty today and to the global economy are the so-called "free trade" agreements. Arguing from a Catholic moral perspective — one that is not inconsistent with the values of other religious traditions, including those recently articulated by former U.S. president Jimmy Carter in his book *Our Endangered Values*[5] — ethicists have concluded that, if allowed to take root, the proposed Free Trade Areas of the Americas (FTAA) agreement threatens to make more extreme the poverty, injustices, and inequalities that people suffer in rural areas and in cities, and to subordinate nations once and for all to the interests of the transnational corporations.

Such has been the conclusion of numerous conferences, colloquiums, assemblies, meetings, and similar gatherings of experts from many professional fields over the past years. One particularly noteworthy conference took place in Havana in January 2004. The participants numbered 1,230 from thirty-five countries in North, Central, and South America. These included not only scholars in theology, economics, political science, engineering, and other varied professions, but also politicians, environmentalists, labor leaders, elected officials, church workers, health workers, and others. The most significant attendees, however, were representatives from the working classes and the poor themselves, including the working poor, indigenous peoples, farm workers, factory workers, the underemployed, and the jobless. Their multitude of personal stories and individual testimonies provided firsthand witness to the daily lived experience of millions. As in other such ventures, the resultant socio-political and economic analysis and moral evaluation produced a less than positive critical assessment of the proposed FTAA.

Among the most formidable critiques of the proposed FTAA is the argument that the proposed agreement has been constructed without the participation of the people who will be most affected by it. It was composed without public knowledge or input, primarily by corporate attorneys. Like the North America Free Trade Agreement (NAFTA), the proposed FTAA clearly favors corporate profits disproportionate to the social needs and human rights of citizens and irrespective of a viably sustainable environment.

Nobel laureate and former World Bank vice president Joseph Stiglitz recently noted that economic policy today is perhaps the most important interaction the United States has with the rest of the world. He warned, however, that the culture of international economic policy in the world's most powerful democracy is not in fact democratic. This he further explicates in his well-known best-selling book *Globalization and Its Discontents,* and in his two recently published texts, *Fair Trade for All* and *Making Globalization Work.*[6]

Free trade agreements can also transcend democratic legislation. The often less than analytical U.S. media typically limits the public debate about free trade to the sole issue of tariff reduction. Officially, the free trade goal is to lower tariff and non-tariff barriers to trade and investment. Thus, local laws that, for example, protect the quality of water, require just wages for employees, give preference to wood harvested in an environmentally sustainable way, or protect domestic jobs, can be judged as "state interference" and be struck down as a non-tariff barrier.

A case in point is NAFTA's chapter 11 section on investment. It specifically accords private investors and corporations the right to challenge environmental, worker safety, and health regulations. In short, free trade means freedom from any democratically established laws that in any way hinder the maximization of profit for international corporations.

Free trade policy and practices facilitate the privatization and deregulation of the energy sector, health care, education, and water resources. Within the framework of free trade, these human services cease to be seen as necessities to which every person has a right. Rather, they become commodities to be traded for profit. Society's poor and marginalized are often forced to go without life's necessities. Thus, free trade agreements undermine the ability of governments to fulfill their responsibility to ensure basic services to their respective peoples.

Free trade agreements like NAFTA not only cost the United States jobs, but also fail to provide good employment opportunities in developing nations. The U.S. Department of Labor certified that by the end of 2002, a total of 525,094 workers lost their jobs as a result of NAFTA. Other studies put the figure as high as 3 million. And while Mexican unemployment rates may have dropped, poverty increased and minimum wages fell 25 percent. Thus, while free trade may be good for profits, it is bad for workers. One AFL-CIO report reached the conclusion that globalization has spawned a race to the bottom for workers in both developed and developing nations alike.

Free trade impacts almost all sectors of society, including workers, small farmers, small business owners, environmentalists, women's organizations, unions, indigenous rights groups, members of religious communities, international solidarity groups, government employees, and many others. But the free trade emphasis on market supremacy meets the needs of only a select few. From the Christian ethical perspective, free trade ought to balance the needs of business, communities, and democratic governance.

An additional negative criticism of NAFTA, and also of other free trade agreements, concerns the investor-state suit provisions. In the view of the legal professionals, they are nothing short of a blatant departure from both domestic and international legal norms. First, it is argued, they provide corporations with the right to directly enforce an international treaty to which they are neither parties nor under which they have any obligations. Second, they allow private industry to oppose longstanding U.S. laws that have nothing to do with commercial contracts and everything to do with public policy. And third, they create substantive legal rights concerning expropriation and national treatment that go far beyond those available to local citizens and small businesses.

Few economists disagree with the view that trade and investment agreements are crucial to both developed and developing nations, with the potential to benefit both business and people alike. But morally, trade agreements must meet everyone's needs and respect everyone's human rights. Unfortunately, current trade agreements emphasize the priority of market supremacy over and above the needs of the greater community.

To fulfill the moral objective of the common good, what is needed are trade agreements that seek to alleviate poverty by educating the poor, offering opportunities for living-wage jobs, and making long-term social development a top priority. Trade agreements must also protect the environment and offer incentives to innovative businesses seeking new, eco-friendly methods of production.

The Catholic Church, together with so many religious, economic, political, and academic leaders, has continued to provide critical analysis and moral assessment of the economic impact of globalization. In response, the singular most common reaction heard from almost all sectors is the question: "So what's the alternative?"

Various scholars have individually begun to suggest possible alternatives to the current state of global poverty vis-à-vis globalization. Two books of note are John Cavanagh and Jerry Mander's edited text, *Alternatives to Economic Globalization,* and the more popular best-selling volume, *The End of Poverty: Economic Possibilities for Our Time,* by Jeffrey Sachs.[7]

The foundational moral basis for a realistic alternative specifically to replace the proposed FTAA can be found both in sacred scripture and in contemporary Catholic social thought. In particular, as already noted, the U.S. Catholic bishops teach that "every economic decision and institution must be judged in light of whether it protects or undermines the dignity of the human person." In short, "the dignity of the human person . . . is the criterion against which all aspects of economic life must be measured."

Does a realistic alternative to the proposed FTAA exist today? It does. It was developed by the Hemispheric Social Alliance (HSA) directly in response to the proposed FTAA. The HSA is a coalition of labor unions, environmentalists, family farmers, economists, scholars, and other coalitions representing more than one hundred organizations throughout North, Central, and South America. It was created in 1999 to facilitate information exchange and joint strategies and action to build an alternative democratic model of development in the face of proposed international trade agreements within overall economic globalization.

The Alternatives for the Americas details the HSA guidelines that would make the economic integration process of hemispheric globalization more inclusive, democratic, environmentally and culturally sustainable, and equitable.[8]

The *Alternatives* document is well within the sphere of Catholic social teaching. The plan proposes economic development based on democratic citizen participation, local control over resources, and the reduction of economic and social inequalities. It proposes a more responsible proactive role for the state and increased regulation of the economy both nationally and internationally in the pursuit of social justice, public services, and public security.

The economic purpose is moral: to achieve just and sustainable development. The *Alternatives* proposal affirms that trade and investment should not become ends in themselves, but rather the instruments (means) to promote economic justice for all. The report details three guiding principles: democratic participation, the role of the state, and the reduction of inequalities.

First, the *Alternatives* document states that local communities affected by economic policies should be involved in drafting, approving, and monitoring those policies. This includes involvement in creating a national development program, developing free trade policies, approving development projects, managing mining, encouraging biodiversity, and so forth. Policy development should be a widely participatory process utilizing broad-based consultation. Local community rights to veto or reject a project must be respected and honored.

The document also outlines how the sovereignty of states should be preserved by any trade agreement so states maintain authority to ensure their citizens' well-being. The objectives of such responsibility would include: to ensure that social needs supersede corporate interests, especially regarding education, housing, and health care; to control investment hazards to workers, the environment, and national development plans; to promote just and sustainable development; to ensure that the export market not sacrifice the domestic market; to evaluate and define rules and regulations of free trade agreements within frameworks of national development plans; and to protect natural resources including small family farms.

Lastly, in order to reduce and eventually eliminate social and economic inequalities, the following alternatives are proposed: promote improved standardization of rights and laws, including those pertaining to insecticide use, emissions and transfers of pollutants, and labor standards; institute a tax on revenues from international financial transactions to endow investment in education, health, and job training; forgive foreign debt; promote aid to developing countries; compensate women and various racial and ethnic groups previously exploited; and recognize indigenous rights to land and resources.

Following Catholic social teaching on the economy, the *Alternatives* document also includes directives on the following categories: human rights, labor, investment, agriculture, gender, environmental protection, and immigration.

First, the report states that human rights should be promoted by economic integration. These rights constitute civil, political, economic, social, cultural, and environmental rights including rights specific to women, children, and indigenous peoples.

Next, labor issues should be included in trade agreements. Basic workers rights should be guaranteed, ensuring adequate social assistance to those negatively impacted by globalization. Labor standards and living standards should be improved.

Third, investment should be productive rather than speculative, should transfer appropriate technology, and should create high quality employment. Governments should have the right to curtail investments that do not further development or are detrimental to human labor and environmental rights.

Fourth, agriculture should have high priority in trade agreements. To ensure food security, nations should have the right to protect or exclude various foodstuffs from agreements. Property rights need to be respected. Small-scale farming needs special protection regarding land conservation, appropriate technology (including biotechnology), agricultural research, credit, and subsidies. Also, trade agreements must improve the standardization of financial assistance for agriculture.

Fifth, women from all levels of society should be included and engaged in trade debates and negotiations. Trade agreements should ensure that women have equal access to needed resources such as credit, technological training, and land. Likewise, laws and policies should provide assistance to promote education, technological training, and skills development for women.

Sixth, environmental protections should be prioritized over corporate interests. Trade agreements should recognize government rights to direct investment toward environmentally sustainable activities, prohibit the privatization of natural resources, and eliminate policies that subsidize fossil fuel energy.

And finally, all trade negotiations should address immigration issues. Governments should grant amnesty to undocumented workers, demilitarize border zones, and support international subsidies for regions and countries that are major exporters of labor.

In conclusion, the challenge is not insurmountable. The change of priorities requires a change of heart. And a change of heart brings a change of mind.

When the world's economic leaders are converted so that they see every man, woman, and child as brothers and sisters, then the genius of our human history and the insight of our moral wisdom will guide our transformation from an economy of the few to an economy of the many. It is then that we will have begun to build the road to an economic justice for all.

Notes

1. National Conference of Catholic Bishops, *Economic Justice for All: Pastoral Letter on Catholic Social Teaching and the U.S. Economy*, 1986.

2. Walter M. Abbott, ed. *Documents of Vatican II* (New York: America Press, 1966); Pope John XXIII, *Mater et Magistra*, 1961.

3. United Nations Development Programme, *Human Development Report,* 2006.

4. John Iceland, *Poverty in America: A Handbook,* 2nd ed. (Berkeley: University of California Press, 2006).

5. Jimmy Carter, *Our Endangered Values: America's Moral Crisis* (New York: Simon & Schuster, 2005).

6. Joseph E. Stiglitz, *Globalization and Its Discontents* (New York: W. W. Norton, 2002); idem, *Making Globalization Work* (New York: W. W. Norton, 2006); and Joseph E. Stiglitz and Andrew Charlton, *Fair Trade for All: How Trade Can Promote Development* (New York: Oxford University Press, 2005).

7. John Cavanagh and Jerry Mander, eds., *Alternatives to Economic Globalization: A Better World Is Possible,* 2nd ed. (San Francisco: Berrett-Koehler Publishers, 2004); Jeffrey D. Sachs, *The End of Poverty: Economic Possibilities for Our Time* (New York: Penguin Press, 2005).

8. *The Alternatives for the Americas.* Available from *www.art-us.org/Alternatives _for_the_Americas.*

5

Setting Aside
Some Economic Paradigms

ALEJANDRO C. LLORENTE

Our economies have often become a scenario for the use of abusive power and hidden violence: an impersonal, anonymous setting that favors alienation from oneself and from everyone else, where the Other in any transaction becomes an instrument of one's own economic interests.

Why do people behave differently in the world of business than among their families and friends? We might say, at first glance, that the prevailing scientific theories model the behavior of economic agents. But I think the issue is more complex. The theories themselves are modeled by human phenomena.

This presentation, from the viewpoint of a moral theologian, seeks to interpret critically the background underlying the prevailing way of conceiving and conducting the economy in my country (Argentina). In the words of Duncan Foley, a different way of describing reality can lead to a different way of living it:

> It will not be easy to create a social science that transcends the antinomies and limitations of rational-actor theory. Certainly we cannot depend on the "usual" processes of scientific self-criticism to accomplish much in this direction. No accumulation of its empirical anomalies or demonstration of its logical inadequacies will somehow magically dispel the power of rational-actor theory. Its power does not rest in the last instance on the adequacy of its explanations or the consistency of its logic. The creation of a more fertile economics will require us to live differently. As Hegel points out, this means essentially to think differently, since those who think differently are already living a different life.[1]

The Economy, a Product of Meaning

Economic activity is characterized by the logic of equivalence. In the last analysis, the search for equivalence in the quantities to be exchanged reveals the presence of "difference." We seek equivalence because the goods to be exchanged are not entirely symmetrical. Exchange is made possible by reducing unequal things to a measurable, quantifiable unit. Although this is a necessary operation, we should not forget that it always involves a reduction of the economic event.

The economy as a human interaction is a cultural event, which generates meaning with reference to the production and consumption of the goods brought together in the exchange: it is part of the cultural-symbolic activity of human beings. What makes societies different (primitive, bourgeois, etc.) is not their symbolic nature, but the focal points of their symbolism. Whereas the symbolic focus in primitive societies was family relationships and religion, in bourgeois society it is the economy.

Many economists share the illusion that economies are constituted pragmatically, that is, exclusively on the basis of their material goods. This "naïve ignorance" of other goods is worth analyzing. In Western culture, the economy is the first and most important arena of symbolic construction. That is, the economy itself is the symbol: it is what determines the structure of our lives.[2]

The cultural-symbolic nature of the economy is like its creator: human beings are symbolic animals. All their activities take place within the production of meaning. This nature is also rooted in the "economic" dimension of human life: people need to express their inexhaustible desire for "being-unto-death" in interdependence with others. Economics and symbols are existential traits of human nature.[3]

Economics and Modernity

The problem of reducing the meaning of the economy as science and as praxis must be seen in the context of modernity. By adopting doubt as a method, people came to believe only in what they could subject to reason. For the first time, they could not go beyond themselves.[4]

The advent of modernity in the scientific arena was characterized by the search for objectivity through method. Attention shifted from content (ends) to forms: the constitutive procedures, rules, and methods of knowledge. In the first half of the twentieth century, economics, politics, and sociology dominated the field of praxis in place of practical philosophy.

The distinction was made between "facts" and "values." One cannot have the certainty with regard to values that science has when it studies the facts and explains them in terms of laws. For Max Weber, the social sciences are unevaluative: they must remain neutral with regard to values. The concept of economics as a "value-free" science meant, among other things, replacing practical reason with theoretical reason in the Aristotelian sense.[5]

The paradigm adopted by the neoclassical theory of a competitive market was based on a static, closed, and deterministic world. Its mechanistic approach postulated a narrow and rigid anthropological model whose only motive was self-interest, identified as economic benefit: *homo oeconomicus.* Economic interests were related to a poorly and narrowly understood self.[6]

When the motive of activity is postulated in this way, choice becomes something mechanical. Economic science is made equivalent to a "hard" science and human freedom, the principal escape of the system, is assured.

A Theological-Existential Hermeneutic

Homo oeconomicus, the symbol of modernity in the economic field, is the very antithesis of gratuitousness. That is, it represents a "reductionist" interpretation of economic phenomena in two ways. It reduces economic events to a quantitative measure, and it explains the motivation of economic activity exclusively in terms of egoistic self-interest.

We might wonder with Marcel Hénaff whether this icon of modernity masks the pretension of doing away with gods, gifts, and debts. Perhaps reducing everything to the quantifiable is an attempt to do away with "the priceless." Perhaps it represents a veiled search for a state of material innocence in which there is no fault or sin, no gift or pardon.[7]

If the phenomenon of *homo oeconomicus* is interpreted existentially, we encounter three fundamental problems: identity is walled off, otherness is denied, and meaning is exhausted.

The naked Adam (Gen. 3:1–24) is the result of the perennial human attempt to take control of one's origins: "You will be like gods." When Adam tries to take what cannot be taken, what can only be given, he distorts his image. His flesh is no longer the carrier of an original otherness, of a "presence beyond himself." Reduced to oneness, he owes no one anything and carries only a self-referential desire.

The symbiotic Adam (Gen. 4:1–16) is the metaphor for the unbearable otherness to which human beings are called. Abel reminds Cain that he is not the only son. Killing one's brother is a way of rejecting difference. What is involved here is the question of the different other and the fantasy of the omnipotent "I."

The Adam of Babel (Gen. 11:1–9) shows the problem of language as a vehicle of the meaning of existence. The goal of a single language represents the wish to silence the resonance of difference in words, the illusion of exhausting the meaning of reality by totally identifying the signifier with the meaning.

We must ask whether these reductions are also present when we understand the motive of economic activity exclusively as selfish interest (the anthropological reduction), competition as warfare (overwhelming the

Other), and the other spheres of human life exclusively within the logic of self-interest (the economy as a single meaning).

Thinking in Terms of Gratuitousness

Economic Activity

Economic activity has multiple aspects; complex thinking about it depends on the underlying epistemology. Certain limitations of economic science can be overcome only by thinking about economic activity beyond the quantitative terms of equivalency (prices expressed in currency).

Even under ideal bargaining conditions between the parties, an exchange involves more than price. The terms of exchange are only one way to bring together goods or services that do not fit a quantitative measure: evaluating a good means entering the world of subjective appreciation. Quantification obviously makes the exchange possible. Nevertheless, it should not be understood in absolute terms. The price is only a tangible approximation of a good that — although it is material — always carries the symbolic value we attribute to it.

Thinking about an exchange in terms of this "asymmetry" of the unit of measurement does not mean denying its validity, but rather relativizing it. We are not denying the practical value of the measurement, but acknowledging that it is imperfect. In this perspective there are no closed transactions. Economic actions are characterized by a fundamental, ontological asymmetry, to which the asymmetries of the market are only appendages.

If the transaction is not entirely covered by the established price, then we can say it remains in some way open. This opening is the space for a different way of thinking about the action. In thinking about the epistemology of economics, it is important to remember that this is an inexact science that attempts to explain realities that go beyond quantitative measurement.

The Motives of the Rational Agent

It is useless to postulate the complexity of economic activity unless we do the same with the motives of the rational agent. What is involved here is the underlying anthropology.

If an action can have more than one logic, we should be able to think articulately about both self-interest and gratuitousness. Gratuitousness is a kind of "wound" at the heart of self-interest, which opens it to other dimensions and prevents it from selfishly closing in on itself.

Self-interest is the unavoidable motive of action; this does not mean it is the only motive, or that it cannot be combined with other interests. Human "subsistence," unlike that of animals, is called to be transfigured into "existence," and this in turn can become "pro-existence." If subsistence is open to pro-existence, perhaps that opening is the place to think about interest as relational or reciprocal interest (*inter-esse*).

Thinking about gratuitousness poses a series of "disconnects" in our concept of economic activity and motives. These breaks highlight some thought-provoking aspects: transcendence, debt, and relationship. Such thinking transcends measurement that equalizes the goods of exchange, leaving the economic relationship open to other possible types of linkage; it relativizes the price as a quantitative measure, showing that there is always an unresolved remainder; it factors into the motive a reference to the other, without whom life would be mere subsistence.

Policies Supporting Gratuitousness

The way to encourage another way of doing economics must be based above all on "policies" that guide, motivate, and energize specific economic measures. But these measures will be useless until society resolves the question of how it wants to live.

If we want to change our way of life, we must accept the risks and costs that this entails. To move in this direction may involve a level of "exposure" that we are not all prepared to assume. The struggle for survival feeds the imagery of death and strongly affects the economic behavior of individuals and countries.

This raises the unconscious aspects of decision-making as a fundamental theme. Although we cannot directly change this dimension, we can influence it indirectly. It is possible to inspire and reward certain ways of doing business that help to channel energy toward more cooperative ends.

Today we see increasingly clear signs of the need to relate business with the needs of society. Demands for corporate citizenship or social responsibility suggest that a well-formed and informed society requires certain standards. These are not measured by business profitability, but by the way such a society wants to live. The ecological issue is a clear example, but not the only one.

Thinking about policies is above all a cultural undertaking, to influence the direction we want the culture and the economy to take. So in order to think about specific economic measures, we must first ask about the way we want to live our lives.

Some Presuppositions

To affirm the possibility of a new vision, paradigm, strategy, or attitude does not mean affirming its reality. Theoretical possibility is one thing, facts are another.

Since the economy is a system of interconnected channels, change will be possible and sustainable only if these policies work across national borders. To think of the economy in a planetary perspective means proposing and agreeing on better ways of life for everyone. This is not an easy task if we also consider cultural differences. It is, so to speak, a "top-down" politics.

A strategy of basic interregional, intercontinental, or international agreements is absolutely necessary. Nevertheless I believe that the most important part begins from below. Preference should be given to a "bottom-up" politics, influencing such leading actors as consumers, investors, and corporations. The best regulations are useless without prior change in everyday behavior.

Measures Supporting Gratuitousness

By "measures" I mean that which leads to a change of mentality, the soil in which specific economic measures grow. The decision to live in a different way is both cause and effect of a great educational task, whose principal agents are the family, the state, educational institutions, and the economic and other institutions of civil society. They are the source of the lifestyles, public and private, that lead to economic decision-making. Here I shall suggest some actions which, although diverse, are complementary and involve some of these agents.

Teaching

Let us look at the reasons for teaching and promoting certain economic models. Economists are not immune to the influence of their own cultures: worldviews, interests, and powers. Also, economics is a human science and its models are fallible. Many early economic axioms presupposed certain scenarios, contexts, and anthropological models as indispensable for the verification of those axioms. If the presuppositions change, the result of applying the axiom will also change.

Economic rationality is definitely rooted in human decision-making. This means that the economy is not a *fatum*, destiny, but a human creation. Thus there is no one model of a rational decision-maker; there may be as many rationalities as there are people. The reasons why people choose depend on their real possibilities: human (real personal freedom), cultural (education for responsibility), economic (access to goods), the information they possess, and the level of real freedom in the market.

Demythologizing

Where I live, certain "myths" have become uncritically established as dogma. To mention a few at random: competitiveness and the maximization of benefit are held sacred as the only criteria by which to judge the health of a corporation; competitors are demonized and threatened with elimination; more corporate growth is always considered good, so long as regulations and the markets allow it; lower profit is seen as a sign of failure even when it means a better life; what cannot be measured is considered irrelevant, and economic incentives are seen as the leading motivation for all people; inefficiency is seen as the only cause of displacement from the market.

These and other myths — along with technological progress and the idea of the self-sufficient subject — have slowly erased the idea of limits, balance, cooperation with others, and self-renunciation. In its place — along with a developed, western anthropological type — we see the imagery of Narcissus and Prometheus, hybridized into a new genetic species: *homo oeconomicus,* detached from everything but its insatiable hunger for more.

Informing

The responsible formation of persons must go together with clear information about the consequences of the small economic decisions we make every day. Human history shows again and again that the separation of decision-making from its consequences diminishes and even erases personal responsibility. Decisions by millions of uninformed persons, both as consumers and as investors, are the breeding ground that generates unjust economic structures.

Transforming

Is it possible to transform certain economic axioms? Yes, if we work simultaneously on both the internal and external aspects of persons. Negative economic behaviors result from a disconnect between the scarcest resource — life — and the most unlimited desire — to live. The pressures of greed, accumulation, incest, and self-defense merely reflect a fearful and ill-conceived resolution of the anguish we feel in the face of our own mortality. In the life of the market, this manifests itself as monopolization, savage marketing, lobbying, false advertising, fraud, harassment, etc.; that is, an alienated way of life in which the people do not know the true reasons behind their actions.

Thus, education must help us to accept our own finiteness and to integrate others into our subjectivity. This requires self-renunciation, dependence on others, and concern for their well-being. It does not deny such values of economic rationality as efficiency, productivity, development, etc.; rather, it integrates them into a broader worldview. However, in view of human weakness, any educational policy must be accompanied by measures to encourage and reward good practices and to discourage and punish bad practices.

— *English translation by Margaret D. Wilde*

Notes

1. Duncan K. Foley, "Rationality and Ideology in Economics," *Social Research* 71, no. 2 (Summer 2004): 341.

2. Marshall Sahlins, *Cultura y razón práctica* (Barcelona: Gedisa, 1997), 204–9.

3. Christian Arnsperger, *Critique de l'existence capitaliste: Pour une ethique existentielle de l'economie* (Paris: Cerf, 2006), 34–37.

4. Hugo Mujica, "La nueva era del viejo yo," in *La etica del compromiso: Los principios en tiempos de desvergüenza* (Buenos Aires: GEA-Fundación OSDE, 2002), 118–19.

5. Ricardo Crespo, *La economía como ciencia moral: Nuevas perspectivas de la teoría económica* (Buenos Aires: Educa, 1997), 116–43.

6. Peter Koslowski, *Principes d'economie ethique* (Paris: Cerf, 1998), 70–71.

7. Marcel Hénaff, *Le prix de la vérité: Le don, l'Argent, la philosophie* (Paris: Editions du Seuil, 2002), 33.

A Ringing Endorsement of Capitalism?

The Influence of the Neo-liberal Agenda on Official Catholic Social Teaching

JOHAN VERSTRAETEN

One of the most striking developments in official Catholic social teaching[1] since the pontificate of John Paul II is its more positive attitude with regard to capitalism, the market, profit, and competition.

In this essay I will demonstrate that both *Centesimus annus* (*CA*) and the *Compendium of the Social Doctrine of the Church* (*CSDC*) offer no "ringing endorsement," but express only a very conditional approval of capitalism based on the priority of work and the universal destination of the goods. This, however, does not exclude the fact that the neo-liberal agenda has gained influence, particularly with regard to the Magisterium's teaching on the state and justice. We will demonstrate that a striking parallel exists between the radical rejection of the social-assistance state and the subordination of justice to a discourse on love and solidarity defined as social love.

Centesimus Annus: A Turning Point

In a triumphant article published in the *Wall Street Journal* of May 3–4, 1991, Richard John Neuhaus labels *Centesimus annus* as "a ringing endorsement of the market economy," an endorsement in which capitalism would have become "the economic corollary of the Christian understanding of man's nature and destiny." Despite the impact of this interpretation on the business community, it is a far from correct presentation of the encyclical's nuanced vision.

Chapter 4 of Centesimus annus on "Private Property and the Universal Destination of the Material Goods"

The explicit positive attitude of chapter 4 of *Centesimus annus* with regard to capitalism, the free market, and profit is obviously a new development in official Catholic social teaching, particularly when compared with the predominantly negative approach in the encyclical *Populorum progressio* (*PP*).

Despite its "elitist" approach, *Populorum progressio* paved the way to incorporating the "third world" agenda into Catholic social teaching ,[2] while liberal capitalism is criticized in extraordinary sharp terms.

With words that recapitulate almost literally the judgment of *Quadragesimo anno* (part 3), written two years after the Wall Street crash, Paul VI rejects "unbridled liberalism" because it would pave "the way for a particular type of tyranny" and lead to "the international imperialism of money" (*PP* no. 26). According to him "the principle of free trade, by itself, is no longer adequate for regulating international agreements." And he expresses great doubts regarding the justice of price mechanisms: "Market prices that are freely agreed upon, can turn out to be most unfair" (*PP* no. 58).

When compared with *Populorum progressio*, *Centesimus annus* marks a real difference. As most commentators have rightly observed, it is the first time that the Magisterium explicitly praises the free market as an efficient tool for the utilization or allocation of resources (*CA* no. 34) and it interprets profit as a legitimate indicator of a well-run company (*CA* no. 35).

Capitalism is explicitly justified insofar as it is "an economic system which recognizes the fundamental and positive role of business, the market, private property, and the resulting responsibility for the means of production, as well as free human creativity in the economic sector" (*CA* no. 42). More than a decade after *Centesimus annus* the *Compendium of the Social Doctrine of the Church* reinforced the viewpoint of *Centesimus annus* by adding a reflection in which not only the market, but a "*competitive* market" is justified as an effective instrument "for attaining important *objectives of justice*" (*CSDC* no. 347). This interpretation does not rely on previous papal texts, but is justified by a hermeneutic of the word *cumpetere* as "a seeking together of the most appropriate solutions for responding in the best way to needs as they emerge" (*CSDC* no. 343).

None of the above mentioned documents, however, supports the free market unconditionally. On the contrary, particularly in *Centesimus annus*, the judgment is very conditional and framed in a most interesting reflection on work as the origin of property. This reflection is articulated in a communitarian language. Work is defined as "work with others and work for others" or "doing something for someone else," and the text refers also to the fact that a person's work is "naturally interrelated with the work of others" (*CA* no. 31). Work is also framed in terms of "a community of work" and "the cooperation of many people in working for a common goal." This is a significant reinterpretation of the possessive individualistic interpretation of work and property by Locke.

We can, moreover, discern several nuances in the text on the free market.

First, the language is very prudent. John Paul II does not write that the market *is* the most efficient means, but: "It *would appear that* the market is the most efficient instrument for utilizing resources and effectively responding to needs" (*CA* no. 34). This nuance has disappeared in the compendium.

The first remark is followed by a double condition: it is only true "for needs that are solvent," meaning: needs which people can meet only if they have purchasing power, and the efficiency of the market is valid only for "marketable goods" (*CA* no. 34). The first nuance reflects Amartya Sen's insight that famines are not caused by a lack of food but by the lack of purchasing power to buy food or by a lack of empowerment to provide oneself with food. The second nuance echoes Michael Walzer's idea of blocked goods, those that are not legitimate objects of market transactions such as weapons or human organs.[3]

A third argument is both that there are needs that the market cannot meet and that, prior to the logic of fair exchange of goods together with their forms of justice (which is an implicit reference to the limits of commutative justice), there is something that must be accorded to people on the basis of their dignity as human beings (*CA* no. 34). This is an implicit reference to distributive justice.

A fourth argument is that the pope clearly states that of itself an economic system does not posses "criteria for correctly distinguishing new and higher forms of satisfying human needs" from "artificial new needs which hinder the formation of a mature personality" (*CA* no. 36). It is therefore necessary to develop new lifestyles.

A fifth argument refers to both the human and the natural environment (*CA* nos. 38–40). Pope John Paul II fully acknowledges the weaknesses of the market, and more or less in contradiction with the spirit of what he wrote on the state in chapter 5, he affirms that "it is the *task of the state to provide for the defence and preservation of common goods* such as the natural and human environments *which cannot be safeguarded simply by market forces*" (emphasis added). He even adds: "Just as in the time of primitive capitalism, when the state had the duty of defending the basic rights of workers, so now, with the new capitalism, the state and all of society have the duty of defending those collective goods which . . . constitute the essential framework for the legitimate pursuit of personal goals on the part of each individual" (*CA* no. 40).

Sixth, with regard to the property of the means of production (that is, the ownership of land or stocks), he prioritizes the creation of useful work over profit. His words are extraordinarily sharp:

> Ownership of the means of production . . . is just and legitimate if it serves useful work. It becomes illegitimate, however, when it is not utilized or when it serves to impede the work of others in an effort to gain a profit which is not the result of the overall expansion of work and the wealth of society, but rather is the result of curbing

them or of illicit exploitation, speculation or the breaking of solidarity among working people. *Ownership of this kind has no justification and represents an abuse in the sight of God and man.* (CA no. 43; emphasis added)

This critical judgment is a logical consequence of the encyclical's interpretation of the theory of the market in light of a communitarian theory of work as the source of property. It is also a consequence of the traditional subordination of private property to the *usus communis rerum* (Thomas Aquinas) or the universal destination of the goods (clearly reaffirmed in official Catholic social teaching since Pius XII). In the *Compendium,* the priority of the common destination of the goods is explicitly and directly linked to the principle of the common good, a point of view that is also maintained by the *Catechism of the Catholic Church.*

Seventh, precisely in the paragraph on profit, John Paul II states that profitability is not the *only* indicator of a firm's condition, since it is possible that the financial accounts are in order while people "who make up the firms most valuable asset" are "humiliated and their dignity offended" (*CA* no. 35). The goal of a business "is to be found in its very existence as a community of persons who in various ways are endeavoring to satisfy their basic needs and who form a particular group at the service of the whole of society" (*CA* no. 35). Again, the theory of work defined as "working with and for others" is crucial here.

Based on all the aforementioned arguments we can conclude that chapter 4 is far from a *"ringing* endorsement of capitalism." Chapter 5 of the same encyclical, however, is a different case.

The Condemnation of the Social-Assistance State in chapter 5 of Centesimus annus: A Neo-liberal Correction?

In this chapter the tone changes, despite the fact that its core is still expressing the best of the social tradition of the church insofar as it rightly rejects the reduction of politics to merely a relationship between individuals and the state (*CA* no. 49). It reflects the classical concern for a living civil society based on the principle of subsidiarity.

But, in a rather astonishing manner, this interpretation is linked to a highly problematic criticism of the *social assistance* state. The *Compendium* later extends this criticism to the whole of the *welfare* state: "Solidarity without subsidiarity can easily *degenerate* into the *welfare state*" (*CSDC* no. 351). This judgment, one assumes, will not be given a warm welcome in the Scandinavian countries. This criticism is followed by the suggestion that *active charity* and *volunteer work* are the most adequate solutions.

Volunteer work is of course necessary, especially because there are always needs and tears the bureaucracy cannot see. Likewise, is it meaningful to criticize some of the negative effects of bureaucratization and the increase of costs in social assistance states.

But what disquiets me the most is the fact that on the level of a universal text (an encyclical) the social assistance state is criticized without any attempt at nuance or adequate definition, and without paying attention to its historical background and real context. Is it fair to condemn *the* social assistance state, knowing that in some countries not even the most essential forms of a health care system or of social protection are realized? Is this radical rejection of the welfare state, combined with a plea for voluntary work, not pouring grain on the mill of neo-liberals and libertarians who oppose absolutely any sort of state intervention in the sphere of distributive justice?

Moreover, the description of the social assistance state is so alien to its reality that only a sort of straw-man image is in fact rejected. In countries like, e.g., Belgium or Germany, the social assistance state is the historical result of precisely free self-organization on the level of the civil society, and even in its actual form it combines state intervention with the contribution of health care insurance organizations based on a plurality of religious and ideological convictions, such as Catholic health care insurances (mutualities) and unions. In other terms, the real social assistance state is, at least in Europe, not necessarily incompatible with the requirements of subsidiarity, as was wisely acknowledged in *Mater et Magistra* (*MM*). According to Pope John XXIII, state intervention is sometimes necessary for the sake of the realization of social rights. His key word in this regard was "socialization," defined as "an increase in social relationships" (*MM* no. 59) and "a symptom and a cause of the growing intervention of the state" (*MM* no. 60). John XXIII was inspired to use the concept of *socialization* by the Semaines Sociales de France, where it was introduced by Pierre Bigo. Although both acknowledge that socialization is not devoid of risk, the main point of John XXIII was that it "brings many advantages in its train" and that it makes "it possible for the individual to exercise many of his personal rights, especially those which we call economic and social and which pertain to the necessities of life, health care, education . . . professional training, housing, work, and suitable leisure and recreation" (*MM* no. 61). A not unimportant detail in this regard is that in the *Catechism of the Catholic Church* and in the *Compendium of the Social Doctrine of the Church,* the meaning of socialization has been changed into "the objectives of *voluntary associations*" where "the qualities of the person, especially the sense of initiative and responsibility," are developed (*CSDC* no. 151, quote from the Catechism 1882).

Last but not least, voluntary work as suggested by *Centesimus annus* is necessary but not sufficient: problems of distributive justice require adequate legislation and intervention (as *Centesimus annus* acknowledges explicitly in chapter 4). For example, a free market of health care insurances will tend to exclude people with high health risks or those whose health care becomes too expensive.

The problem behind an unnuanced condemnation of the social assistance state is not only that it matches the liberalization agenda of neo-liberal capitalism and the ideology behind the former structural adjustments programs of the IMF, but that *Centesimus annus* appears to be influenced by the text of *Towards the Future*. Written as a critique of the first draft of the U.S. bishops' letter *Economic Justice for All*, this text reflects the ideas of Michael Novak, William Simon, and "twenty-nine other Catholic laypersons,"[4] a pressure group with clear links to the American Enterprise Institute and its interests. The similarities are striking: the lay letter declares itself to be "sceptical of entrusting planning to the state," for according to the writers there is no government on the planet capable of directing free men and women,"[5] and it insists on the primacy of freedom over justice as well as on the primacy of the "liberty of *voluntary* cooperation." I will return to this striking parallel later.

The crux of the matter: the partially neo-liberal critique of the social assistance state running parallel with a tendency to sacrifice the discourse on justice to a discourse on love and solidarity defined as social love.

This is especially visible in the *Compendium of the Social Doctrine of the Church*.

The Compendium of the Social Doctrine of the Church: Charity as Substitute for Justice?

Chapter 4 of the *Compendium* develops an idea that is quite alien to both the history of official Catholic social teaching and Catholic social thought as tradition. A remarkable distinction is made between principles and values. According to the *Compendium*, the principles of "Catholic social doctrine" are the dignity of the human person and the common good; linked in a most interesting manner to it, the universal destination of goods; subsidiarity; in an original manner linked with participation; and solidarity.

These "principles" are subsequently distinguished from "fundamental values of social life," which are defined quite vaguely as "an expression of appreciation to be attributed to those specific aspects of moral good that these principles foster, serving as *points of reference* for the proper structuring and ordered leading of life in society." They are: truth, freedom, justice, love.

I consider this distinction to be problematic in more than one regard.

First, in classical Catholic ethics, justice and love are interpreted as virtues and not values.

Second, in order to justify its distinction, the *Compendium* refers to the *Catechism of the Catholic Church* paragraph 1886. But this text refers to the necessity of a hierarchy of values in general and does not refer to the distinction between values and principles.

Third, the *Compendium* is not always consistent when it applies its distinction. At least once, justice is called a criterion (283) and elsewhere solidarity is called a value.

Fourth, it is strange that only two pages are devoted to justice (and even there the text partially refers to solidarity), while social justice is summarized in less than two lines. This is quite far from the teaching of *Quadragesimo anno*, in which, despite its focus on solidarity and the peaceful cooperation of classes, "social justice" is a key concept linked to the common good. Moreover, while there are only two lines on social justice, there are, in the *Compendium*, twenty-five pages on the family. This can hardly be considered a very balanced treatment of *social* ethics.

Fifth, the link between freedom and justice follows the suggestion made by the already mentioned lay letter *against* the first draft of the U.S. bishop's letter *Economic Justice for All*. In this controversial letter Novak et al. write: "We humbly propose as a motto for the church in this new age, *not solely justice and peace, but liberty, justice and peace*. The liberty of *voluntary* cooperation. The liberty of providence. Liberty under law, liberty suffused with moral purpose. Liberty, in the end, is *the contribution of the experience of the United States to the social teaching of the Catholic Church*."[6]

The problem is not that justice is linked with liberty, nor that the *Compendium* would offer a libertarian interpretation of freedom. But it is disquieting with regard to the theme "justice with freedom," that more attention is paid to representatives of a U.S. pressure group than to *Economic Justice for All*, the excellent document of the National Conference of Catholic Bishops. In this regard, the *Compendium* is, unfortunately, consistent with its own ecclesiological vision, since it reasserts that, although the bishops are carrying "the primary responsibility for the pastoral commitment to evangelize social realities," they have *only* the task of *"promoting* the teaching and diffusion of the Church's social doctrine" (539; emphasis added). This is a denial of the consensus reached during the 1993 conference at the University of Fribourg, organized on the occasion of the presentation of the *Répertoire des documents épiscopaux des cinq continents* (1891–1991).[7] During that conference, Cardinal Etchegaray, former president of the Pontifical Council for Justice and Peace, gave his explicit support to taking the bishops' "ministry" with regard to social teaching more seriously. He criticized the unilateral focus on papal texts.[8] He also declared that the social teaching of the bishops will be "more and more continental and regional" and suggested the possibility of documents "edited by both the bishops of the North and the South."[9] Moreover, he explicitly criticized the fact that the social discourse of the church is "still too much western," and he proposed a new conference, one that would pay attention to the texts of the laity. And he even pleaded for more ecumenical initiatives. According to

Cardinal Etchegaray, speaking in the spirit of *Gaudium et spes* and *Octogesima adveniens,* "Ecumenical declarations are not less from the Church than a strict catholic declaration."[10]

Is it not surprising that, despite the consensus among many of the most prominent bishops and experts in Catholic social thought, the *Compendium,* moving away from the spirit of the post–Vatican II era, appears to have learned nothing from the bishops, particularly with regard to justice? And on the basis of that criteria can a letter of a pressure group command more authority than the U.S. bishops' letter *Economic Justice for All,* in which perhaps the most interesting re-interpretation of the Thomistic justice triad was made (with special attention to contributive and social justice)?

This brings me, last but not least, to the problem of the explicit subordination of justice to love. In the *Compendium,* love is described as "the highest and universal criterion of the *whole* of social ethics" (204), as something that "presupposes and transcends justice" (206). The *Compendium* also contends that *"only* love, in its quality of form of the virtues [this part refers to Thomas Aquinas, ST, IIa-IIae q. 23 a. 8] *can animate and shape social interaction"* (emphasis added).

This approach differs fundamentally from earlier encyclicals, such as *Populorum progressio,* where solidarity, justice, and love are mentioned as equivalent principles expressing different aspects. In this encyclical, solidarity is defined as "the aid that the richer nations must give to developing nations" (44), while social justice is described as "the [structural] rectification of trade relations between strong and weak nations" (44) and as "equality of opportunity" (61). Universal charity is defined in terms of "the effort to build a more humane world community, where all can give and receive" (*PP* no. 44).

After *Populorum progressio,* under the influence of the Consejo Episcopal Latinoamericano (Latin American Episcopal Conference) meeting at Medellín in 1968 and liberation theology with its awareness of structural injustice, there was perhaps a tendency to focus too exclusively on justice. But in the final text of the general synod on justice, *Justice in the World (JW),* there is still a clear balance between justice and charity. On the one hand the text proclaims that "action on behalf of *justice* and participation in the transformation of the world fully appear to us as a constitutive [erroneously translated in Dutch and German as 'essential'] dimension of the preaching of the gospel, or, in other words, of the Church's mission for the redemption of the human race and its liberation from every oppressive situation" (*JW* no. 6). On the other hand, the synod fathers of 1971 proclaimed liberation and *justice* from the perspective of the insight that "unless the Christian message of *love and justice* shows its effectiveness through action in the cause of *justice* in the world, it will only with difficulty gain credibility with the men of our times" (*JW* no. 35).

The problem is that the discourse of the 1971 synod on social structures and on "the observance of the *duties of justice*" (*JW* no. 30) has been gradually replaced by an almost exclusive discourse on solidarity and love in which the institutional and structural approach is made subordinate to a more individual and intersubjective approach.

I am not suggesting that the justice discourse became completely neglected, nor that the enthusiasm for the free market and the corporate world completely dominates Catholic Social Teaching. On the contrary, even in the *Compendium* — and particularly in the chapters and paragraphs on work, the universal destination of goods, and peace — the attitude is and remains critical.

Nor do I want to suggest that the synod text of 1971 has been the last great text on justice: this would be denial of the fact that the justice discourse of 1971 has continued to resonate, for example in *Evangelii nuntiandi,* paragraph 30, where a paragraph from *Justice in the World* on the duty of the church to bring liberation is repeated, and paragraph 31, which clearly states that charity cannot be proclaimed without promoting in justice and in peace the true, authentic advancement of man. Moreover, during his entire pontificate, John Paul II continuously repeated that justice and love cannot be separated from one another.

The point, however, is that the Magisterium appears to have moved away from a balanced approach and has gradually subordinated justice to love and solidarity (often defined as "social love" or "political love"). In the *Compendium,* the task of "organizing and structuring society" has become mainly a matter of "social love."

Conclusion

Contemporary Christian social ethics has demonstrated that the relationship between love and justice cannot be adequately understood without acknowledging their dialectics. From the perspective of both Thomistic thinking and Ricoeur, Catholic social teaching must acknowledge that it is not sufficient to build communities based merely on charity and love, since for their realization, *just institutions* are necessary. Social ethics refers not only to intersubjective relationships, as the *Compendium* suggests, since it is rooted in the longing to live a good life with and for others *in the context of just institutions.*[11] Without these just institutions no human *polis* can be built.

On the other hand, official Catholic social teaching is right when it warns against the fact that just institutions often abstract from the concrete "face of the other." While justice is oriented toward the "everyone" of the institutions, charity personalizes the abstract relationships of social justice. "In order to avoid that the 'to each' of just distribution would be reduced to the anonymous level of 'everyone' or to the reification of social relationships, the imagination of charity and its singularizing regard must see that the privilege of the face to face is extended to all relations with the others without face," which implies: charity requires justice.[12] Charity also radicalizes justice. As a Christian virtue, it can be a source of inspiration and continuing vigilance in view of a more just order, leading to a dynamic state of law that responds to the real needs of all citizens (including the development of their "capabilities to function"). In this regard, it is not correct to make justice subordinate to love.

A too exclusive discourse on charity or solidarity, defined as "social love," is problematic and, willingly or unwillingly, grain on the mill of the neo-liberal agenda, as is the tendency to pay more attention to documents written by interest groups serving the corporate world than to bishops' conferences articulating a genuine concern for the poor and for just structures. In fact, the influence of these bishops' conferences on official documents of the Magisterium appears to have become severely limited.

If the Magisterium of the Catholic Church would continue to focus on charity and love at the cost of a discourse on justice, this might become an ultimate victory of the neo-liberal agenda on Catholic social teaching. It would imply a shift from a genuine concern for justice and the real needs of people to a discourse that can be summarized in terms of the libertarian device articulated by Robert Nozick as: "from each as they choose to each as they are chosen." It would make the poor again the objects of paternalistic benevolence and no longer the carriers of inherent rights that must be protected by the state and the civil society (including social rights as proposed by *Mater et Magistra* and *Pacem in terris*).

I am strongly convinced, however, that the wisdom of Catholic social thought as a living social tradition will lead to the necessary corrections being made in the spirit of the words of Cardinal Etchegaray: "The Church offers simply a meeting with the Risen [Christ], with Him who both generates and fulfils a hunger for *justice* that is deeper than that of men."[13]

Notes

1. For a clarification of the difference between official Catholic social teaching and Catholic social thought, see Johan Verstraeten, "Re-thinking Catholic Social Thought as Tradition," in *Catholic Social Thought: Twilight or Renaissance?* ed. Jonathan S. Boswell, Frank P. McHugh, Johan Verstraeten, BETL 157 (Leuven: University Press/Peeters, 2000), 59–77.

2. See Donal Dorr, *Option for the Poor. A Hundred Years of Catholic Social Teaching* (Dublin: Gill and Macmillan, 1992; Maryknoll, N.Y.: Orbis Books, 1992): 179–204.

3. Michael Walzer, *Spheres of Justice* (New York: Basic Books, 1983).

4. Michael Novak, "The Two Catholic Letters on the U.S. Economy," in *Challenge and Response: Critiques of the Catholic Bishops' Draft Letter on the U.S.*

Economy, Ethics and Public Policy Essay 57 (Washington D.C.: Ethics and Public Policy Center, 1985), 31.

5. Michael Novak et al., "Toward the Future, Lay Commission on Catholic Social Teaching and the U.S. Economy," reprinted in abbreviated form in Novak, *Challenge and Response,* 27–28.

6. Novak, *Challenge and Response,* 29. Emphasis added.

7. The conference took place in Fribourg, Switzerland, from April 1–3, 1993. The proceedings were published: Roger Berthouzoz and Roberto Papini, eds., *Ethique, économie et développement: L'enseignement des évêques des cinq continents* (1891–1991), Etudes d'éthique chrétienne 62 (Fribourg: Editions Universitaires, Paris: Cerf, 1995). The reason for the conference was a project that was later published by Roger Berthouzoz, Roberto Papini, Carlos J. Pinto de Olivera, Ramon Sugranyes de Franch, eds., *Economie et developpement: Répertoire des documents épiscopaux des cinq continents* (1891–1991), Etudes d'éthqiue chrétienne 69 (Fribourg: Editions Universitaires; Paris: Cerf, 1997).

8. Berthouzoz and Papini, *Ethique, économie et développement,* 257.

9. Ibid., 258.

10. Ibid., 259.

11. Alain Thomasset, *Paul Ricoeur: Une poétique de la morale,* BETL 124 (Leuven: Peeters/University Press, 1996), 574.

12. Ibid., 572; Referring to Ricoeur's book *Théonomie et/ou autonomie* (p. 32), Thomasset writes "Pour éviter que le 'chacun' de la distribution ne glisse sur la pente de l'anonymat du 'on', ne revient-il pas alors à l'imagination de l'amour et à son regard singularisant d'étendre le privilège du face à face à tout les rapports avec les autrui(s) sans visage?"

13. Cardinal Roger Etchegaray, in Berthouzoz and Papini, *Ethique, économie et développement,* 262.

Compendium of the
Social Doctrine of the Church
and the Ethic of the Environment

KARL GOLSER

A Shared Vision

The new *Compendium of the Social Doctrine of the Church* (CSDC) attributes great importance to the environment. This is notable, especially if
one draws a comparison with the *Catechism of the Catholic Church* (CCC)
published twelve years earlier. The CCC dedicated four entire numbers
(2415–18) in the treatise of the seventh commandment — "You shall not
steal" — to "respect for the integrity of creation." The *CSDC*, however, has
dedicated the whole of chapter 10, covering almost twenty pages, to the
environmental question. The chapter is even longer than the one reserved
for the very important question of "the promotion of peace" (chapter 11).
Moreover the classical themes of the social doctrine of the church such as
"economic life" (chapter 7) or "the political community" (chapter 8) do not
even cover thirty pages.

The *CSDC* has chosen the "literary genre" of a "compendium," that is
to say, a kind of collection of the doctrine of the universal church. Although
a lengthier essay might explain the relation between moral theology and the
church's social doctrine, this is not something that we can provide here. [1]
Nevertheless, it is important to note that the *CSDC* does not intend to be an
aggregation of citations of the church's Magisterium, but rather an organic
exposition of the church's social doctrine. Its theological core is Christian
personalism, that is, a view of the human person as part of the human family
that is in solidarity with all other human beings (introduction, nos. 13–19),
one whose ultimate purpose and destination is Christ, the Word made flesh
(see *Gaudium et spes* 22). And it is in this context of love for all humanity
that the church has the mission, especially through its social doctrine (chapters 1 and 2), to announce the good news. Thus, the other social principles
are deduced from the personalist principle (chapters 3 and 4).[2]

The fact that the historical exposition of the evolution of the social doctrine is missing means that some of the complex philosophical, theological, and social dimensions of this emphasis on the "integral" human person are not made explicit. Moreover, this is seen in the *Compendium*'s treatment of the environment. For example, there is no reference to the "principle of sustainability," despite the fact that it has become a core unifying principle (arising from the Brundtland report of 1987 and from the International Conference of Rio de Janeiro in 1992). The principle of sustainable development begins with a vision of the global dependences and connects our responsibility for the present with that of future generations, and the problems of the developed countries with those of the developing. It proposes an action that, from the beginning, integrates economic, social, environmental, and political aspects, admitting therefore an integral vision between nature and culture. The human person, the cultural being par excellence, is seen as embedded in natural orders and structures, or — said in theological terms — the human is presented as God's creature together with other creatures also created by God and therefore having their own dignity.

The *CSDC* says correctly in no. 459 that the "respect of man and women ...must also be accompanied by a necessary attitude of respect for other living creatures," that "one must take into account the nature of each being and of its mutual connection in an ordered system," and "that we cannot interfere in one area of the ecosystem without paying due attention both to the consequences of such interference in other areas and to the well-being of future generations." Therefore, the concept of sustainability is implicitly present in some chapters, even if it is not made explicit.

It is interesting to point out that, unlike the CCC, the *CSDC*, even by emphasizing this human relationship to all creatures, has literally forgotten about animals. They are not mentioned in chapter 10 and the "analytical index" includes no reference to animals. By contrast, in its treatment the CCC has dedicated three out of the four paragraphs devoted to the respect for the integrity of creation to respect for animals (nos. 2416–18). It is difficult to understand this gap in the *CSDC*, especially given the contemporary importance of the animal question, including the much discussed problems of animal breeding and animal experiments.

One last observation on the shared vision: the ecological question, being a transversal argument, has been correctly treated also in other chapters of the *CSDC* in order to evolve a theological anthropology of responsibility for all creation.

Therefore, already in the first chapter "man and woman" are presented "in the garden where God has placed them as cultivators and custodians of the goods of creation" (26) and the following number (27) enumerates as one of the consequences of evil the "rupture... of the harmonious relations between mankind and other creatures." Once again, in the third chapter the text comes back to the relation between human beings and the other creatures, stating that "their dominion over the world requires the exercise of responsibility; it is not a freedom of arbitrary and selfish exploitation" (113). The same notion of common good also includes the protection of the environment (166), and in 170 there is even talk about the "universal common good of the whole of creation."

The Individual Arguments of Chapter 10

Chapter 10 is divided into four parts, presenting first the biblical aspects (451–55), considering afterward "man and the universe of created things" (456–60), highlighting as a third point "the crisis in the relationship between man and the environment" (461–65), and as a last argument confronting different specific ethical problems in a section entitled "a common responsibility." In this part, having emphasized that the environment is a common good (466–71), the text elaborates on the use of biotechnologies (472–80), on the relationship between the environment and economics (481–85), and finally on "new lifestyles" (486–87).

Given the vastness of the problem, I concentrate here on what is considered the foremost duty of the church: evangelization and testimony. In doing so, I will focus on two aspects: first the biblical foundation and, second, some aspects of our common responsibility.

The Biblical Foundation

The biblical part of chapter 10 of the *CSDC* dedicates two numbers to the Old Testament and three to the New Testament. Besides the already mentioned anthropological aspect of creation (that is to say that the relation with the world is a constituent element of human identity and that humanity bears responsibility for creation that is always an object of praise to the Lord), this section also emphasizes the eschatological aspect. This section focuses on the new creation and, most of all, on its finality, that is to say that everything has been created with regard to Jesus Christ and that therefore nature also participates in the drama of the Son of God and takes part in the renewal that takes place in the Easter of the Lord. "Nature, the work of God's creative action, is not a dangerous adversary. It is God who made all things, and with regard to each created reality 'God saw that it was good'" (451).

Here it is noted that some exegetes of great relevance (such as Gerhard von Rad) have contrasted the faith of Israel in a historical God, the "God of the armies," with the divinities of nature and fecundity, such as the Baal from the country of Kanaan, emphasizing that the biblical theme of creation entered the Bible quite late and has therefore been regarded as of secondary importance. One might say, as Paolo Carlotti did, that "the fact of creation, is chronologically first and theologically second,"[3] because the believer, embedded in a relationship with the God of the salvation, is praising him also for all the gifts connected with his existence. And one has to emphasize on the basis of recent exegetical studies that the theme of benediction is present from the beginning. "The Bible, in fact, does not...talk only of the God who comes in history, but also of the God who is present in daily life as benediction and lies at the origin of the same real good that we live in."[4]

Another point that needs emphasis is the issue of theodicy, which, according to the exegete Zenger, is the original *Sitz im Leben*. The first pages of the Bible rightly emphasize that both humanity and the world are counter-marked by evil, wickedness, and violence. Therefore the story of creation is intimately connected to the story of the deluge. While Genesis 1 describes and legitimates what is and what needs to be, Genesis 6–9 speaks to what doesn't have to be, which is to say the return to chaos because of human sin. God the Creator presents himself as God the Savior or, better yet, faith in creation is to be interpreted as faith in redemption. One can have faith in the fundamental order of the universe because it is founded on a good and merciful God who bestows salvation on us. Indeed, it is not by chance that many of the biblical texts referring to creation seem to have been written in difficult times, as for example with Genesis 1 and most of all Deutero-Isaiah having been written during the exile, or Job being written during his experience of personal misfortune.

This redemption is definitely completed in Jesus Christ, Son of God, "for in him and through him and for him all things were created" (Col. 1:15–20); therefore "the creation itself will be set free from its bondage to decay and obtain the glorious liberty of the children of God" (Rom. 8:19–23). Because the Bible considers "all things" as the unique work of God the Creator and Savior, redemption and creation are to be seen as two sides of one coin. I would like to emphasize this because Catholic priests and pastoral workers often announce redemption in their daily pastoral duties and celebrate it during liturgy, whereas they are tempted to consider an engagement with creation as secondary and also as ambiguous (usually because creation is often regarded as too closely connected with certain political movements that do not start exclusively from Christian assumptions).[5]

It would have been important to also introduce in our *Compendium* a reference to the theology of creation, to the relationship between creation and the sacraments, to a spirituality of creation, and also, alluded to in no. 464, to talk about Benedictine and Franciscan spirituality.

Number 464 is inserted in the third part, which confronts the crisis in the relationship between human beings and the environment, that is to say, the tendency toward an "ill-considered" exploitation of the created resources. "The aspect of the conquest and exploitation of resources has become predominant and invasive, and today it has even reached the point of threatening the environment's hospitable aspect: the environment as 'resource' risks threatening the environment as 'home' " (461).

One can argue correctly that such an attitude toward nature is the result of a long historical and cultural process. It is not a consequence of the biblical anthropocentrism as it derives from "scientism and technocratic ideologies" (462). The remedy cannot be a divinization of nature, but rather a return to an attitude of gratitude toward the Creator and of responsibility toward the created. "It is the relationship man has with God that determines his relationship with his fellow men and with his environment" (464). In this context "the intimate connection between environmental ecology and '*human ecology*'" (emphasis in original) is also mentioned.

The Common Responsibility

The fourth point of the chapter on the environment in the *CSDC* also alludes to different complex arguments that we are not able to examine in their entirety. We cannot enter into the problem of the fundamental relationship between ecology and the economy, discussed under the aspect of a partition of the goods (481–85). Had we the space, it would be important to discuss a "sustainable" administration of the goods of the world.

Within these space constraints, however, I wish to point out that this "common responsibility" refers to the common good of the environment or, better, to the created as the "common heritage of mankind" (467). The value of biodiversity (466) is expressly declared in this text, along with the importance of the Amazon region. The text also notes the problem of desertification[6] and appeals to "universal solidarity" (there is a bond between the environmental crisis and poverty, 482–83). Finally, it urges that responsibility toward the environment find "an adequate expression on a juridical level" in order to arrive at a gradual elaboration of those international norms that protect "the right to a safe and healthy natural environment" (468).

In this context, 469 is inserted, presenting clearly the "precautionary principle" and correctly stating that it "does not mean applying rules but certain guidelines aimed at managing the situation of uncertainty." It asks that there be a "comparison of the risks and benefits foreseen for the various possible alternatives, including the decision not to intervene," and notes that there will always be uncertainties and provisional solutions that will require transparency in the decision-making process. This precautionary principle, which is concerned with articulating calculable risks together with strategies to overcome these risks, has not yet fully entered into the social doctrine of the church. Thus it does not yet have a role in the declarations of the Magisterium of the church. Nonetheless, it has been used in many of the diverse international and national legislative acts (as, for example, in the conventions of the global summit of Rio de Janeiro, in the treaties of Maastricht and Amsterdam of the European Union, and in the Charta of Nice) and may have an impact on future declarations.[7]

This precautionary principle is in many respects a political principle, although elements of this principle are evident throughout the tradition of moral theology, especially those aspects that have emphasized the role of prudence and, of course, in the tradition of casuistry. However this precautionary principle has acquired new value in the context of the complexity of the alternatives possible today, especially when we consider the long-term consequences of certain actions on the environment and on human health. Indeed, it requires a sustained effort to continue to inform the population, to consider different forms of knowledge, and to implement transparent procedures in the pursuit of democratic participation in important decisions.

The question of climate change is discussed in no. 470, which quotes one of the Holy Father's statements to a group of the Pontifical Academy of Sciences[8] — "The climate is a good that must be protected and reminds consumers and those engaged in industrial activity to develop a greater sense of responsibility for their behavior." The climate is considered to be in the public domain and it is recognized that the mechanisms of the market are not able to defend or to foster it properly.

Here we touch the complex problem of energy resources. The CSDC rightly says that the non-renewable resources have to be in the service of all people and that it is necessary to continue to identify new alternative sources of energy. In regard to atomic energy, it notes that there are security issues that need to be properly addressed (470). Moreover, the elaborate discussion of the use of biotechnologies (paragraphs 458–59 and again in numbers 472–80) notes ambiguities. Thus, after having given a substantially positive judgment on the use of these biological and biogenetic techniques, the text raises the ethical problem of evaluating "accurately the real benefits as well as the possible consequences in terms of risks" (473). The following section clearly states that "one must avoid falling into the error of believing that only the spreading of the benefits connected with the new techniques of biotechnology can solve the urgent problems of poverty and underdevelopment that still afflict so many countries on the planet."

Of greater consequence than the feared risks in using genetically modified organisms are the problems of social ethics. Therefore, the principle of the "universal destination of goods" is strongly emphasized in the following numbers and the text puts its finger on "the environmental crisis and poverty . . . connected by a complex and dramatic set of causes" (482). Furthermore, it discusses the serious problems of the large number of poor people who live in crumbling and unsafe houses in cities in developing countries, of unfair international trade, of demographic problems, and, as in no. 471, of indigenous people and their critical relationship to the land. In particular, it states that the principle of the universal destination of goods has to be applied to water, which, being a public good, "cannot be treated as just another commodity among many" (485), and goes on to note that "the right to safe drinking water is a universal and inalienable right."

I conclude with a comment on the last two numbers of chapter 10, dedicated to "new lifestyles." In this context the treatise on virtue is also relevant.

The "ecological conversion" desired by Pope John Paul II[9] asks foremost for a sincere change in humanity's attitude toward nature, in the sense that one should consider the created world no longer as a source of resources to be exploited for our needs, but rather as a prodigious gift of our Lord Creator and Savior — a gift that must be handled with care, a feeling of thankfulness, and praise toward our Lord Creator of life. The church and, in a broader view, the diverse religions can find an alliance in a new educational and spiritual approach toward the environment, which should be reflected in new lifestyles.

What closing opinion can we offer on chapter ten? First of all, we should be full of gratitude that the *CSDC* contains such an elaborate treatise on the environment, especially since the *CSDC* talks to the whole church. There are ecclesiastical regions in which the sense of responsibility toward the created has grown noticeably in the last decades, but there are also other regions in which the responsibility is not yet felt.

This chapter will therefore act as a strong stimulant for projects in theological education and also for church initiatives that can answer major problems in that region. Concerns for environmental ethics are not only complex, but also constantly changing. For this reason one cannot expect a synthetic compendium to fully present all the different aspects of the problem. Rather, what we expect, and what we get, is an invocation to integrate environmental concerns with faith in God the Creator and Savior.

Notes

1. Paolo Carlotti, *"Un chiarimento decisivo": DSC and Moral Theology*, in *For a Humanism Worthy of Love: The "Compendium of the Social Doctrine of the Church,"* ed. P. Carlotti and M. Toso (Rome: LAS, 2005), 157–80.

2. This "strong anthropological and theological foundation" is well emphasized in the annotation of Simone Morandini, "L'ambiente nel *Compendio della Dottrina Sociale della Chiesa,*" *Studia Patavina* 53 (2006): 218–19.

3. Paolo Carlotti, "Ecologia e DSC: Compendium of the Social Doctrine," *La Società* (2006): 237.

4. Put into words by Simone Morandini, *Ecologia e teologia* (Morcelliana: Brescia, 2005), 119.

5. The Second European Ecumenical Assembly of Graz (1997) had formulated the following functional commendation: "We recommend to the churches that they consider and foster the integrity of creation as a vital part of life on all levels."

6. Pope Benedict XVI in the homily for the feast of Corpus Domini 2006 (June 15) said: "In a time in which we talk of desertification and in which we always hear anew warnings of the peril that people and animals die of thirst in regions without water — in this time we again become aware of what a gift water is and how much we are incapable of generating it on our own"; text in *L'Osservatore Romano,* June 16 and 17, 2006.

7. See Carlo Petrini, "Il principio di precauzione: Nuovi sviluppi scientifici e politici," in *Bioetica, ambiente, rischio,* ed. Carlo Petrini, Ateneo Pontificio Regina

Apostolorum (Rome: Logos Press, 2002); see also Karl Golser, "Globalizzazione e sviluppo sostenibile: principi di dottrina sociale," *Bioetica e Cultura* 12, no. 24 (2003): 245–68.

On March 4, 2006 The Italian Episcopal Conference organized a seminar in Rome on this principle, with lectures by A. Bondolfi, M. Tallacchini, and L. Butti, which have been published in the *Bulletin of the National Office on Social Problems and on Labour* 10, no. 2 (May 2006): 109–53.

8. See John Paul II, Address to a Study Group of the Pontifical Academy of Sciences (November 6, 1987).

9. See his speech at the General Audience on January 17, 2001, in *L'Osservatore Romano*, January 1, 2001.

Reflections on the Relationship between Ecology and Theological Ethics

SIMONE MORANDINI

Theology and ecology — an improbable juxtaposition? Surely not: it is an incontestable fact that the study of environmental themes has assumed a considerable importance in theological research in the last decades. It has become steadily more impossible for a reflection that is attentive to "the joys and the hopes, the griefs and the anxieties of people today" (*Gaudium et spes* 1) and that intends to ponder these matters in the light of faith in Christ, to prescind from the earth as a common house (*oikos*) that is *under threat*.[1] For we live in a "risk society,"[2] which sees environmental menaces assuming global dimensions and assailing the existence of each one of us and of our children. We cannot close our eyes to the fact that climatic changes have now attained a scale that is relevant to the planetary ecosystem itself. It is certainly not by chance that the Nobel prize winner for chemistry describes this age as "anthropocene," in other words, the era in which human action is one of the principal factors that determine the evolution of the planet.

A Context for Theology

In this context, theology is invited to a profound new reflection on the existence of the *humanum* and on its role, in a dialogue with ecology, which aims to understand its dynamics, its logic, and its nuances. In the case of fundamental theology, it is certainly true that it does not intend to offer practical tips about how we should care for creation; its proposal consists rather of conceptual instruments that may permit humankind to understand the created world and to dwell in it. Theology's attention is focused primarily on the "ecological idea," which asks critical questions about the very modern image of human existence as that of a pure thinking subject, and which points out how deeply the human person is embedded in the "eco-auto-organization" of all that lives.[3] The English-language world is particularly active in this area, as we see for example in the existence of a periodical specifically dedicated to "ecotheology"[4] and in the research project of the "Earth Bible."[5] It has thus been possible to speak of a "greening" of theology, or even of the Christian faith itself.[6] These expressions may be somewhat naïve, but they reveal a climate of interest and of cordial dialogue between theology and ecology, as well as a relationship marked by a positive reciprocal interrogation in their common concern for a threatened planet. We have come a long way from the accusations in the 1960s and 1970s, which saw Christianity as an anthropocentric and anti-ecological religion that was so obsessed with the importance of the *humanum* that it forgot the earth on which we dwell.[7] Recent decades have helped us to move beyond such a partial perception; and one significant factor in this development has been an exact analysis of the biblical theme of creation in its relationship both to redemption and to eschatology. This has made it possible to rediscover all the richness of this theme and has demonstrated that it cannot be reduced to the robust anthropocentrism of the modern age. Besides this, the same period has seen attention to the earth become the object of a promising dialogue among the great world religions, all of which are challenged by a topic that of its very nature concerns the entire planet.[8]

What Path Ought the Church to Take?

This means that the specifically ethical reflection by theologians on the environment also takes place today in a context of greater serenity, free from pseudo-problems. Its starting point is the discovery of a special responsibility for a world that is sorely tried by an unsustainable development, and it goes on to appeal to a new dimension of the praxis of faith.[9] This research takes two principal paths. On the one hand, the perception of the power over nature that is put in our hands by modern technology has made it clear that ethics must be articulated anew on a planetary scale;[10] on the other hand, an attentive fresh reading of scripture has led to the discovery (or rediscovery) that care for the earth is a constitutive dimension of biblical ethics.[11] The need to reply to the cry of a threatened creation, of a planet that is damaged in its most vital structures, has thus prompted theologians to propose profound transformations in personal and ecclesial praxis that go so far as to affect our lifestyles.[12] Such reflections have found an echo in concrete ecclesial praxis, and this movement has found a sympathetic welcome among the most discerning environmentalists.[13]

Another indication of how widespread such reflections have become is the importance of the concept of "creation care," which the ecumenical movement employs to express its own specific attention to environmental topics, thus confirming the essential harmony — already obvious on the etymological level — between *oikoumenê* and *oiko-logia*. In its recent document *AGAPE*,[14] the World Council of Churches too has expressed its concern about the vicious circle of injustice and environmental degradation that is typical of the age of globalization; this document is a development of reflections that go back to the 1970s. In the assemblies at Basle, Seoul, and Graz, in the *Charta Oecumenica*,[15] and in the preparatory material for the Third European Ecumenical Assembly at Sibiu, the environment is one of the focal points of a shared sensitivity that crosses confessional borders. This is also expressed symbolically in the document signed by Pope John Paul II and the Orthodox Patriarch of Constantinople, Bartholomew I, in 2002.[16]

Besides this, in numerous speeches and documents John Paul II strongly encouraged a renewed attention to environmental topics on the part of Catholic ethics.[17] More recently, in an address on the Vigil of Pentecost 2006, Pope Benedict XVI emphasized the relevance of an ethic of responsibility that is genuinely capable of caring for the earth.[18] The *Compendium of the Social Doctrine of the Church* contains an extremely important section on the environmental question. This broad treatment is surely one of the major new aspects in the structure of this text.[19] On the national level, the Catholic Church in Italy has recently expressed its concern for this subject by adopting the proposal — originally suggested by the Ecumenical Patriarchate of Constantinople — of celebrating a Day for the Creation on September 1 each year, beginning in 2006 (September 1 is the beginning of the Orthodox liturgical year).

The Debate in Theological Ethics:
Data about Which Consensus Exists

The growing diffusion of a specifically ecclesial attention to this theme has now reached a phase where ethical-theological reflection is becoming more detailed; in other words, we have moved beyond the initial explorations, and there is a consensus that some elements in the theological reflection are certain.[20] Space does not permit me to present here an analysis of the paths that have led to this situation, nor to discuss the contributions of individual scholars. I mention only some concepts about which a consensus now exists.

The first element is the spread everywhere in the world of theological attention to "creation care." In the northern hemisphere, this research is particularly intensive in the German-speaking area, but we also find it in North America and Australia. It is also a major theme in the theologies of the Christian third world, meaning Asia and Africa, as well as Latin America, where it began in Brazil. There is a considerable variety of perspectives, but this cannot obscure the emergence of something completely new: a common conceptual sphere.

This is not surprising, since the ecological question is increasingly perceived as the *locus* of a new ethical experience of solidarity within the human family. We understand clearly that we are all in the same boat. We share the same condition of threat and of joint responsibility, although our tasks and roles may differ. An ethical-theological reflection on this question must offer a hermeneutic of this experience that is capable of showing the profound dimension that this experience contains if it is read in the light of faith in the triune God. What is at stake is the creation of God, the place where the Word became incarnate, and the breath of the Spirit. This splendid "house of life" is threatened by a pervasive violence. The vocation of humanity must be conceived as a collaboration in the action of the Creator God, as a share in his providential action which always maintains all things in being. The reality of his creation is menaced by chaos, but God guarantees that it will remain inhabitable for all living things.

The second element to which I wish to draw attention is the interdisciplinary dimension that must be a structural element in ethical-theological reflection in this field, since it can perform its proper task only in a close and competent interaction with the environmental sciences (and more in general, with the sustainability sciences), with environmental sociology, with philosophy, etc. If I may permit myself a play on words: the sapiential dimension characteristic of the theological point of view must take the form here of a meditation that is oriented to that praxis of the knowledge (*sapere*) of the environment, which finds expression in the consensus of the various sciences.[21]

Third, against this epistemological background, the approach of theological ethics will be able to demonstrate more effectively how the emphasis on the value of the human person that typifies the perspective of faith is highly relevant to the construction of an ethical-environmental position. Obviously, this is not an *absolute* anthropocentrism like that of the modern period, and it is important to make the difference very clear. What we must do is express the centrality of the *humanum* in relational terms that are capable of recognizing the intrinsic value of non-human realities, but without falling into the trap of an undifferentiated biocentrism. Above all, we must concentrate on *responsibility,* which is a typically human trait, namely, the capacity to assess the consequences of one's actions over a wide space of time, without yielding to the temptation of looking only at the present day.

Drawing on the language of scripture, we may say that human beings are not to be seen as lords of the creation, but rather as *oikonomoi,* responsible stewards who are called to cultivate it and guard it (Gen. 2:15); as the image of the provident God who gives his blessing to all, the human person is called to bear witness to his life-giving love in the community of his creatures (Gen. 1:27–28). This perspective suggests how we might develop a rich spirituality of creation.[22] We should also rethink the virtues in ecological terms, integrating this dimension thoroughly into our personal moral experience. Here justice is particularly important. The praxis of justice must be developed both within each generation and between the generations.

Fourth, when responsibility is given a central position, we will be able to overcome the antithesis between the integrity of the creation and justice that was typical of the first phase of ethical-theological research into this subject.[23] Today we understand well the need to see the relationships between the environmental and socio-economic dimensions of sustainability, between justice within each generation and justice between the generations, and between the cry of the earth and the cry of the poor, in terms of a positive correlation.[24] In an age of globalization, an effective fight against poverty is impossible without an attentive consideration of its environmental dimension. Similarly, the ecological crisis cannot be resolved without attention to the factor of economic asymmetry.

Fifth, the interconnectedness of these perspectives shows that a challenge of such global proportions demands an equally global response. The responsibility must be put into practice on many levels, in keeping with the principle of subsidiarity, from the personal level to that of local institutions and of national governments, as well as the supranational institutions that are genuinely capable of coming to grips with the environmental problems.

This means that theological ethics is called to take up anew the great conciliar theme of the human family, demonstrating the constitutive relationship between this family and the "house of life" in which it dwells. It is in this house that we must promote an encounter between the various cultures, so that these may become more attentive to the earth; and it is in this house that the various faiths of humankind are called to meet and to engage in a dialogue where they learn from each other how to share their responsibility for the earth.

The Debate within Theological Ethics:
Areas for Future Research

The common elements listed in the previous section constitute an important point of reference that will enable us to take up some open questions where the debate does not yet appear to have reached the stage of convergence. I am not thinking here of topics in fundamental theology such as the relationship between the immanence and the transcendence of God with regard to his creation, although this subject is not irrelevant to moral theology, and there is in fact an ample ongoing debate here. I have in mind more immediately ethical topics that have a more direct influence on concrete behavior, for it is here that theological ethics is summoned to offer its own contribution to a debate that concerns the entire human family. We must find better categories to express our responsibility vis-à-vis the future generations; we must find words that effectively express our relationship to the non-human component of creation.

The first question here is primarily terminological — but on a level in which the words that we use are highly significant. I am referring to the language in which we express the centrality of the human person (as I have done above). My impression is that the word "anthropocentrism," which is often found in Catholic reflection, requires too many nuances in the environmental field to be genuinely helpful.[25] The numerous problematical connotations that have become attached to this concept in the course of history mean that an appropriate ethical-theological reflection must employ other expressions (such as "personalism," "humanism," or "ecologically responsible").

Second, the affirmation of the centrality of the human person, with the accent on human responsibility, obliges us to specify more precisely the co-ordinates that enable us to evaluate human activity, with particular reference to the relevance of this activity to the environment. Since the human person is a cultural being, he or she is the subject of *technical action* that introduces elements of novelty and speedy change into the slow evolution that characterizes the eco-systemic structure of our planet. How is reflection on "creation care" to evaluate this component of human existence? How are we to regard the technological structure that now constitutes such an important dimension of our life on earth?

Is this technological structure an illegitimate disturbance of the integrity of the creation, something that ought to be reduced to a minimum? Or are such actions inherently positive, since they allow human persons who are the image of God to express their participation in the creativity of the Lord by making the earth in their own image? Or ought we perhaps to move beyond such antitheses and identify more precisely the parameters of an ethical evaluation that is not aprioristic, but rather local (in the sense that it pays heed to the *specific* consequences of the individual actions of human beings)?

I believe in fact that we must elaborate some kind of evaluation of the environmental impact as one element in the ethical-theological evaluation of *every* action. The environmental dimension must become a constitutive component of *every* ethical-theological discernment. It is certainly not by chance that the *Compendium of the Social Doctrine of the Church,* which dedicates twenty pages to the explicit treatment of environmental topics, also refers expressly to them in relation to many other themes by means of a network of cross-references that covers the entire book. It is clear that the environmental theme can no longer be limited to one chapter (and still less, to the last chapter) of moral teaching: today, it can be seen as a dimension that influences *all* ethical reasoning.

Third, however, it is clear that the theological elaboration of environmental ethics faces the challenge of *a more detailed articulation of one's own perspective.* In view of concrete problems (controversial large-scale environmental works, handling problems such as waste or mobility, environmentally relevant decisions that must be made in conditions of uncertainty), the debate is complex and many-layered, and thus requires the development of a complex and many-layered conceptual network. How far has Catholic theological ethics developed conceptual categories and instruments that allow us to take part constructively in a research that is both one and manifold, and that is a constitutive element of reflection in late-modern society? To what extent is Catholic theological ethics able to enter effectively and competently into a dialogue that by now embraces the entire body of society and sometimes becomes the focal point for latent conflicts?

Fourth, we may take the example of a term such as "sustainability," which is central to the consideration of environmental themes. The *Compendium of the Social Doctrine of the Church* seems to have adopted this term to some extent, via the idea of the "environmental compatibility" of development. But does such an interpretation go far enough? Ought we not to listen more carefully to the criticism that comes from other churches and points out the risk of reducing this idea to a mere adjective incapable of attacking in a serious way the tendency of the global economy to a growth that devastates the environment? In other words, is sustainability truly sustainable? Personally, I believe that it is; but I also believe that we need a more analytic elaboration of a category, which is extremely valuable for an environmental ethics in the age of globalization, as well as for a "local" reflection that seeks to identify forms of society and lifestyle that are environmentally compatible.

Another example is the *principle of precaution,* which is likewise adopted explicitly by the *Compendium,* but which also appears to require a more sophisticated elaboration, in order to grasp its relationship both to the other axioms of the social doctrine of the church and to the categories of ethical-theological research.

These are only two examples, but they suffice to demonstrate how much work remains to be done in order to reflect theologically on principles that — let me emphasize this point — were not born in the theological field, although they can probably find ample points of reference in various elements of the Christian tradition. These principles must be given their place with all due care in the conceptual network that supplies the structure of the social doctrine of the church and indeed of theological ethics as a whole, while preserving the specific character of this network — and without losing sight of the relationship between these principles and the other components.

Fifth, I believe that this work is only the first step toward a construction of environmental ethics *in a hermeneutical perspective.* Here, the principles that guide our reflection must have theological foundations and provide orientation for understanding and interpreting a complex reality, and then for action. Here, even more than in other fields, the variety of factors involved demands that we define our perspective thoroughly, without taking undue shortcuts. The temptation of a fundamentalist interpretation of "creation care" poses a threat because such an interpretation seems both ethically consistent and effective; but in the present context, we must express this requirement in such a way that we do not forget other requirements that complement it.

Conclusions

I believe that the challenge to theological ethics in this field is that of defining its own inspiration in the hard work of detailed and nuanced reasoning. We need a reflection that is deeply rooted in theology, but is also flexible and capable of responding to the new challenges. The breadth of the global horizon must go hand in hand with the "local character" of specific environmental problems; the radical passion for the integrity of creation must go hand in hand with the discernment of the *variety* of factors that make up the total picture.

This hard work on the elaboration of concepts bears witness to the fruitfulness of faith in a God who becomes flesh in order to give a creation that groans and suffers in the pangs of birth an orientation to glory (Rom. 8:19ff.) — in a God who works through the assumption of the human form by his Word, in a dynamic action that invites men and women to think, to speak, and to act out of love for creation.

— English translation by Brian McNeil

Notes

1. For a precise general description of the ecological crisis, see the reports of the Worldwatch Institute.

2. U. Beck, *La società del rischio* (Rome: Carocci, 2000).

3. An exemplary study in this sense is the reflection by E. Morin, *Il pensiero ecologico* (Florence: Hopefulmonster, 1988); see also E. Morin and A. B. Kern, *Terra-Patria* (Milan: Raffaello Cortina, 1994).

4. Published by Sheffield Academic Press. The periodical was founded in 1992 as *Theology in Green;* the title was changed to *Ecotheology* in 1996.

5. See especially the second volume, which studies Genesis: N. C. Habel and S. Wurst, eds. *The Earth Story in Genesis* (Cleveland: Pilgrim Press, 2000).

6. S. Bouma Prediger, *The Greening of Theology: The Ecological Models of Rosemary Radford Ruether, Joseph Sittler and Jürgen Moltmann* (Atlanta: Scholars Press, 1995); J. E. Carrol, P. Brockelman, and M. Westfall, eds., *The Greening of Faith* (Hanover: University Press of New Hampshire, 1997).

7. Here I refer in particular to the famous essay by Lynn White, "The Historical Roots of Our Ecological Crisis," *Science* 155, no. 3767 (March 1967): 1203–7. On the debate that this essay generated, from a variety of perspectives, see A. A. Auer, *Umweltethik: Ein theologischer Beitrag zur ökologischen Diskussion* (Düsseldorf: Patmos, 1984); A. Simula, *In pace con il creato: Chiesa Cattolica ed ecologia* (Padua: Messaggero, 2001), 30–37. Among those who disputed this wholly negative interpretation of Christianity, the best-documented contributions are by J. Barr, "Uomo e natura: La controversia ecologica e l'Antico Testamento," in *Etiche della terra: Antologia di filosofia del'ambiente,* ed. M. C. Tallacchini (Milan: Vita e Pensiero, 1998), 61–84; R. Attfield, *The Ethics of Environmental Concern* (Oxford: Basil Blackwell, 1983); U. Krolzik, "Die Wirkungsgeschichte von Genesis 1:28,"

in *Ökologische* Theologie: Perspektive zur Orientierung, ed. G. Altner (Stuttgart: Kreuz Verlag, 1989), 149–63.

8. On this, see K. Golser, ed., *Religioni ed ecologia: La responsabilità verso il creato nelle grandi religioni* (Bologna: EDB, 1995); D. Hervieu-Léger, *Religion et écologie* (Paris: Cerf, 1998); L. Musu, ed., *Uomo e natura verso il millennio: Religioni, filosofia, scienza* (Bologna: Il Mulino, 1999); S. Morandini, *Creazione* (Bologna: EMI, 2005).

9. S. Morandini, *Nel tempo dell'ecologia: Etica teologica e questione ambientale* (Bologna: EDB, 1999).

10. The fundamental work here, for theology as much as for other disciplines, is H. Jonas, *Das Prinzip Verantwortung: Versuch einer Ethik für die technologische Zivilisation* (Frankfurt a. Main: Suhrkamp, 1979).

11. On this, see especially K. Golser, "Custodire la casa della vita anche per le generazioni future," in *La casa della vita*, ed. R. Altobelli and S. Privitera (Cisinello Balsamo: San Paolo, 2006), 68–112; Karl Löning and Erich Zenger, *Am Anfang schuf Gott: Biblische Schöpfungstheologien* (Dusseldorf: Patmos, 1997).

12. S. Morandini, *Il tempo sarà bello: Fondamenti etico e teologici per nuovi stili di vita* (Bologna: EMI, 2003); S. Morandini, ed., *Etica e stili di vita* (Padua: Lanza and Gregoriana, 2003).

13. The 2003 edition of the *State of the World Report* by the prestigious Worldwatch Institute dedicated its closing section to the path taken by "the religious world toward sustainability," with particular attention to the Christian world: see chapter 8 of this report by H. Youth, "Engaging Religion in the Quest for a Sustainable World."

14. Available at *www.coe.org*.

15. M. Mascia and R. Perogaro, eds., *Da Basilea a Graz: Il movimento ecumenico e la salvaguardia del creato* (Padua: Lanza and Gregoriana, 1998). The ecumenical reflection on the European level is extensively documented on the home pages of the European Christian Environmental Network (*www.ecen.org*) and the Council of the Episcopal Conferences of Europe (*www.ccee.ch*).

16. The text can be found on the home pages of the Vatican and the Ecumenical Patriarchate.

17. An anthology of texts with an introduction has been edited by A. Giordano, S. Morandini, and P. Tarchi, *La creazione in dono: Giovanni Paolo II e l'ambiente* (Bologna: EMI, 2005).

18. See the Vatican home page.

19. Published by the Pontifical Council for Justice and Peace in 2004. For a presentation and an analysis, see S. Morandini, "L'ambiente nel compendio della Dottrina Sociale della Chiesa," *Studia Patavina* 53 (2006): 217–25.

20. In addition to M. Rosenberger, *L'albero della vita: Dizionario teologico di spiritualità del creato* (Bologna: EDB, 2006), I refer to my book *Teologia ed ecologia* (Brescia: Morcelliana, 2005), for a broad survey and a bibliography. There is a more specifically ethical approach in L. Biagi, ed., *L'argomentazione in etica ambientale* (Padua: Lanza and Gregoriana, 2000).

21. This is the conclusion of the essays in S. Morandini, ed., *Sostenibilità ed antropologia* (Padua: Lanza and Gregoriana, 2007).

22. S. Morandini, *Terra splendida e minacciata: Per una spiritualità della creazione* (Milan: Ancora, 2005).

23. An example is the book by T. Sieger Derr, *Ecologia e liberazione umana: Critica teologica dell'uso e dell'abuso del nostro diritto di primogenitura* (Brescia: Queriniana, 1974).

24. This is the view taken in G. L. Brena, ed., *Etica pubblica ed ecologia* (Padua: Messaggero, 2005); see also L. Boff, *Grido della terra, grido dei poveri* (Assisi: Citadella, 1996).

25. In the ecumenical texts that still employ this term, one leitmotif is the need to distinguish it from "anthropomonism," a term that has a clear meaning, but is even less elegant than "anthropocentrism."

PART TWO
GENDER

9

Becoming Better Samaritans

The Quest for New Models of Doing
Social-economic Justice in Africa

TERESIA HINGA

In mapping the geographical spread of global poverty, many analysts have identified that conditions in Africa constitute a desperate situation that requires urgent attention. In many cases, basing their reports on eyewitness accounts, analysts have indicated that the levels of poverty in Africa verge on sheer indigence. According to virtually all the indicators of poverty, namely, hunger, disease, malnutrition, homelessness, and lack of education, Africa ranks at the bottom of the pyramid, and the situation is not improving.[1] Nor, according to many concerned, is adequate action being taken to address the crisis. Responding, for example, to the fact that fifteen thousand people die in Africa each day from treatable diseases, Bono commented:

> What is happening in Africa makes a fool of the idea [of equality] many of us hold very tightly.... What is happening in Africa mocks our pieties, and questions our commitment to equality.... If we were honest, there is no way we could conclude that such mass death day after day would be allowed to happen anywhere else.... An entire continent [is] bursting into flames.... If we really accept that their [African] lives are equal to ours, we would all be doing something to put out the fire.[2]

It is not only outsiders looking in who draw portraits of these extreme levels of poverty. Much of the reporting comes from African countries themselves. For example, in an interim *Poverty Reduction Strategy Paper* dated July 13, 2000, the government of Kenya reported that over 50 percent of the Kenyan population lives in extreme poverty and hunger. Considering that the total population of Kenya is over thirty million people, this means that a staggering fifteen million Kenyans are affected. The country is among the most impoverished countries in the world, and the majority of these indigent millions are women and children.[3]

Against this background, this essay will examine the crisis of poverty in Africa and outline the ethical challenges it presents. I will argue that poverty in Africa constitutes a leading if not *the* leading bio-ethical issue of our times. I will also endeavor to show that poverty is not a defining feature of Africa in any generic sense. Rather, it is intricately linked to forces in history, and particularly to colonialism, as well as to the multiple systems of domination, including racism and sexism, all of which persist. Thus rather than merely being poor, Africa has become and continues to be impoverished by the forces and systems of domination operative in history. Furthermore, I will show that these forces have a cumulative, multiplicative, debilitating, and often lethal effect on African peoples. Thus hunger and malnutrition, for example, compromise the physical well-being of the people so much that they become easy prey to what has been referred to as "the diseases of the poor." These include the opportunistic diseases related to HIV/AIDS that attack the immune system and also thrive on the compromised health of the victims. Moreover, being weakened by disease leads in turn to their inability to work, thereby compounding their impoverishment. The cumulative effect of hunger and disease in Africa is what Jeffrey Sachs refers to as "the perfect storm," in other words, "a lethal combination of climactic disasters, impoverishment, the AIDS pandemic and the longstanding burden of malaria and other diseases."[4]

Sachs came to this deepened insight into African poverty after visiting a number of African countries, after which he denounced the hitherto preferred simplistic explanations of Africa's poverty. As he put it, "politics, at the end of the day simply cannot explain Africa's prolonged economic crisis. The claim that in Africa corruption is the basic source of the problem does not withstand practical experience or serious scrutiny."[5]

It is worth pointing out that women are the majority of the impoverished, as has been noted by analysts who speak of the feminization of poverty. Feminist analysts confirm Sachs's assessment that the impoverishment of women is the consequence of multiple and interlocking systems of injustice. Elisabeth Schüssler Fiorenza coined the term "kyriarchy" to highlight the fact that "gender oppression is multiplied by racist dehumanization, multiplied by economic exploitation, multiplied by heterosexist prejudice and multiplied by ageist stereotypes."[6]

In view of these insights regarding the feminization of poverty, this essay will apply a gendered lens while outlining ethical challenges and analyzing alternative ethical responses to the scandal of poverty. In particular, I will focus on one such alternative response that I call the "better Samaritan model."

Defining and Naming the Ethical Scandal of Poverty

One of the difficulties in identifying viable responses to poverty is with conflicting ways in which poverty is both defined and measured. In many cases, poverty is defined with reference to an often arbitrarily determined, statistical standard. In recent decades the most common measure has been articulated in terms of how far one falls below the "poverty line" or the "poverty threshold." If a family's income falls below the designated threshold, then a family is *considered poor*. The poverty line as a measure of poverty was first developed in 1964 based on data collected in a 1955 survey by the U.S. Department of Agriculture. However the adequacy of this measure has recently been challenged,[7] as have other measures, for example, the "market basket measure" (how much income is needed to meet not just bare subsistence needs, but needs for a livelihood that approaches respectable community norms).[8] However, in the case of Africa and other third world countries where extreme poverty is rampant, the World Bank has proposed yet another definition of extreme poverty. According to this definition, those who subsist on one dollar per day are extremely poor while those who subsist on incomes between $1 and $2 per day are considered relatively poor. Using this criterion, it has been estimated that over one billion people in the world are living in conditions of extreme poverty.[9]

For his part, Jeffrey Sachs prefers a qualitative definition of poverty, namely, one that takes account of the degree of deprivation experienced by the poor. While acknowledging that there is controversy about the exact numbers of poor people, he distinguishes between extreme poverty, moderate poverty, and relative poverty. According to Sachs, moderate poverty generally refers to "conditions of life in which basic needs are met but just barely while relative poverty is construed as household income level below a given proportion of average national income."[10]

While Sachs accepts an income poverty line and other statistical measures of poverty as indicators of relative poverty, there are conditions that he calls "extreme poverty" for which "poverty lines" and "market baskets" are no measure. Extreme poverty for him is a condition where the poor are unable to meet their basic needs for the survival. "They are chronically hungry, unable to access health care, lack safe drinking water and sanitation, cannot afford education, lack even rudimentary shelter or a roof to keep the rain out and even basic articles of clothing."[11]

Regardless of which measure of poverty is applied, analysts point out that the overwhelming majority of the extremely poor live in the global South, and while the majority of these live in rural areas, increasingly, massive urban poverty is escalating all across the global South, including Africa.[12] It is this extreme poverty that is the target of the ongoing Millennium Development Goals intended to end poverty.

Probing Behind Statistics: The Human Face of Poverty and the Scandal of Its Feminization

Statistical definitions of poverty give us very little help in answering the question "Who are the poor?" They tell us little about the human faces, often those of women and children, of poverty or the human tragedies behind the statistics. What the one dollar per day scenario camouflages, for example, is that in many households, even at this level of abject poverty, the survival of the family is often at the expense of the unquantified (not unquantifiable) labor of women. If the work of women were to be quantified and paid, it would become apparent that whole families subsisting on one dollar per day is primarily fiction. As Mercy Amba Oduyoye has pointed out, women in Africa do not exactly fall into the category of underemployed.[13] She reminds us that when one speaks of the impoverishment of women in Africa, one is referring to persons whose physical labor is used to fetch sustenance for themselves and for their families, but "who can no longer cope because the market value of their products has fallen" or the land that they used to deploy is no longer accessible.[14] Women continue to be expected to fend for their family often at their own risk, a situation that Oduyoye, drawing a comparison between the condition of impoverished and exploited women in Africa and that of the Hebrews under Egyptian bondage, compares to being forced to make "bricks without straw."[15]

Neither do the statistics tell us about the tragedy of modern-day slavery. In fact, as many researchers are beginning to discover, the conditions of extreme poverty in which millions live, though real, are often hidden. In many cases, the conditions are so harsh that even the term "poverty" is a misnomer or a travesty. Increasingly, however, it is recognized that extreme poverty is frequently indistinguishable from slavery and bondage. In his 1999 book *Disposable People*, Kevin Bales describes with a keen sense of compassion what he calls the "new slavery in the new global economy,"[16] and in a set of compelling case studies he persuasively documents this unspoken scandal of our time.[17] The "slaves" are mainly women and often (girl) children whose work and bodies have been commoditized and who are referred to in innocuous terms like "nanny," "hospitality worker," "house girl," or "commercial sex worker." For example, Bales reports that in Thailand, where in the past small numbers of children, mainly girls, may have been sold into slavery by impoverished families, today there is a flood of enslavement due to rapid industrialization and changes in consumer patterns and values. Bales also documents the impact of the forces of global capitalism, which turns this trafficking into a global industry, in many ways comparable to the routine trafficking in other goods such as cotton and sugar. Around the world many people have unwittingly invested in the trafficking industry and reap the benefits of their investment in ignorance, while others deliberately cash in. The anonymity of it all makes it possible.[18]

Similar stories of enslavement of women from Africa abound. Pushed by rural poverty into major towns, many end up working in "sexploitative" situations either as nannies or in brothels run by others who profit from their enslavement. Increasingly, the sexual enslavement of African women has gained momentum in a globalized world, as women, pushed by extreme poverty, are lured into cities at home and abroad by false promises of more lucrative jobs. They find themselves enslaved in places as far-flung as Paris, Riyadh, Amsterdam, and New York. It is this sexploitation of women, entangled with the global tourist industry, that has been referred to by one analyst as a strange phenomenon where we have victims without crime, since rarely do we hear of government outcry or intervention.

Usually slavery is hidden, deliberately camouflaged, or simply ignored. Such is the lot of thousands of immigrant African women who are often held as slaves in homes abroad where they work as nannies and often end up worse off than when they started. The enslavement of such women as nannies or as domestic workers is well-documented by Joy Zarembka in the collection entitled *Global Woman*.[19] Zarembka concludes that each year thousands of domestic workers come to the United States under special visas and are then at the mercy of their employers turned slaveholders. According to her, many women suffer in silence because they do not know their rights and they do not know where to go to seek help. Some may leave an abusive relationship only to find themselves in even worse circumstances. This was the case with Tigri Beleke, who found herself in jail for (alleged) child endangerment when she escaped from her abusive employer for whom she had worked as a live-in maid.[20]

Such is the human tragedy with a woman's face that hides behind statistics and rhetoric about poverty. Such is the tragedy and scandal that some try to capture by using the term "feminization of poverty" but which, in truth, is often also the "feminization of enslavement."

Responding to Extreme Poverty:
The Case for a Clinical Economics
and a "Better Samaritan" Ethics

Faced with this tragic phenomenon of enslavement and impoverishment, particularly of women and children, Sachs notes that "the world community so far has displayed a fair bit of hand wringing, even some high-minded rhetoric but little action."[21] Moreover, even where there has been some intervention, it seems to have had little effect. Sachs believes this is because the interventions are disproportionately meager, with the improvement being from "almost nothing to almost nothing." Sachs claims that part of the problem lies in the failure to make the proper diagnosis in advance of implementing remedies. Indeed, he claims that misdiagnosis often leads to remedies that exacerbate the situation. As he puts it:

> In some ways, today's development economics is like eighteenth-century medicine when doctors used leeches to draw blood from their patients often killing them in the process of trying to cure them. In the past 25 years, when impoverished countries have pleaded with the rich for help, they have been sent to the world's "economic doctors,"

the IMF/World Bank. These have prescribed budgetary belt tightening to patients much *too poor to own belts.* . . . IMF-prescribed austerity measures have frequently led to riots, coups, and the collapse of public services.[22]

Sachs proposes an alternative model of dealing with poverty, one that draws on the example of the world of medicine, which he describes as "clinical economics." He suggests that the following lessons can be learned from the evolution of medical knowledge: first, economists must recognize that economic scenarios and systems are complex, just as the human body is. As with the complex systems of the body, failure in one corner of the system can cascade into failure in other parts of the body and lead ultimately to total failure; second, economists must learn the science of differential diagnosis and cure so the root causes of poverty and of failing economies must be properly diagnosed; third, clinical economics like clinical medicine should view treatment in terms of "family" rather than in terms of the "individual"; fourth, like in good clinical medicine, good developmental practices demand constant monitoring and evaluation; finally, the development community like that of the medical profession needs to develop an ethical code of conduct. They should take on their work with a sense of ethical responsibility, particularly to their chief clients, the poor.[23]

Sachs' concludes that such a form of clinical economics is needed to replace the past twenty years of development practice, which often based remedies for poverty on simplistic misdiagnoses. Previous policies, particularly the structural adjustment measures, assumed that bad governance underlay all economic distress — the prescription being belt-tightening combined with market liberalization and privatization. However these "remedies" led to further impoverishment. Sachs's solution of a "clinical economics" emphasizes the importance of identifying the root causes of poverty instead of merely treating the symptoms.

Christian Reponses to Poverty:
The Bible, Catholic Social Teaching,
and Good Samaritanship

It would be fair to conclude that although many Christians have been involved in hand-wringing when faced with poverty, they have also often done something to ameliorate poverty. Christian faith mandates compassion and charity to the poor. This is endorsed in biblical teaching both in the Old and New Testaments.[24] The poor feature in a variety of ways in the Bible, but mainly as objects of compassion. At times poverty is extolled as a virtue to be aspired to while materialism is to be avoided. For example, the Beatitudes state that "blessed are the poor, for theirs is the kingdom of God" (Luke 6:20), while later on Jesus says that it is going to be as difficult for a rich person to enter heaven as it is for a camel to go through the eye of a needle (Luke 18:25). Elsewhere the parable of the rich man and Lazarus (Luke 16:19) emphasizes the problem of the arrogance of the rich who neglect and exploit the poor. The Bible is clear also that compassion for the poor is as a matter of religious duty. In answer to the rich young man's question of "What must I do to be saved?" Jesus summarizes the central theo-ethical imperative of biblical faith: "Love your God with all your heart and your neighbor as yourself" (Luke 10:27). Probing further to try to understand his mandate, the rich young man asks for clarification: And who is my neighbor? It is in this context that Jesus told the story of the Good Samaritan, at the end of which he recommended to the enquirer to go and do likewise (Luke 10:37).

This story underwrites many of the responses to poverty in Christian circles. Like the young man in the parable of the Good Samaritan, Christians have "gone and done likewise." They have tended to the wounded, fed the destitute, housed the homeless, and given alms generously to support the many works of charity. This model is perfectly legitimate and well-grounded in biblical teaching. As an ethicist, however, I suggest that given the complexities of the phenomenon of poverty and the multiple and cumulative factors underlying it, the Good Samaritan model is necessary but not sufficient for two related reasons. First, the Good Samaritan model focuses on immediate relief and, while this is necessary, it is not sufficient to make a dent in the massive scandal of poverty facing the world today.[25] Second, the charitable model fails to acknowledge that the poor have often become impoverished through the exploitative practices of those seeking to make profit and to enrich themselves quickly. Thus the Good Samaritan model fails to address the ethical issue of injustice rooted in systematic and systemic exploitation of humans by others determined to profit from such exploitation. The model of charity would be utterly inadequate, for example, as a response to the scandal of modern-day slavery.[26]

Given the inadequacies of the Good Samaritan model, I argue for what I call the "better Samaritan model," namely, a model that involves the use of clinical economic tools and that focuses on proper diagnosis (a process that theologians call discernment) and then developing appropriate theo-ethical and practical responses to the scandal of poverty today. Instead of merely being "good" Samaritans, I suggest we need to become better Samaritans in order to address the fundamental factors that impoverish, dehumanize, enslave, and kill millions every day, particularly in Africa and the global South. Clinical economics and theo-ethical discernment would allow us to identify the multiple and intersecting systems of injustice that work in concert to impoverish people and keep them trapped. As theo-ethicists, we should borrow a leaf from the medical world and learn to address root causes, make differential diagnoses, connect the dots between the causes and the effects of poverty, and probe the historical and social contexts and forces that underlie the mass impoverishment, particularly of women and girl children.

Toward Alternative Ethical Reponses to Poverty: Clinical Economics and "Better Samaritan" Ethics at Work

In order to illustrate how the methods recommended here can work, I will now discuss how these approaches can be or indeed have been applied to address the key objective of the Millennium Development Goals of ending poverty and hunger. I will revisit the scandal of poverty in Africa using the lens of "clinical economics" and "better Samaritan" ethics in order to identify effective practices. While one can identify several examples of clinical economics and "better Samaritan" ethics in the last decade, I want to consider the two examples of the Jubilee 2000 debt-cancellation campaign and the work of African feminist ethics as embedded in the projects of the Circle of Concerned African Women Theologians.[27]

Jubilee 2000

The Jubilee campaign can be regarded as an example of clinical economics coupled with better Samaritan ethics that has yielded substantive and tangible results. The Jubilee 2000 movement crystallized toward the year 2000 as a global movement and campaign to end poverty. Applying the methods of clinical economics, activists diagnosed the debt crisis as a root cause of poverty in Africa. While this diagnosis was itself not new, what was new was the recognition of the fact that the debt crisis did not result from any failure of Africans to manage their wealth. Rather the Jubilee 2000 campaign connected the dots between the activities of other players in the global community and the impoverishment of the African continent. They noted that structural adjustment programs exacerbated rather than alleviated the debt crisis and consequently further impoverished nations. Moreover, they noted that the escalation of Africa's impoverishment was directly tied to a country's attempt to try to discharge its debts to the World Bank and/or the IMF.

Jubilee 2000 also recognized that massive poverty and hunger were related to the fact that in order to raise foreign exchange to service the loans, much of Africa's agricultural production was redirected to the production of foreign-currency-generating crops (in other words, cash crops such as coffee, tea, and cotton), which in turn took away valuable land that could have been used to grow crops like millet and beans, which provided food for the people. Clinical economists are increasingly connecting the dots between the growing of such crops (cotton in West Africa, for example) and the sustained crisis of hunger and poverty. Such a scenario of impoverishment through the cash-crop economies, controlled by the first world and for the benefit of the first world (through transnational corporations, many of which control agribusiness in Africa), is well captured by Jean-Marc Ela in *African Cry.* Speaking of his home country of Cameroon Ela points out that

> in black Africa, on the edge of the Sahel, in that tropical region where farmers reap but one harvest a year, where sowing is always diffi- cult, and where women and children live in a state of chronic famine, thousands of peasants are being forced to pull up millet that is just sprouting and to plant cotton in its place. In societies where millet is a staple, that deed forced upon landless peasants is a veritable dag- ger in the heart. It is all done so quietly, under the watchful eye of the agricultural monitors employed by a large development company investing in cash crops.
>
> And so the peasants have to devote the best land, rented each year from their traditional superiors, to a crop that, they are told, will bring in foreign currency. But the illiterate farmers watch the machinery roll by every year with pangs of anguish, for they can be sure they will be robbed of what they sow. After the multiple claims of a series of inter- mediaries have been satisfied, the peasants, who labor extraordinarily hard though they live in deplorable conditions, find themselves once more in the ever-recurring cycle of cotton, taxes, debts.[28]

The end result of this differential diagnosis was the realization that sending aid, though necessary, was not sufficient. Equipped with a better understand- ing of debt as a major root cause, among other causes, of poverty in Africa, and recognizing the connivance of multiple and intersecting forces through- out history, Jubilee 2000 activists demanded the cancellation of the debts that were keeping Africans stuck in the trap of poverty. Moreover, recogniz- ing the cumulative and multiplicative effects of other forces, particularly the forces of colonialism and global capitalism, a global movement to counter these effects has, in the last decade, crystallized in the World Social Forum. This forum is determined to put people, rather than capital, center stage, and it insists on working toward an alternative world in which the indignity and the violence of poverty and its multiple symptoms will no longer exist. They are convinced that a better world is possible.[29]

The Circle of Concerned African Women Theologians

As noted above, poverty in Africa and in other contexts in the global South has increasingly acquired a feminine face. While colonialism and global- ization can explain the impoverishment of the continent, it does not quite explain the feminization of this poverty. Thus for a more complete diagno- sis of this phenomenon we need to examine the insights offered by feminists who have named sexism and patriarchy as complicating factors in the scandal of poverty. It should be noted, though, that much of the feminist analysis has operated within a secular framework and has been marked at times by a suspicion of religion.

In the African context, however, the indifference toward the role of religion in fostering women's oppression, or nurturing their empowerment, has been identified as a problem by the Circle of Concerned African Women. By contrast, members of the Circle insist on giving adequate attention to the impact of the sexism embedded in and nurtured through patriarchal interpretations of Africa's triple heritage of religion and culture, namely, Indigenous African Religions, Christianity, and Islam. Moreover, they insist that diagnoses must proceed with reference to women not as victims, but rather as persons, as moral agents capable of working to transform society and of participating in the construction of a better world where women do not suffer the violence and indignity of poverty fueled by the injustices of racism and sexism.

Constraints of space do not allow a comprehensive account of the Circle and its work since 1989. Suffice it to note that for the last three decades reclaiming their moral agency that has at times been stifled by colonialism, sexism, and racism, members of the Circle have embarked on a sustained initiative of research and publication in an attempt to diagnose and to name the root causes of the plight of women on the continent caught at the intersection of these multiple systems of domination. Having engaged in this diagnostic research, these African women theologians conclude that in order to respond adequately to the ethical scandal posed by the feminization of poverty, its legitimation by religio-cultural traditions must be recognized.

Under the leadership of Mercy Amba Oduyoye, African women have made the analytical connection between cultural sexism, patriarchal theologies, and the conditions of indigence, violence, and disease in which many African women continue to live. Their diagnosis has led to a call for gender justice and equality in both church and society as a necessary condition for the eradication of poverty and its feminization. Furthermore, they have noted that although women have endured these intersecting systems of injustice, they cannot be saved if they are regarded as objects in a burning house. They insist that women must reclaim their agency as full-fledged members of church and society and bring their moral agency to bear in eradicating the death-dealing realities of our times and in constructing a humane and just future in the global village. They insist that creating a humane world entails listening to women's own analyses of the issues at stake and working in solidarity to construct and implement practical solutions to the problem of impoverishment. Like many others caught in the painful traps of poverty in the global South, these women also believe that a better world is possible, even for them.

Making Poverty History:
An Enduring Ethical Challenge

There is no doubt that addressing the enduring ethical challenge of poverty in Africa, and beyond, is multidimensional. For starters, both the clinical economics model and the better Samaritan model insist that there is a mandate to properly diagnose the causes of poverty before prescribing cures. Now, given the multiple causes of poverty and its multifaceted dimensions, the enduring ethical task becomes one of continuing discernment and diagnosis of the specific socio-historical contexts in order to better develop appropriate, effective, and sustainable strategies of action in solidarity with the poor. Both clinical economics and better Samaritan ethics also insist that it is important to translate the results of diagnosis and discernment into concrete actions and practices designed to end poverty. Such actions would need to be qualitatively different from many of those of the past, which frequently exacerbated rather than alleviated poverty. Moreover, the mode of engagement needs to be different, so that interveners work in solidarity with the poor and in a way that respects their dignity and agency as persons. Ultimately, then, solidarity with the poor means not action on their behalf, but rather action with and alongside them, perhaps best described by a term used by the late Archbishop Romero: "accompaniment."

Notes

1. Jeffrey Sachs, *The End of Poverty: Economic Possibilities of Our Time* (New York: Penguin Press, 2005), 20.

2. Ibid., xvi.

3. *Kenya Interim Poverty Reduction Strategies Paper: 2000–2003; www.imf.org/external/np/prsp/2000/ken/01/index.htm* (accessed June 27, 2006).

4. Sachs, *The End of Poverty*, 5.

5. Ibid., 190.

6. Elisabeth Schüssler Fiorenza, ed., *The Power of Naming: A Concilium Reader in Feminist Liberation Theology* (Maryknoll, N.Y.: Orbis Books, 1996), xxi.

7. See Nicholas Eberstadt, "The Mismeasure of Poverty," *Policy Review* 138 (September 2006): 2ff; see *www.hoover.org/publications/policyreview/3930481.html.*

8. For details, see "The Market Basket Measure: Constructing a New Measure of Poverty," in *Applied Research Bulletin* 4, no. 2 (Summer/Fall 1998); *www.hrsdc.gc.ca.*

9. Cited in Sachs, *The End of Poverty*, 20.

10. Ibid.

11. Ibid.

12. This is the case for example in Kenya where over 50 percent of the people live in extreme poverty and where urban poverty has escalated to monumental proportions. Kenya "boasts" one of the worlds' largest slums, Kibera (featured in the Hollywood film *The Constant Gardener*). With all its squalor Kibera is home for approximately one-third of Nairobi's population. For details of the rapidly escalating

urban poverty and slums phenomenon in Kenya, see the *East African Standard* (Nairobi) June 29, 2006.

13. Mercy Amba Oduyoye, "Poverty and Motherhood," in *The Power of Naming: A Concilium Reader in Feminist Liberation Theology*, ed. Elisabeth Schüssler Fiorenza (Maryknoll, N.Y.: Orbis Books, 1996), 127.

14. Consider the oddity of defining poverty in Africa in terms of the ability to subsist on a dollar per day when the majority of people will live and die without ever seeing a dollar, let alone using one. Consider also that if one had access to water, food, and other means of subsistence an actual dollar would be redundant. Consider further how the language of the dollar as a measure of poverty shapes our responses to extreme poverty. Thus, some may conclude that if poverty is about subsisting on less than a dollar per day, then if five dollars were given to the poor, they would be doing fine. I submit that behind such understandings and definitions of poverty may be the belief that the impoverished lack the capacity to handle money and therefore that money should be given to them in judicious doses. I suspect too that the whole idea of microfinance, which is now touted as a major strategy to combat poverty, also thrives on the belief that the poor cannot handle "big bucks." For a discussion of how the myth of the incapacity of the poor to handle material wealth has worked in concert with other myths to keep them impoverished, see Jeffrey Sachs, *The End of Poverty*, 310ff. For a critique of the one dollar per day as a mismeasure of poverty in Africa, see "The Myth of Living on One Dollar per Day," in *New African* 447 (January 2006): 18–19.

15. Mercy Amba Oduyoye, *Daughters of Anowa: African Women and Patriarchy* (Maryknoll, N.Y.: Orbis Books, 1995), 171.

16. See Kevin Bales, *Disposable People: New Slavery in the Global Economy* (Berkeley: University of California Press, 1999), and compare it with Barbara Ehrenreich, ed., *Global Woman: Nannies, Maids and Sex Workers in the New Economy* (New York: Henry Holt, 2002).

17. Bales's accounts of Seba and Siri graphically reveal the brutality and barbarity of this new "economy."

18. Bales, *Disposable People*, 49.

19. Joy Zarembka, "America's Dirty Work: Migrant Maids and Modern Day Slavery," in *Global Woman*, ed. Ehrenreich (New York: Henry Holt, 2002), 142–53.

20. Ibid.

21. Sachs, *The End of Poverty*, 10.

22. Ibid., 75. For an analysis of the impact of World Bank–imposed austerity measures (the so-called structural adjustment programs) on the impoverishment of African women, see the documentary *To Be a Woman: African Women and Economic Crisis*, produced by the Women's Desk, All African Conference of Churches, Nairobi.

23. This paragraph summarizes the five lessons discussed in more detail in Sachs, *The End of Poverty*, 79–81.

24. For a relatively comprehensive account of the biblical view on poverty, see Thomas D. Hanks, *God So Loved the Third World: The Bible, the Reformation and Liberation Theologies* (Maryknoll, N.Y.: Orbis Books, 1984).

25. Readers should note here that there are rather generic, ahistorical responses to poverty implicit in earlier documents, while many of the post-conciliar documents are more historically, politically, and economically informed (and therefore closer

to the "better Samaritan" model discussed later in this chapter). For details of this shift in method within the church's documents on social justice, see Charles Curran, *Catholic Social Teaching, 1891–Present: Historical, Theological and Ethical Analysis* (Washington, D.C.: Georgetown University Press, 2002), 55ff.

26. In some cases, Christians have bought slaves from their condition of enslavement, have provided shelter to individual women, or have provided soup-kitchens for the multitudes of homeless people to be found in big cities. While such acts of charity are necessary, they do not address the question of why such homelessness, enslavement, and violence against women occur.

27. The Circle of Concerned African Women Theologians is a pan-African organization of women scholars of religion, founded in 1989 under the leadership of Mercy Amba Oduyoye, with the goal of undertaking sustained research, writing, and publishing on the implications of religion and culture on women's lives in Africa. For a detailed account of the Circle and its goals see my "Between Colonization and Inculturation: Feminist Theologies in Africa," in *The Power of Naming,* ed. Schüssler Fiorenza, 36–44. For a comprehensive list of Circle publications thus far, see the Circle of Concerned African Women's website at *www.thecirclecawt.org/*.

28. Jean-Marc Ela, *African Cry,* trans. Robert R. Barr (Maryknoll, N.Y.: Orbis Books, 1986), v.

29. This was the rallying cry for the World Social Forum held the last week of January 2007 in Nairobi, Kenya.

10

Women's Perspectives in Bioethics

A Case Study from Tribal India

PUSHPA JOSEPH

To commit a crime against the natural world is a sin. For humans to cause species to become extinct and to destroy the biological diversity of God's creation ... for humans to degrade the integrity of Earth by causing changes in its climate, by stripping the Earth of its natural forests, or destroying its wetlands ... for humans to injure other humans with disease ... for humans to contaminate the Earth's waters, its land, its air, and its life, with poisonous substances ... these are sins. We have become un-Creators. Earth is in jeopardy at our hands.[1]

This study has as its context the tribal communities of Chhattisgarh, a state in Central India. Acclaimed as a hot spot for biodiversity, Chhattisgarh has become a haven for new experiments in biotechnology. Women contribute immensely toward the maintenance of the biodiversity of the state. In such a scenario, bioethicists and feminists are wary about the threat to the diversity of the ecosystem with which Chhattisgarh is blessed.

One remarkable example of biodiversity is the diverse, decentralized, and sustainable food security systems that have traditionally existed in the tribal areas of the Indian subcontinent, especially in Chhattisgarh. A unique feature is the important role played by women in maintaining these food security systems. This essay examines those philosophies and worldviews underlying women's approaches and praxis. The essay claims that such an investigation can offer sound philosophical and theological foundations for an ethical approach to biotechnology.

Seeking the Rationale

Diversity is the very texture of nature. God in His/Her wisdom has created a world filled with an authentic variety of species, woven into complex webs of interlocking relationships. Nature as a system is guaranteed to be stable, sustainable, and creative. However, as humans, we have tried to dominate and control nature. As a result, we have violated the core ecological principle of diversity. Whether goaded by greed, ignorance, or compassion,[2] our modern methods of standardization and forceful imposition of uniformity in order to ensure the highest yield from any species or system puts us all at great risk.

The Earth, its flora and fauna, is encountering an enormous crisis in biodiversity.[3] It is possible to witness the spreading dominance of monocultures both in the West and in the East.[4] In the Indian scenario too, studies record the slow spreading of such monocultures.[5]

India has 7 percent of the world's biodiversity and, with it, a treasure of traditional knowledge of the medicinal properties of indigenous plants. However, the reality is that current environmental public policies and laws are not effectively addressing the crises of biodiversity. We are in need of developing appropriate mechanisms to protect environmental sustainability and provide for environmental stewardship.

The Context

The immediate context of this study is Chhattisgarh, a state in central India. It was formed when the sixteen Chhattisgarhi-speaking southeastern districts of Madhya Pradesh gained statehood on November 1, 2000. Raipur serves as its capital. It is the tenth largest state of India.

Along with being one of the largest states of India, Chhattisgarh is also one of the richest in terms of mineral resources and biospheres and is endowed with about twenty-two varied forest types. These all have naturally occurring varieties of herbs and shrubs, with proven medicinal and aromatic ingredients. The state has thousands of square kilometers of virgin forest that have yet to be scientifically surveyed. A wealth of varieties of indigenous rice, an unexplored gene pool, occurs naturally. Established traditional knowledge systems of self-healing and nutrition based on a deep understanding of the bio-wealth are a unique feature of various communities of the state.

One area in which the biodiversity of Chhattisgarh is manifested is in the decentralized and alternate food security systems visible in the state's tribal communities. This particular factor is the theme of our study.

Decentralized Food Production System

Traditionally known as the rice bowl of India, Chhattisgarh is renowned for its great variety of food production systems. These include many varieties of rice germ plasm, a wide range of millets, and other dryland crops, pulses, oilseeds, fruits, edible flowers, tubers, mushrooms, and other gathered foods. Many of these are dependent upon access and close proximity to the forests. The pathbreaking research of Dr. R. H. Richaria, the pre-eminent rice scientist of the region, demonstrated that there are more than fifteen hundred varieties of indigenous rice available in Chhattisgarh. These include indigenous rice varieties capable of giving the equivalent of, or even higher yields than, the green revolution varieties. These yields have been achieved using indigenous seeds and local resources and skills, without the use of chemicals.

The farmers of Chhattisgarh use a wide range of technical and production practices. The procedures and techniques employed are directly dependent on the land cultivated. For example the techniques used in lowlands differ from those used in middle lands.[6]

There are also a variety of sowing practices known to the farmers. Al-though Chhattisgarh is chronically drought-prone, the farmers here are the inheritors of a rich heritage of biodiversity in rice and dry-land crops, and this, together with great resilience, has helped them survive. Thus variety is ingrained in the very fabric of the agricultural and cultivation processes in the state.

Biodiversity is also visible in the number of crops grown.[7] The diversity in rice crops found in Chhattisgarh is very extensive. The world's longest rice, for example, "Dokra-Dokri," is found in Chhattisgarh. Unfortunately, the variety is now suffering attrition because of the organized promotion of monocultures.

Farmers in Chhattisgarh are well aware of the drought resistance and ecologically wholesome nature of indigenous varieties and practices. Nor-mally each farmer grows four or five varieties of rice. There are a number of reasons behind the practice. First, if one variety fails to grow during a particular season, another would make up for it. Beside this, the farmers grow different crop varieties for their different uses and preferences.

Dry-land crops are a major aspect of the food security of the region, as assured irrigation in the area is only 13 percent and supplementary irriga-tion is available in only 35 percent of the area. It is therefore of paramount importance to develop dry-land crops in the region. A positive feature is that there exists a rich tradition of dry-land agriculture in the region. How-ever, seeds and skills have been lost due to the penetration of market forces and capital in agriculture. Many dry-land crops are nutritionally very valu-able, though their market value may be low. Their loss has meant serious deterioration in the diet of peasant families, as well as a loss in terms of knowledge base.

It is not possible to have a discussion on biodiversity in food resources without referring to the many kinds of uncultivated foods used in Chhat-tisgarh. These include a multitude of roots and tubers, greens, and seasonal edible mushrooms. There is also a large range of leaves from trees, bushes, and shrubs that are eaten here as *bhaji*s (vegetables). Some of these, like the *tinpania* and *chanori bhajis*, grow naturally in the many rice fields after the harvest. As a matter of fact, the distinction between what is a *bhaji* and what is a "weed" is a product of the culture of agricultural monoculture that is in complete contradiction to the culture of biodiversity prevalent in Chhattisgarh. These foods lend richness to the diet, and in times of drought and food scarcity, these food resources have sustained generations of people of Chhattisgarh.

Women's Role in Food Security in the Tribal Regions

The role that women have played in maintaining these systems is relatively poorly understood.

First, in many tribal regions in Chhattisgarh, for example, women are the major agricultural workers. They work in each and every aspect of crop production, preservation, and storage. In certain parts of the state, women are also known to use the plough, a function that is taboo and prohibited for them in almost all other parts of the country. Apart from crop weeding, maturing, and harvesting, women are the leading players in all post-harvest and storage operations. Women also play a major role in the collection and processing of the many kinds of uncultivated foods found in Chhattisgarh. Many of these foods are collected from the forest and women use them for maintaining household food security and nutrition needs outside the market system.[8]

Second, women are the primary gatherers of all uncultivated foods and inheritors of an ancient knowledge system about food biodiversity.

Third, they are also the gardeners and herbalists with primary knowledge and responsibility for maintaining the home gardens, the *baris/bakhris*.

Fourth, it is the women who take the produce to the primary markets and barter or trade in the items related to primary food needs.

Fifth, women are blessed with knowledge of seed technologies, varietal preferences, and even breeding experiences and procedures.

Finally, women are also the keepers of the seeds. As stated above, women are responsible for all post-harvest operations. An important aspect of these is the preservation of the seeds of biodiversity. Thus, the role played by women in maintaining and preserving the biodiversity is evident. It will benefit us as bioethicists to explore the underlying worldview and approach to life in general of these women's ethos in order to draw ethical pointers as we construct a bioethics that will preserve the diversity of our universe.[9]

Ethical Pointers —
Philosophical and Theological Foundations

In the tribal cultures existing in India, there is no great distinction between religion and culture, and ethical decisions are grounded in both religious beliefs and cultural values. In contrast to the contemporary secular approach to bioethics, which is predominantly rights based, bioethics in the tribal cultures of India is primarily duty based. Traditional teachings deal with the duties of individuals and families to maintain a lifestyle conducive to physical and mental health. These tribal traditions share a culture and worldview that includes ideas of relationality, collective versus individual identity, and a strong emphasis on connectedness to the earth. These basic values form the bedrock or foundation for the construction of an ethic that can ensure the sanctity of life. Neera Mani opines:

> This is an approach that is indeed based on women's ways of seeing and encountering reality. The tribal ethos of the state of Chhattisgarh is primarily feminine and arguably feminist because of its particular approach to the complex phenomenon of the self. Such an approach offers profound ethical challenges for constructing an ethic of life that will be true to the goal of sustainability and stewardship that we humans are called to play.[10]

Based on the context that we have described, sustainability and stewardship can be viewed as two defining principles for developing a bioethical perspective, which could be used to direct further scientific investigation and improve the development and application of public policies.

Sustainability

The global ecosphere, the sacred Gaia, that we depend upon for life is provided to us as a gift. We are responsible for its care and well-being. The goal of sustainability is to achieve the well-being of the ecosystem and the human system together. The responsibility of caring for the ecosystem comes to us because of our capacity to be the most adaptive, while at the same time the most destructive, of all creatures on earth. The sustainability of the earth and the biosphere is ensured when we humans operate on an understanding of "how natural processes are intended to function and the role each species plays within the ecosystem."[11] The ethos of the tribal communities of Chhattisgarh is built on an acute understanding of the interconnectedness, interdependence, and interrelatedness of living systems and all life in general. Such a worldview is based on a particular notion of the self and the universe that is our common home.

Self as a Complex Phenomenon

The understanding of self as a complex phenomenon is based on the *advaitic* view of reality. The theory that best explains this is the *kosha* theory, which understands reality as having many layers. According to the *kosha* theory the self is constituted by different *koshas,* sheaths, or layers — the *annamaya, pranamaya, manomaya, vijnanamaya,* and *anandha maya.* Thus, person-hood is defined in terms of an in-depth and dynamic interaction with the different layers of life as manifested in the universe.[12]

Yet another approach that is constitutive of the complex understanding of the self is seen in the democratic fourfold vision of reality, with its poten-tial for unity and communion building, as depicted by Sri Narayana Guru of the Ezhava tradition, a marginal community of Kerala.[13] The self in this scheme is *Catuspad* — fourfold. The self represents Brahman, the reality as *jagrat* (wakeful), *swapna* (dream), *susupti* (sleep), and *turiya* (silence). It is symbolized in the very sound production "A," "U," "M," and "silence." The wakeful consciousness (*jagrat*) is directed to the world of objects (ex-ternal world), the dreamy half-awake consciousness (*swapna*) to the world of the subject, the deep sleep (*susupti*) state to the hidden world of the preconscious-subconscious, and the "silence" (*turiya*) of the unconscious as the perfect vision of Being as Being or Non-Being; in other words, the self as non-dual.

In the tribal women's worldview, the non-dual self is an interfacing of threefold dimensions — the cosmic, the life principle of the material world; the human, consisting of the economic, political, and social realm; and the link factor, the divine, with its aesthetic religious effervescence. The *Lokam* (world of experience) is a comprehensive conception of the world one experiences, the only realm of "being" in which and through which reality is transmuted to the person and through him or her to fellow per-sons. The *Lokam* of tribal women is a cosmotheandric appropriation of being-in-the-world.

Such an understanding of self offers great dividends for constructing an ethic of responsibility and interconnectedness with nature. In such a scheme, the self is not seen as isolated and individualistic but relational and interdependent.

The Self as Relational, Interdependent, and Narrative

Two views of the self have been prominent in modern and contemporary philosophy — the Kantian ethical subject and the *homo economicus.* Both of these notions see the individual as an autonomous, independent, and rational agent. Whereas the Kantian subject employs pure abstract reason to discover absolute truth, *homo economicus* uses reason to rank desire in sequence for the goal of maximizing desire satisfaction. Feminists argue that these conceptions of the self isolate the individual from personal relationships, larger social forces, and from creation itself.[14] What feminist philosopher Diana Meyers says in this regard is revelatory:

> For the Kantian ethical subject, emotional bonds and social conven-tions imperil objectivity and undermine commitment to duty. For *homo economicus,* it makes no difference what social forces shape

one's desires provided they do not result from coercion or fraud, and one's ties to other people are to be factored into one's calculations and planning along with the rest of one's desires.[15]

The tribal women's understanding of self and personhood is consonant with feminist ethics and metaphysics, which shifts from the self, understood as individual and separate from all others, to a relational conception of the self. It demonstrates, first, that the mind/body emphasis of personal identity debates involves an artificial dichotomy between bodily and psychological aspects of a person, for we are all both embodied and narrative selves. Second, the autonomous self, rather than being an independent rational will, is a relational self that can exist only and persist through relations with others and as a being that can cause change, be recognized, and tell its story.[16] Thus, in such an understanding, the autonomous subject has three important attributes. The specific attributes of the self and agency as delineated by feminism are, (1) its relational and embodied characteristic, (2) its potential for bringing about change, and (3) the emphasis on the "self as narrative" for "it is a being that can tell its story."

Feminist philosophers thus point to the significance of a narrative self. The narrative approach emphasizes the telling to listening others of the story of who one is. The self, it affirms, is constituted by social interaction in the telling. Retelling and being taken seriously as an authority on what has happened can help restore the self, especially in a context where women's words are construed as lies and gossip. Just as one can be reduced to an object through torture, one can become a human subject again through telling one's narrative to caring others who are able to listen.

Such an understanding of the self is consonant with tribal worldviews because it creates a compassion for tortured others, a connectedness that goes beyond mere human interconnectivity, creating thus a new bond and communion with all forms of life — an important prerequisite for the preservation of biodiversity and respect of nature.

Embracing Differences

All patriarchal cultures have looked upon differences with suspicion and construed the one who is different as the Other. A holistic approach will welcome difference and accept wholeheartedly the other who is different, accepting him or her with his or her uniqueness. This will also lead to the preservation of diversity, to a challenge to false standardization in the realm of nature, and to a challenge to monocultures.

Land as an Extension of God's Body

Echoing the same theme, Indian tribal women's worldviews are replete with organic understandings of nature. Various metaphors are used in the Indian context to describe nature and the universe, both the cosmic world and the world of the humans. One of the usages is *lila*, which describes creation as the divine play of God and the universe as a body or a stage in which God's play of continuous creation takes place. The divine *lila* is also the divine mother who creates; *lila* is also seen as the divine play in which *Brahman* is the great creator who uses his "magic creative power" (*maya*) to transform himself into the world, so the world and cosmos are also seen as the extended body of God.[17] This world is our God-given home. It is a good home (although much spoiled by our disastrous disobedience to God). It contains wonderful diversity and beauty. It is a home that has been sanctified by God's son, Jesus, making it his home too. Archbishop William Temple once described Christianity as "the most materialistic religion" because it affirms a good creation and teaches God incarnate in material form. Just as Jesus worked out his relationship with God in the back streets of Nazareth, the roughness of a carpenter's shop, and the deserts of Sinai, so we are to put roots down where God has placed us.[18] The understanding of nature as an extension of self is grounded in a philosophical understanding of the complex nature of the human self.

The Land Belongs to God and Is a Gift from God

In his book *The Land,* Walter Brueggemann states, "Land is not given over to any human agent but is a sign and function in covenant."[19] Land belongs in usufruct, in trust, to the living. The gift of land does not confer absolute ownership on us. It is not a gift in the sense of being ours to use and abuse if we wish — but a gift in covenant, a leasehold rather than a freehold. The clearest example of this is in the gift of the Promised Land to Israel. The land is first promised, and then given to God's people, who have to claim their inheritance with blood and toil. Yet the land still belongs to God.[20] In Leviticus 25, the Lord commands Israel to observe a Sabbath on the land every seven years, and a Jubilee every fifty, when land sold is returned to its original owner's family. God tells the people: "The land is not to be sold permanently, because the land is mine, and you are but aliens and my tenants" (Lev. 25:23). It is important then to maintain a sacred relationship with land because it is holy ground. As humans we are called to be stewards of the land. In the tribal worldview, land is seen as a gift given by God. As such, land is to be respected and adored and not to be misused for our greed.

Stewardship

A crucial area of reflection is the function of stewardship in defining how we are to be involved in the praxis of ecological sustainability. The concept of stewardship offers a "structured approach to the care and management of natural ecosystems, upon which human activities and habitats depend."[21] Stewardship is the assumption of responsibility for the maintenance of the biosphere and the welfare of the world. It is the "recognition that we have been entrusted with the care of the earth and the careful management of its natural and social communities."[22] This reminds us of our responsibility to act as trustees of the earth and its natural resources. We have a responsibility to preserve and protect the life-sustaining ecosystem for future generations. As a phenomenon of the universe, stewardship is a force that acts to preserve the universe from harm.

The diversity of natural and social life is a complex, inter-dependent "gift community" that has been entrusted into our care. For the women of the tribal communities in Chhattisgarh, this trusteeship is to be demonstrated in how they manage effectively the ongoing sustainability of their natural ecosystems and the human communities that depend on those ecosystems. In this way, they view stewardship as a political activity, which should affect the form and function of public policy. For these women, the goal of management of the ecosystem is not simply "sustaining" the quality of life, but actually improving it. This is visible in the words of one of the women of the Gondh community when she says with emotion pointing to the piece of land in front of her hut, "This land is my home. I have grown with it and in it. It is my mother. It cries when I cry, it sucks my tears into its bosom and spreads consolation into my heart in exchange for the tears. This land is my mother. I will not ruin it."

Conclusion

We have explored some of the special aspects of the philosophical and theological features underpinning the approach tribal women of Chhattisgarh adopt in their perspective on nature. As Christian ethicists, our search for developing a clearly stated view of the earth and human responsibility for its care can be informed by the restorative and reconciling perspectives in the indigenous traditions. Whether our endeavors help reinstate nurturance will depend upon our sensitivity in authentically collaborating with the renewing factors inherent in these traditions.

Notes

1. "Address of His All Holiness Patriarch Bartholomew at the Environmental Symposium, Saint Barbara Greek Orthodox Church, Santa Barbara, California, November 8, 1997," in *Cosmic Grace, Humble Prayer,* ed. John Chryssavgis (Grand Rapids, Mich.: Eerdmans, 2003), 220–21; quoted in Neddy Astudillo et al., *God's Earth Is Sacred: An Open Letter to Church and Society in the United States* (*www.nccecojustice.org/openletter.html*).

2. The "green revolution" sacrificed diversity in a technological drive to feed the hungry. For such an analysis see Timothy Peterson, "Bio-Regional Ecosystems and the Form and Function of Public Policy: Improving the Quality of Natural and Social Life," in *Coalition for Christian Colleges and Universities: Global Stewardship Initiative* (Canton, Ohio: Malone College, 1996) and *http://cesc.montreat.edu/GSI/GSI-Conf/discussion/Peterson.html*.

3. The dire consequences of the loss of biodiversity have been explored by many ecologists. See for such an analysis Darryl R. J. Macer, "Bioethics Education, Awareness of Ethics and Dissemination of Knowledge," in *Human Genome Research: Emerging Ethical, Legal, Social and Economic Issues,* ed. Mambillikalathil Govind Kumar Menon et al. (New Delhi: Allied Publishers, 1999), 99–208.

4. The analyses by scientists show that in many nations whole counties are planted with a single strain of corn or soybeans. Rather than a mix of different crops and pasture, a crowd mentality (fueled by seed companies, land grant universities, and lenders) stakes the life of farms and communities on a single crop. Not only does that uniformity raise the risk from a quirk of weather or market forces; it actively encourages the spread of damaging insects and fungal blight.

5. See the analysis of C. Pandian and D. Macer, "Bioethics Education in High Schools: An Investigation in Tamil Nadu with Comparisons to Australia, Japan and New Zealand," in *Bioethics in India,* ed. J. Azariah, H. Azariah, and D. R. J. Macer (Ibaraki, Japan: Eubios Ethics Institute, 1998), 390–400.

6. For example, the *biyasi* system of rice cultivation was very beneficial for the farmers cultivating on lowlands. Under the broadcasting method, the farmers kept the seeds ready for sowing just before the onset of rains in June. After the seeds germinated for a little more than five weeks and the water reached the height of the seedlings, the fields were ploughed with the standing crop to take care of weeds in around July and August. Thereafter, the crop was left to grow with the villagers guarding it till harvest. The Marias of Abhujmarh practiced this type of rice cultivation under the shifting system of cultivation where these tribes burnt the trees in the forests to convert a strip of forests into cultivable land just before the rains. They then spread the ashes on the ground and waited for the rains to come before they broadcasted the paddy seeds. After this they practiced the *biyasi* system as described by Dr. Richaria, the only difference being that the Marias shifted their fields every two or three years. They came back to the same fields only when the forest cover had regenerated, after a gap of thirteen or fourteen years. For an analysis see Ilina Sen, "Decentralized Food Security Systems and Women: An Examination of Viable Alternatives in Food Security Arrangements among Forest Communities in Chhattisgarh and Possibilities for Their Recreation" (paper presented at the Conference on Ethical and Gender Issues in Biotechnology, Madras University, Chennai., April 2005), 17–19.

7. For the amazing variety of crops see Sen, "Decentralized Food Security Systems and Women," 18.

8. Ibid., 17–19.

9. Ibid., 20.

10. Neera Mani, "The Earth Our Dwelling Place" (paper presented at the Conference on Ethical and Gender Issues in Biotechnology, Madras University, Chennai., April 2005), 14.

11. Dave Bookless, "Theology of the Land: Foundational Principles," online at *www.arocha.org/resources/uk/2002/env-sunday/b1-theology.doc.*

12. This is a remarkable way in which the lower castes and women try to appropriate the claims made by the upper classes and interpret them for their own benefit.

13. George Thadathil, "The Vision of Sri Narayana Guru Movement in the Literature of Nitya Chaitanya Yati," Ph.D. dissertation (University of Madras, 2002), 179 (forthcoming).

14. Pushpa Joseph, "Philosophizing from Feminist Perspectives," in *Subaltern Perspectives: Philosophizing in Context,* ed. George Thadathil (Bangalore: ATC Publications, 2005), 218.

15. Diana Meyers, "Feminist Perspectives on the Self," in *Stanford Encyclopedia of Philosophy, http://plato.stanford.edu/entries/feminism-self/#BM2*; also see Elisabeth Porter, *Feminist Perspectives on Ethics* (New York: Longman, 1999), 11.

16. Susan Brison, "Outliving Oneself: Trauma, Memory and Personal Identity," in *Feminists Rethink the Self,* ed. Diana Tietjens et al. (Boulder, Colo.: Westview Press, 1997), 4–50.

17. Sankara, the exponent of *advaitic* philosophy, affirms that our extended body is the environment and it contains the never-ending supply of energy and information that is available to us. There is no boundary between our body and our extended bodies. Each breath that we inhale and exhale is a reminder of the continuous conversation taking place between our physical body and our environment.

18. The event of the Chipko women hugging the trees can be seen as a kairotic moment (I mean God's moment of intervention/incarnation, *sambvami yugé yugé*) because simple rural women who were considered to be "powerless and faceless entities" unite together in the simple act of "hugging trees." Ramachandra Guha, in his narrative of the Chipko movement, underscores that these women were placing their bodies between the trees — their extended bodies since, according to Sankara, nature is your extended body — and the hackers who were ready with sharp axes. The sharp axes, symbolizing the might of the empire, could at any moment go down on the backs of the "hugging women" tearing their flesh into pieces by the might of the empire. I would like to enter into a critical theologizing with the very intention of bringing to our critical awareness the kairotic impact of this moment on Indian culture (dominant), on the lives of Indian women under the yoke of cultural codifications, and on the project of theologizing at large. See Githa Hariharan, "Second Thoughts: Embracing Other Selves," *The Telegraph* 24 (May 21, 2006): 8.

19. Walter Brueggemann, *The Land as Gift, Promise, and Challenge in Biblical Faith* (Minneapolis: Fortress Press, 1978), 96.

20. Bookless, "Theology of the Land."

21. Peterson, "Bio-Regional Ecosystems and the Form and Function of Public Policy."

22. Ibid.

11

Gendered Identity Formation
and Moral Theology

CHRISTINE E. GUDORF

Almost fifty years ago, Valerie Saiving, perhaps the first theologian of the contemporary feminist movement, published an article in which she proposed that Christian formulations of sin and virtue served the moral interests of men but not women.[1] She argued that definitions of sin in terms of pride and selfishness serve to set limits on the secular socialization of males to be ambitious competitors for power, wealth, and control, and to thus make possible a male moral self open to concern for neighbor. But that same definition of sin in terms of pride and selfishness, she suggested, reinforce the socialization of females to be passive and self-sacrificial nurturers of others, thus often obstructing, if not preventing, in females the possibility of responsible agency.

Saiving's article thus argued both for expanding definitions of sin to cover types of moral passivity more common among women, and for more androgynous socialization processes that would encourage both sexes to be both nurturing and ambitious. Saiving's article was written at the beginning of a period when socialization was considered the basis of sex differences. Today the pendulum has swung, and both biological and social scientists are clear that sex differences draw on a complex interweaving of genetic and environmentally influenced processes that unfold at various stages in development.

I would like to propose an argument similar to Saiving's in some ways, one expanded beyond Christian definitions of sin and virtue, but still dealing with sex differences and morality. I should stress that I am being pushed by research findings to formulate questions with which I am not at all comfortable, but to which I feel driven by intellectual honesty. My initial interest in returning to Saiving's argument was aroused by Linda Holler's *Erotic Morality,* in which she demonstrates that autistics and persons with various kinds of brain injuries are not capable of moral behavior based in empathy for the sufferings or welfare of others because they are unable either partially or completely to recognize the emotions of others.[2] Autistics' desire to act morally induced them to demand specific, objective deontological moral rules. I was, and still am, disturbed that large groups of persons seem incapable of empathy. The most basic moral precepts of religion and philosophy — love your neighbor, do no harm — are based upon reading the emotions of others. Even applications of the Golden Rule — do unto others as you would have them do unto you — are actually first learned in terms of not making "Jimmy" hurt if you don't like to hurt. If one cannot tell when "Jimmy" is hurt, the rule has little effect. If the authority of rules depends not on shared commitment to human flourishing, but on the source of the rule, then the prospects for the Reign of God seem infinitely more remote.

Connecting Holler's work with recent research in biology and psychology on sex differences exacerbated my concern. Part of her argument was that many persons share with autistics and brain damaged persons some degree of disability in reading the emotions of others, and thus of one's effects on others. Recent research has established fairly well that males as a group, compared to females as a group, share with autistic and brain damaged persons some degree of difficulty with discerning the emotions of others. Even more remarkably, male-type difficulty in recognizing and responding to emotions, particularly emotions of distress, is present in the first months of life and remains throughout adulthood. This is not to say that no males or all females share an ability to read emotions of others, or that men or women cannot or do not learn to improve their ability to read others' emotions. Yet sex group differences are significant and persistent. In the last forty years, more than thirty studies conducted on infants and children show that boys are more oriented toward objects and girls to people, as measured in duration of eye contact, empathetic response to distress in others, recognition of faces, and time spent looking at faces or objects.[3] Several studies found that infant girls are more responsive to and more sensitive to social cues than infant boys. For example, when infants of six months were placed in the presence of an unfamiliar and potentially threatening toy (a monkey), both sexes would approach the toy if their mothers' cues were positive and encouraging.[4] But when the mothers' cues were negative, despite the fact that mothers' warning cues to boys were significantly more intense than those directed at girls, boys tended to approach the toy and girls to withdraw.[5] In another study of six-to-twelve-month-olds, mothers were found just as likely to initiate social interactions with sons as daughters, but daughters were much more responsive than sons to these overtures.[6] When this study was repeated across a wide variety of cultures with twelve-month-olds, girls responded to mothers at a rate of 52 percent and boys with a 25 percent rate.[7] Girls also initiated communication 30 percent more often than boys.[8] It was found that boys orient themselves more often to geometric shapes, to colored objects, blinking lights, and non-human three dimensional objects than to other persons.[9]

One 1988 study of children conducted in Liberia, Kenya, India, Mexico, the Philippines, Japan, and the United States concluded:

Of the five major categories of interpersonal behavior explored — nurturance, dependency, prosocial dominance, egoistic dominance, and sociability — two emerge as associated with sex differences. Across the three older age groups (knee, yard, and school-age children) girls on average are more nurturant than boys in all dyad types . . . while boys are more egoistically dominant than girls.[10]

These early differences seem to be strengthened by the voluntary sex segregation that Eleanor Maccoby documents as occurring cross culturally between the age of three and late puberty.[11] With different interests, skills, and social strategies, boys and girls have different play styles. Initially boys try to involve girls in rough and tumble play, but girls shy away; girls try to influence boys through verbal requests and suggestions, but boys are unresponsive.

Sex differences revealed in standard personality tests normed in the United States and given to 105,742 adults from six different nations from the 1940s through the 1990s showed a clear pattern, with only minor differences in magnitude across nations. Six of seven women showed higher levels of "tender-mindedness" (defined as nurturance and empathy) than the average man, and seven of ten men scored higher than the average woman on measures of assertiveness.[12]

There are related sex differences in the ability to interpret and send nonverbal social messages, including differences in processing facial expressions of others, as well as interpreting body posture and changes in intonation independent of actual speech content. In cross-cultural studies, these differences always favor girls and women, though the advantage of females is most pronounced for facial cues, less pronounced for body cues, and least pronounced for vocal cues.[13] When all nonverbal cues are combined, seventeen of twenty females were more skilled at decoding nonverbal cues in real world settings than the average male.[14]

But this same study showed that seventeen of twenty females also regularly conveyed more information in facial expression than did the average male.[15] Other research shows that males also express much less emotion verbally than do females, with the exception of anger.

Women have a significant advantage over men in reading emotions of disgust, fear, and sadness in others, and tend to read equally well expressions of anger in men and women.[16] Men are significantly better at reading anger in other adult males, especially when that adult gazes at them directly, than they are at reading any other emotion, or at reading anger in women or adolescent males.[17] In fact, recent studies suggest that men might be particularly insensitive to women's sad facial expressions.[18] The anger of adult males is the only emotion that men read better than women from nonverbal cues. The general interpretation is that men are more sensitive to negative dominance cues as the result of millennia of male-male competition for advantage in sexual selection.[19]

The sexual basis of this ability to read emotions of others is clarified by a number of other studies. The processing of facial expressions in women responds to hormonal fluctuations in the female menstrual cycle: females' processing of facial expressions is at its height when estradiol and progesterone levels are near peak, and such processing also increases when post-menopausal women are put on hormone replacement therapy.[20]

Furthermore, studies of Turner Syndrome women, who have only one sex chromosome, an X, determined that women who received their X from their mothers performed at lower male-type levels in processing nonverbal social cues, but that the 29 percent of Turner Syndrome women who received their X from their fathers performed at or above the higher female-type level.[21] This suggests one reason why male processing levels are lower: these skills are carried on the paternal X chromosome, and boys' only X chromosome comes from their mothers, not from their fathers.

There is a great deal more to be learned about sex differences, though we need to be critical of research design and interpretation of findings. A number of well-touted studies about sex differences suffer from major defects in research design — too few subjects, unsupported assumptions about sexual orientation, unaccounted for intervening variables — as well as from over-interpretation of findings. At the present moment, however, it appears that most females have a significant advantage in interpreting what actions "love your neighbor" or "do no harm" require in specific situations, because they are better able than most males to read the feelings of others. Responding to suffering is at the heart of the Christian imperative. Male-types seem not only disadvantaged in their ability to recognize and therefore respond to suffering in others, but also disadvantaged in that they are significantly less expressive of emotions than female-types, and therefore less likely to have their suffering recognized and responded to.

Thus, existing sex differences within human anthropology raise interesting questions for moral theology:

1. Should we be insisting on formal statements of sexual consent — among the married as well as the unmarried? Over the last few decades, many of us have been advocating a shift from objective rules of behavior toward greater formation of individual conscience based on sensitivity to the needs of an Other. In sexuality, for example, we have been arguing for the normativity of mutuality and consent but, given differences in perceptions of others, male-type persons and female-type persons interpret these concepts differently. As sociological studies have long shown, many males' notions of consent to sex assume female consent unless forcibly prevented.[22] New evidence suggests they assume this not only because of socialization, or self-interest, but also because they are not wired to read social cues.

2. Should we be teaching male-types to be more expressive, so that others can better recognize the suffering of male-types? This proposal, of course,

assumes that male-types recognize their own suffering, but merely fail to express it. This assumption is far from demonstrated in the research. To the contrary, we have many medical studies that show that males are much less likely to see doctors for either physical or mental problems, and that when life-threatening conditions are discovered in men they are often discovered later and at more advanced stages, producing higher mortality rates. Perhaps instead of assuming that we all recognize our own suffering and that of others — that empathy is a capacity that all humans share — and building moral education on that assumption, we need to begin moral education with specific training in reading both our own emotions and the emotions of others. Some have suggested that we should be educating male-types to be more expressive of emotion, to shed the warrior's façade of invincibility to pain that developed within sexual selection from male-male competition. Most of the other male characteristics produced through male-male competition — such as larger size, bigger hearts, more upper body strength, and muscles more adept at neutralizing the effects of exercise — are largely now, in postmodernity, no longer advantageous, and the aggressiveness connected to high testosterone levels has clearly become problematic.

But training in recognizing, expressing, and reading emotions is not only necessary for male-types. Female-types may be more adept at reading emotions of others because relative powerlessness has made this an important survival skill almost certainly subject to sexual selection too. Female-types may also express more emotion in face or body posture than men. But female-types could also benefit from training in not only recognizing their own emotions, but discerning the causes of them, as psychological surveys on happiness in men and women have shown for many decades. In much of traditional marriage there seems to be an emotional co-dependency that is often treated in terms of complementarity: men have felt a need for women as emotional outlets, and women have felt a need for successful relationships with men in order to feel fulfilled as women.

3. How well can intellectual approaches to justice function without the empathy that so often alerts us to some lack of justice around us? There is a cruel irony in the concentration of power and authority around the world in the hands of male-types with a deficit in recognizing and responding to human distress. This is perhaps even more poignant in the church, where ordained ministry is restricted to males on the grounds that only males can resemble Jesus, the compassionate one. And as Paul Valadier pointed out here in the Intercontinental Panel on the *Sensus Fidelium,* the Magisterium needs to "read" the receivers of their teaching tradition in order to assess what has been understood. When the Magisterium does not (or cannot) "read" the laity, church teaching easily becomes irrelevant. Today in the Catholic Church, the Magisterium at both papal and episcopal levels seems to have severe difficulties "reading" the *sensus fidelium* around issues of

sexuality, not only on ongoing issues such as the ban on contraception, but more recently and dramatically in the priest pedophilia scandal. Nothing before this scandal has so alerted the laity to the Magisterium's problematic focus on individual sin and the administration of repentance and forgiveness — here on forgiving the sin of priests in breaking their celibacy vows — rather than on issues of justice, suffering, and ecclesial responsibility for the common good.

4. The genetically and biologically based sex differences discussed above can be and are attenuated in specific environmental situations. Many adaptations have long been in place unconsciously. For example, mothers have cross-culturally adapted to sons' lesser responsiveness. Despite the fact that daughters of one year or less are twice as responsive to physical or verbal initiatives from mothers as are sons, mothers initiate with sons as often as with daughters, but adapt to sons' lesser responsiveness through greater intensity — raising their voices, creating a face-to-face link, or using an object to gain sons' attention.[23] It also seems that male-types with significant childcare experience are better at reading emotional cues, especially of children, than are other male-types. Because there does seem to be some learning involved in this skill, despite its genetic base, many of the suggestions that emerged from earlier studies that assumed socialization was the foundation of sex differences are still relevant: involve male-types in childcare and continue to change the power differential between men and women in society.[24]

Conclusion

Since the Second Vatican Council, many of us moral theologians have pointed to physicalism as the fundamental problem with church approaches to sexuality. Biology, we said (by which we meant anatomy), is not destiny. Meanwhile, developments in the biological sciences, and their intersection with findings in the sociological and psychological sciences, have changed the situation so that biology is no longer a prop, but a problem, for traditional moral teachings of the church on sexuality.[25] Whether we speak of sexual orientation, sexual identity, or sex differences, biology and related sciences present us with complex data that cannot be reduced simply to a dimorphic, complementary human sexuality; instead it calls into question not only what we teach at church about sexuality and morality, but also how we teach it. This research demands new attention to the process of human moral development with serious attention to the possibility that the persistence of different models for the exercise of moral development among humans is related to the complex and varied nature of the hardwiring in humans.

Notes

1. Valerie Saiving [Goldstein], "The Human Situation: A Feminine View," *Journal of Religion* 40 (1960): 100–112.

2. Linda Holler, *Erotic Morality: The Role of Touch in Moral Agency* (Piscataway, N.J.: Rutgers University Press, 2002).

3. David C. Geary, *Male, Female: The Evolution of Human Sex Differences* (Washington, D.C.: American Psychological Association, 1998), 218–21.

4. M. R. Gunnar and C. Stone, "The Effects of Positive Maternal Affect on Infant Responses to Pleasant, Ambiguous and Fear-Provoking Toys," *Child Development* 55 (1984): 1231–36.

5. W. D. Rosen, L. B. Anderson, and R. Bakeman, "An Experimental Investigation of Infant Social Referencing: Mother's Messages and Gender Differences," *Developmental Psychology* 28 (1992): 1172–78.

6. M. R. Gunnar and M. Donahue, "Sex Differences in Social Responsiveness Between Six and Twelve Months," *Child Development* 51 (1980): 262–65.

7. Beatrice B. Whiting and Carolyn P. Edwards, *Children of Different Worlds: The Formation of Social Behavior* (Cambridge: Cambridge University Press, 1988).

8. Ibid.

9. D. McGuiness and K. H. Pribram, "The Origins of Sensory Bias in the Development of Gender Differences in Perception and Cognition," in *Cognitive Growth and Development: Essays in Memory of Herbert G. Birch,* ed. M. Bortner (New York: Brunner/Mazel, 1979), 19.

10. Whiting and Edwards, *Children of Different Worlds,* 270.

11. Eleanor Maccoby, *The Two Sexes: Growing Up Apart, Coming Together* (Cambridge, Mass.: Harvard University Press, 1998); David C. Geary, *Male, Female: The Evolution of Human Sex Differences* (Washington, D.C.: American Psychological Association, 1998), 240.

12. A. Feingold, "Gender Differences in Personality: A Meta-Analysis," *Psychological Bulletin* 116 (1994): 429–56.

13. J. A. Hall, *Non-Verbal Sex Differences: Communication Accuracy and Expressive Style* (Baltimore: Johns Hopkins University Press, 1984), 27.

14. Robert Rosenthal, Judith A. Hall, M. R. DiMatteo, P. L. Rogers, and D. Archer, *Sensitivity to Nonverbal Communication: The PONS Test* (Baltimore: Johns Hopkins University Press, 1979); J. A. Hall, "Gender Effects in Decoding Nonverbal Cues," *Psychological Bulletin* 85 (1978): 845–57; Hall, *Non-Verbal Sex Differences.*

15. Hall, *Non-Verbal Sex Differences.*

16. N. G. Rotter and G. S. Rotter, "Sex Differences in the Encoding and Decoding of Negative Facial Emotions," *Journal of Nonverbal Behavior* 12 (1988): 139–48.

17. Rotter and Rotter, "Sex Differences in the Encoding and Decoding of Negative Facial Emotions"; H. L. Wagner, R. Buck, and M. Winterbotham, "Communication of Specific Emotions: Gender Differences in Sending Accuracy and Communication Measures," *Journal of Nonverbal Behavior* 17 (1993): 29–53.

18. R. J. Erwin, R. C. Gur, R. E. Gur, B. Scolnick, M. Mawhinney-Hee, and J. Smailis, "Facial Emotion Discrimination: I. Task Construction and Behavioral Findings in Normal Subjects," *Psychiatry Research* 42 (1992): 231–40; R. C. Gur, B. E Scolnick, and R. E. Gur, "Effects of Emotional Discrimination Task on Cerebral Blood Flow: Regional Activation and Its Relation to Performance," *Brain and Cognition* 25 (1994): 271–86.

19. Rosenthal et al., *Sensitivity to Nonverbal Communication;* Geary, *Male, Female,* 295–98. Women's advantage in virtually every aspect of individual level social competency is similarly explained by evolutionists as the result of predominantly patrilocal residency patterns combined with female's parental investment pattern: women most often lived with the kin of their mate and wanted stable social communities in which to rear children. Therefore, selection pressures would favor those females successful at developing and maintaining social relationships.

20. G. Heister. T. Landis, M. Regard, and P. Schroeder-Heister, "Shift of Functional Cerebral Asymmetry during the Menstrual Cycle," *Neuropsychologia* 27 (1989): 871–80.

21. D. H. Skuse, R. S. James, D. V. M. Bishop, B. Coppin, P. Dalton, G. Aamodt-Leeper, M. Bacarese-Hamilton, C. Creswell, R. McGurk, and P. A. Jacobs, "Evidence from Turner's Syndrome of an Imprinted X-Linked Locus Affecting Cognitive Function," *Nature* 387 (1997): 705–8.

22. Charlotte Muehlenhard is one of the best known researchers in this area. See her "Misinterpreting Dating Behaviors and the Risk of Date Rape," *Journal of Social and Clinical Psychology* 6 (1988): 20–37; see also C. Muehlenhard and S. Andrews, "Open Communication about Sex: Will It Reduce Risk Factors Related to Rape?" presented at the Annual Meeting of the Association for Advancement of Behavior Therapy (Houston, November 1985); C. Muehlenhard, A. Felts, and S. Andrews, "Men's Attitudes toward the Justifiability of Date Rape: Intervening Variables and Possible Solutions," presented at the Midcontinent Meeting of the Society for the Scientific Study of Sex (Chicago, June 1985); C. Muehlenhard, M. Goggins, J. Jones, and A. Satterfield, "Sexual Violence and Coercion in Close Relationships," in *Sexuality in Close Relationships,* ed. K. McKinney and S. Sprecher (Hilldale, N.J.: Erlbaum Publishing, 1991); C. Muehlenhard and L. Hollabaugh, "Do Women Sometimes Say No when They Mean Yes? The Prevalence and Correlates of Women's Token Resistance to Sex," *Journal of Personality and Social Psychology* 54 (1989): 872–79; C. Muehlenhard and M. Linton, "Date Rape and Sexual Aggression in Dating Situations: Incidence and Risk Factors," *Journal of Consulting Psychology* 34 (1987): 186–96; C. Muehlenhard, Z. Peterson, L. Karwoski, T. Bryan, and R. Lee, "Gender and Sexuality: An Introduction to the Special Issue," *Journal of Sex Research* 40 (2003): 1–3; C. Muehlenhard and C. Rodgers, "Token Resistance to Sex: New Perspectives on an Old Stereotype," *Psychology of Women Quarterly* 22 (1998): 443–63; C. Muehlenhard and J. Schrag, "Non-Violent Sexual Coercion," in *Acquaintance Rape: The Hidden Crime,* ed. A. Parrot and L. Bechkhofer (New York: John Wiley & Sons, 1991).

23. Rosen et al., "An Experimental Investigation of Infant Social Referencing."

24. For example, Nancy Chodorow, *The Reproduction of Mothering: Psychoanalysis and the Sociology of Gender* (Berkeley: University of California Press, 1974); Carol Gilligan, *In a Different Voice: Psychological Theory and Women's Development* (Cambridge, Mass.: Harvard University Press, 1982).

25. Janet Shibley Hyde, ed., *Biological Substrates of Human Sexuality* (Washington, D.C.: American Psychological Association, 2005), 171–78.

PART THREE
WAR AND PEACE

12

A Tale of Two Presumptions

The Development of Roman Catholic Just War Theory

WILLIAM WERPEHOWSKI

Contemporary theological ethical reflection on the morality of warfare has included a debate about how one ought to understand the nature and purpose of just war theory. On one side, and presumably in keeping with the U.S. Catholic bishops' 1983 Pastoral Letter, *The Challenge of Peace,* just war reflection takes its point of departure from a moral "presumption against war," and normative criteria are employed to set stringent conditions for overriding that presumption. Critics of this approach, on the other side, insist on historical and logical grounds that this effectively corrupts just war ethics by, for example, inconsistently and otherwise disastrously allying it with a bankrupt "practical" or "functional" pacifism (or pacifism *simpliciter*), and by evading the meaning and character of a viable political ethic of "statecraft" for a world still effectively made up of sovereign nation-states. Over against the "presumption against war," these critics urge that just war thinking begins with a "presumption against injustice," that is, with the "presumption to restrain evil and protect the innocent"[1] by the "use of the authority and force of the rightly ordered political community."[2]

A good example of the latter view is the ongoing challenge of one of our most important just war theorists, James Turner Johnson. In a recent study on the "war to oust Saddam Hussein," Johnson contrasts contemporary Catholic just war doctrine, which begins "with a general 'presumption against war'" and presents "jus ad bellum criteria as guidance for determining whether this presumption should be overruled in particular cases or not," with the "classic tradition's" understanding of the use of force as "morally neutral" yet "good" when a war is determined to be just in terms of the interconnected primary norms of just cause, sovereign authority, and right intention. Referring specifically to *The Challenge of Peace,* he explains this apparent departure from the classic tradition in terms of its aiding the Catholic bishops in their categorical opposition to the use of nuclear weapons, its marking out a middle ground among both "just war" and "pacifist" Catholics (since both are taken to share the presumption), and its indebtedness to James Childress's interpretation of just war theory as defining a set of criteria that would override a prima facie duty not to kill or injure.[3] Johnson is convinced that this position "has essentially turned into a rejection of war, that is, a functional pacifism,"[4] and cites as exemplary Bishop Wilton Gregory's letter to President George W. Bush in September 2002 regarding the question of waging war with Iraq. But Johnson fails to note that at the beginning of that letter, Gregory, then President of the U.S. Conference of Catholic Bishops, refers to an earlier communication to Bush written by his predecessor, Bishop Joseph Fiorenza, in which the bishops judged that "the use of force against Afghanistan could be justified, if it were carried out in accord with just war norms and as one part of a much broader, mostly non-military effort to deal with terrorism."[5] I believe that this claim belies any sweeping assertions about "the rejection of war" and "functional pacifism." Johnson, moreover, never considers adequately enough, in my understanding, the theological arguments underpinning the so-called "presumption against war" view.

Defenders of the "presumption against war" perspective, however, do at times appear to argue for too much by trading on controversial matters of general ethical theory and its relation to just war doctrine.[6] Just to that extent, and thus like their counterparts, they may be arguing too little from relevant grounds rooted in Christian faith. Generally, one can reasonably worry that the energy in this debate may be based on parties merely jousting with phantoms or caricatures of their opponents, who are taken to be, after all, either realists or pacifists in just-warrior dress. I do not deny that the contest has yielded valuable insights; but I do question whether the clarity and volume of further insights might be improved if all the parties involved reoriented their respective viewpoints.

In what follows, I will argue that there are in fact sound reasons for endorsing *in part* the "presumption against war" position as one feature of a developing Roman Catholic political ethic that seeks to locate just war thinking more nearly within a fitting theological context and, in particular, in line with an eschatological vision of human persons and peoples in relation in the world under God in Jesus Christ. If we understand and affirm these reasons, we may be in a position to know better how to proceed in critically advancing and testing this ethic. I will also suggest that Roman Catholic reflection on war does not at all exclude positive attention to the way in which a "presumption against injustice" figures in moral assessments of armed conflict.

Consider the following reading of the U.S. bishops' 1983 claim in *The Challenge of Peace* that just war theory "starts from" a "presumption against war." First, just war theory "begins with the presumption that binds all Christians," a norm of neighbor love that consists of a general duty not to do harm, the "key test" of love of enemies, and a stance of deep moral seriousness, even horror, toward any act of killing.[7] Second, one moves from this presumption (which is important but not yet, remember, the one or other we are stalking) to the just use of lethal force by way of the "Augustinian insight" that the former yields to the overarching and authorizing "command of love"; the meaning of this command is now deepened by the understanding of the need in a fallen world "to restrain an enemy who would injure the innocent (par. 81)." The bishops identify this as the "central premise" of just war argument in Catholic theology; as such, it can fairly be named its "starting point" and also *renamed* a "presumption against injustice." Third, the bishops claim that just war teaching has *evolved,* after its proper and continuing affirmation of war's legitimacy concerning a government's right of self-defense in a "decentralized international order," "as an effort to prevent war." Just war criteria require "extraordinarily strong reasons for overriding the presumption *in favor of peace and against war* (par. 83, emphasis in original)." Note that the appeal to this presumption is based on a Catholic interpretation of, and contribution to, a developing Catholic just war tradition. Johnson's contrasting appeal to his interpretation of the "classic tradition" in this connection is well-taken; but to resist a religious community's historical efforts before God to faithfully develop its particular moral teaching simply in the name of that "tradition," as Johnson sometimes appears to do, risks a kind of historical positivism.[8] This maneuver would also be odd if it is taken for the sake of vindicating a preferred "presumption against injustice" that, I am suggesting, *The Challenge of Peace* also and already acknowledges.

Thus, within the theory, the "central premise" of which is that love may command protection of the innocent through the use of violent force, there stands a presumption in favor of peace and against war. This position is not incoherent; but it bears within itself and elaborates two severe tensions. One is between the rightful claim to the use of force and an avowed moral pressure, imposed in pertinent part by just war criteria, against using it. This moral pressure comes to light, for example, in the theory's employment of a criterion of "comparative justice" that, as Paul Ramsey observed, "relativizes 'just cause itself.' The bishops stress this in order to add weight to the need to limit war. They say, in effect, we need all the more to *limit* 'limited war,' dampen down its destructiveness, because in a comparison of justices none escapes moral criticism."[9] The other tension has to do with the affirmation of just war theory and pacifist nonviolence as moral responses to injustice inasmuch as they both share *this one* presumption against war and may preserve one another from distortion.

The tensions and the "presumptions" that sustain them are justified by a vision of the relation between fallen human history and the inbreaking Kingdom of God. This vision focuses on the paradox that nonviolent means of "fending off aggression and resolving conflict best reflects the call of Jesus both to love and to justice," while war yet remains a moral possibility, and indeed, necessity, to oppose injustice (par. 78). The pressure against war *within* just war theory is an expression of this paradox, as it is to be embodied in Catholic moral deliberation and judgment, and the tensive relation *between* the theory and pacifist nonviolence is as well;[10] the "complementary" relation between just war and nonviolence is a matter of each strategy honoring a feature of the paradoxical relation between fallen human history and the Kingdom of God for which we wait but is yet present in promise. Both moral approaches to injustice respectively serve the "common good" thereby.

In light of the preceding argument, we can say that a Catholic political witness to the state, in the service of the common good, may have many dimensions. There will be a call to develop the variety of nonviolent approaches to the resolution of conflict (this is a theme implicit in *The Challenge of Peace*, but it is explicitly affirmed in the bishops' 1993 document, *The Harvest of Justice Is Sown in Peace*).[11] There will be pacifist opposition to war as well as arguments to vindicate justice through recourse to it. In time of war, vigilant questions about it and defenses of its justice will go forward. More specifically, I would imagine that a Roman Catholic witness to the state might also include the following four strategies of discernment — strategies in which Catholic theological ethics may constructively participate.

First, there may be, in keeping with an *ad bellum* norm of just intention, an attempt to oppose an "ideology of war" that resists easy claims, not only about the *absolute* justice of war that fosters a crusade mentality (consider here the interaction with "comparative justice"), but also about its inevitability and the impossibility of peace. The effort would also expose ignoble motives of political domination and economic interest and would not shrink from detailing what the horrors of war are and do.[12] This is not a matter of tendentiously parading certain sorts of "worst case scenarios";[13] — it is rather to offer morally reasonable and politically realistic challenges to would-be "best case scenarios" taken on the cheap.

Second, and in accord with seeking the end of war in peace and an *in bello* norm of just intention, there would be the effort to discover how to be (and how it is or is not possible to be), as Augustine had it, "peaceful in warring." That is, how may warriors be "free from the enslaving power of force,"[14] and wage it, when it must be waged, without hatred or the desire for vengeance?[15] One may think that the first strategy is more likely the province of "pacifist" Catholics and the second the concern of "just war" types. But the options may and ought not to be exclusive in this way. The former may learn from and fittingly adapt John Howard Yoder's important and still neglected early monograph, *The Christian Witness to the State*; there he outlines and gives examples of a viable pacifist evangelical word to political and military leaders along a "continuum of increasing tolerability," that proposes ways to make wars *less unjust*.[16] Just war advocates, in their turn, should be concerned about practical employments of the theory that give it a bad name as they also damage the common good of societies.

Third, the common good has increasingly been conceived in Roman Catholic theological ethics as bearing a global referent, based on "the theological truth: the unity of the human family — rooted in common creation, destined for the kingdom, and united by moral bonds of rights and duties" (par. 235). The concept of world order is normatively qualified by a call to solidarity, "a firm and persevering determination to commit oneself to the common good; that is to say, to the good of all and of each individual, because we are all really responsible for all."[17] The case for global solidarity, in turn, affords a basis for interpreting practical employments of a longstanding Roman Catholic *cosmopolitanism* that concedes yet challenges and redirects our "standing" nation-state system toward international agreements honoring forms of legitimate international authority in the name of human rights. Thus Catholic moral theology "accords a real but relative value to sovereign states" (par. 237). Implications for reflection and action for peace and just war theory follow. To take one example, the emergence of a more robust and critical *ad bellum* condition of *proportionality* (which does a good deal of work in exercising the "pressure" against war that I mentioned earlier) drives moral attention toward the global costs (and benefits) of the presence and practice of war for the common good, and also toward these costs (and benefits) as they redound especially *to the poor*, with whom we are called to stand in solidarity. Moral costs to them are relatively greater, to the extent that the evil of their marginalization is increased, and this issue should play a role in considerations of how and why the vulnerable might also need to be protected through the use of force. Further, but more broadly, Catholic cosmopolitanism and its basis in solidarity may find instruction and refinement in proposals such as that of the Princeton Project on National Security, which commends "forging a world of liberty under law" through a "commitment to multilateralism" that "can be realized through a wide range of formal and informal multilateral tools: alliances, institutions, bilateral relations, treaties, public and private networks, rules, norms, and shared expectations — all of which provide multiple arenas for cooperation and action."[18]

These three strategies of Catholic witness and discernment can be understood to emerge from a "presumption against war" that possesses sensible theological backing. They may tend to raise "the threshold for resort to the use of force,"[19] but none of them weaken or exclude the sober acknowledgment that at some time wars for the sake of justice and with the end of peace may and must be waged. In fact, they may strengthen the acknowledgment by removing what impedes discovering its truth in the clear light of day.

As should be clear by now, I do not agree with Johnson's claim that *The Challenge of Peace* "frames peace wholly in terms of the absence of war, despite the threats to peace that remain";[20] the bishops explicitly deny that peace is merely the absence of war, assert that it is an "enterprise of justice," and clearly allow that the struggle for justice may threaten certain forms of peace (par. 68, 60). However, if my reading against his is right, then it should follow, fourth, that Roman Catholic deliberation, judgment, and action regarding war and peace may soundly heed his call to take seriously what it means to place, at the center of just war doctrine, the idea that the end of war is and can only be a justly ordered peace. Such seriousness involves understanding and endorsing the political and military responsibilities that are present before, during, and after armed conflicts regarding the protection of human rights, the provision of basic physical and economic security, respect for the rule of law, the overcoming of enmity, and the importance of "having international involvement as broad as possible in the effort to rebuild and reestablish a peaceful society."[21]

I have tried in this short essay to sketch a picture of a specific and pertinent Catholic witness to the state regarding the matter of war. Such a witness, according to the account proposed above, cannot be described strictly and simply in terms of a *sweeping suspicion in principle* about the use of force to protect the innocent; rather, and again, that force may and should be so used, when it is fitting. So critical attention to when and in what manner it *is* appropriate and necessary ought not to be considered as an effort, as Paul Ramsey put it, merely to discredit all wars one by one. It is instead the attempt to identify what the just use of force is concretely, and to that extent is an enterprise that can in fact strengthen a Catholic moral theory of the just war.

And yet and yet: if the way of nonviolence does best reflect the call of Jesus Christ, then some *sturdy suspicion in fact* about the use of force in this or that historical circumstance is also fitting. Discrediting wars and war — on any number of fronts — may then always and also be an act of faithfulness formed by charity. In this time between the times, to allude for the moment to the well-known Protestant voice of Reinhold Niebuhr, one prays for the wisdom to know the difference.

Notes

I want to thank Thomas Smith and Darlene Fozard Weaver for their comments on an earlier draft of this essay, as well as Linda Hogan and Jean Porter for their helpful remarks during the Padua conference on "Catholic Theological Ethics and the World Church."

1. Paul Ramsey, *Speak Up for Just War or Pacifism* (University Park: Pennsylvania University State Press, 1988), 83.

2. James Turner Johnson, "The Broken Tradition," *National Interest* (1996): 30.

3. James Turner Johnson, *The War to Oust Saddam Hussein* (Lanham, Md.: Rowman and Littlefield, 2005), 26–28. See also James F. Childress, "Just War

Criteria," in *War or Peace: The Search for New Answers,* ed. Thomas Shannon (Maryknoll, N.Y.: Orbis Books, 1980), 40–58.

4. Ibid., 32.

5. Available at *www.usccb.org/sdwp/international/bush902.htm.*

6. For an interesting challenge to figures, such as Lisa Sowle Cahill, who are supposedly wedded to a "prima facie system" in their discussion of just war theory, see Helmut David Baer and Joseph E. Capizzi, "Just War Theories Reconsidered: Problems with Prima Facie Duties and the Need for a Political Ethic," *Journal of Religious Ethics* 33, no. 1 (March 2005): 119–37.

7. National Conference of Catholic Bishops, *The Challenge of Peace* (Washington, D.C.: United States Catholic Conference, 1983), par. 80. Future references to this document will appear in the text.

8. I am indebted to Edmund N. Santurri for helping me to see this point.

9. Ramsey, *Speak Up for Just War or Pacifism,* 90.

10. Todd David Whitmore, "The Reception of Catholic Approaches to Peace and War in the United States," in *Modern Catholic Social Teaching: Commentaries and Interpretations,* ed. Kenneth R. Himes (Washington, D.C.: Georgetown University Press, 2005), 509.

11. National Conference of Catholic Bishops, *The Harvest of Justice Is Sown in Peace;* available at *www.nccbuscc.org/sdwp/harvest.htm;* see also Drew Christiansen, S.J., "A Roman Catholic Response," in John Howard Yoder, *When War Is Unjust: Being Honest in Just War Thinking* (Maryknoll, N.Y.: Orbis Books, 1996), 105–6.

12. *La Civiltá Cattolica,* "Modern War and Christian Conscience," in *Moral Issues and Christian Response,* 5th ed., ed. Paul T. Jersild and Dale Johnson (Fort Worth, TX: Harcourt Brace Jovanovich, 1993), 223–24.

13. Johnson, *The War to Oust Saddam Hussein,* 49, and elsewhere in the volume.

14. Gilbert Meilaender, "War and Techne," *The Atlantis* (Summer 2005): 53.

15. National Conference of Catholic Bishops, *The Harvest of Justice Is Sown in Peace.* Also see James Turner Johnson's moving discussion in *Morality and Contemporary Warfare* (New Haven: Yale University Press, 2001).

16. John Howard Yoder, *The Christian Witness to the State* (Scottsdale, PA: Herald Press, 1964), 48. Stanley Hauerwas turns to this study in his "Epilogue," in Paul Ramsey, *Speak Up for Just War or Pacifism: A Critique of the United Methodist Bishops' Pastoral Letter "In Defense of Creation"* (University Park: Pennsylvania State University Press, 1988), 159ff.

17. John Paul II, *On Social Concern,* 38. Available at *www.osjspm.org/cst/srs.htm.*

18. Final Paper of the Princeton Project on National Security, "Forging a World of Liberty under Law: U.S. National Security in the 21st Century," co-directors G. John Ikenberry and Anne-Marie Slaughter (September 27, 2006), 28. Available at *www.wws.princeton.edu/ppns/report/FinalReport.pdf.* See also the paper's general discussion of the use of force (29–32) and particularly "humanitarian intervention" and United Nations reform (23–25). I am grateful to Jean Porter for her counsel regarding this theme.

19. Christiansen, "A Roman Catholic Response," 112.

20. Johnson, *The War to Oust Saddam Hussein,* 29.

21. Ibid., 141–42.

13

A New *Casus Belli?*
Counterproliferation in an Age
of Terrorism

KENNETH R. HIMES

The just war tradition is an ongoing conversation that responds to, and evolves with, new experiences and ideas. Throughout history a variety of rationales have been offered to justify engaging in war. Due to the horror of World War II, Pius XII narrowed the range of acceptable rationales for war to defense against aggression.[1] More recent times have seen arguments presented that make a case for humanitarian intervention as a legitimate reason to take up arms under certain circumstances.[2] John Paul II gave support to this revision of Pius XII's position, and that change has been incorporated into the *Compendium of the Social Doctrine of the Church*.[3]

Present Catholic teaching on war, therefore, maintains that a just cause for taking up arms is twofold: self-defense against aggression or coming to the aid of defenseless victims of genocide or ethnic cleansing. Due to the nature of a living tradition, however, we ought not be surprised that conversation about the theory of just war continues and a new *casus belli* is again being proposed. My aim in this essay is to offer an assessment of a proposed expansion to the list of legitimating reasons for armed force — a new *casus belli* — the counterproliferation of nuclear weapons.

Armed Force and Counterproliferation

The structure of the argument can be outlined in six steps: (1) the devastation of nuclear weapons is so great that they must not be used; (2) nations with nuclear weapons have refrained from using them due to a system of deterrence; (3) classical schemes of deterrence do not work against terrorists nor against so-called "rogue states"; (4) therefore, such nations and terrorist organizations must not be allowed to possess nuclear weapons; (5) furthermore, the key ingredient in making nuclear weapons is enriched uranium or plutonium and verifiable control of these substances is the only effective way to avoid the spread of nuclear weapons; (6) consequently, dangerous nations or groups seeking to acquire existing fissile material or the capability to produce such material must be stopped, through diplomacy if possible, but through force if necessary.

How might just war theorists think about the case for counter-proliferation as an expansion of just cause beyond self-defense and humanitarian intervention?

The most notable case for the new cause to justify armed force was the 2002 National Security Strategy of the United States where it was argued that the nexus of global terrorist networks and Weapons of Mass Destruction (WMD)[4] forced those states likely to be terrorist targets to adopt a new strategy of initiating armed attacks to protect themselves.[5] Since then critics and supporters of the policy statement have subjected it to close scrutiny.

Duties to Protect (and Prevent?)

The crises of Rwanda, Bosnia, and Kosovo challenged the ability of the United Nations to protect the fundamental human rights of vulnerable populations. The failure to act in a timely manner in these cases led the U.N. secretary general to ask government leaders to establish a working policy that might guide action in future crises. In response to Kofi Annan's 1999 call for a consensus policy on humanitarian intervention, an international commission sponsored by the Canadian government proposed a new doctrine called "The Responsibility to Protect."[6] The essence of the doctrine is that "populations at risk of slaughter, ethnic cleansing and starvation" should be protected by the membership of the United Nations if individual "states are unwilling or unable to do so themselves."[7]

The responsibility to protect emerged from what the commission saw as a gap between the reality of massive human suffering and the existing rules and mechanisms for managing international order. To fill this gap the commission identified an international obligation, the responsibility to protect, which requires states to intervene in the internal affairs of other states to end the most extreme humanitarian crises.

In a later publication two influential members of the U.S. foreign policy elite made their case for counterproliferation intervention by proposing a corollary principle to the duty to protect. The Americans proposed a "duty to prevent." This new duty would entail preventing "nations run by rulers without internal checks on their power from acquiring or using WMD." In defending their position, Lee Feinstein and Anne Marie Slaughter suggest that, as with the duty to protect, "the premise is that the rules now governing the use of force, devised in 1945 and embedded in the U.N. Charter, are inadequate."[8]

According to the authors, the international commission's proposed revision of sovereignty and its rationale for a communal duty to protect are relevant to the issue of proliferation. With the growth of international terrorism, there is a new international obligation to address the dangers of nuclear weapon proliferation in a way that parallels that of the duty to protect. The "duty to prevent" evokes a responsibility incumbent upon states to act in concert to prevent governments lacking internal accountability from acquiring nuclear weapons. Where the weapons are in the hands of such non-accountable regimes, action must be taken to halt nuclear production and avoid transfer of nuclear capabilities, or actual weapons, to terrorist groups.

In sum, the argument for revising just cause to include counterproliferation is that it is an extrapolation from recent developments in the discussion of humanitarian intervention.

Response to Intervention for Counterproliferation

Criticisms of this proposed revision to the *jus ad bellum* are several.

First, there is the matter of setting the trip wire at the right place. Is the possession of nuclear weapons, or the infrastructure to produce them, satisfactory reason to go to war? Traditionally, suspicion or fear about another's intentions is not adequate reason to justify the use of force. If fear can serve as a justification for assault, then the possibilities for attack become near limitless.

Second, the uncertainty of assessing threats has been underlined by the aftermath of the Iraqi war. While the United States and its allies argued that Iraq was producing and storing WMDs, the post-invasion investigations have conclusively demonstrated that this was not the case at the time that the charges were being made at the United Nations and in other venues. The uncertainty of intelligence reports underscores the danger of confusing pre-emptive and preventive uses of armed force. The former has been accepted under conditions articulated by many just war theorists and developed over time.[9] The latter remains highly controversial and lacks anything resembling a supportive consensus.[10]

A third concern is that the Bush administration's policy is one of selective opposition to nuclear weapons, based on the simple criterion of whether you are a friend or foe. The new policy shifts the distinction from good and bad weapons to good and bad actors. However, a core presumption of the majority of those who oppose proliferation is the belief that all nuclear weapons are problematic. This constituency sees the recent pact between the United States and India as mistaken, for it tells other nations that it is okay to have nuclear weapons as long as you are not an enemy of the Americans. Should China or Russia follow this precedent, approving or at least tolerating new nuclear arsenals held by regimes friendly to them, there is little hope for advancing a consensus to stop North Korea or Iran. And what principle will then be left to dissuade others from developing nuclear arsenals as regional rivals of these nations — such as Japan, Saudi Arabia, or Turkey — consider joining the nuclear club?

A fourth criticism of the duty to prevent is the possibility of alternatives to a military assault. The new doctrine puts the emphasis in the wrong place. The shift to counterproliferation against "rogue states," a military option, and away from nonproliferation, a diplomatic strategy, is a major departure.[11] After all, nonproliferation has worked relatively well for many years while the counterproliferation approach is untested. Since the group of five (the United States, U.S.S.R./Russia, Britain, France, China) emerged in the 1950s, there have been only a few additions to the nuclear club (Israel, South Africa, India, Pakistan, and North Korea, with South Africa since disarming) to make a confirmed group of eight nations. Numerous other countries could develop nuclear weapons if they so chose (Germany, Sweden, Switzerland, Saudi Arabia, Egypt, Turkey, Japan, and Brazil, to name those who have had programs in the past or who could start them with relative ease). A world with fewer nuclear nations makes for an easier system of monitoring and control of fissionable material. If the worry is about such material falling into the hands of terrorists, why increase the number of possible sources? Further, if regional stability is a goal, why open up the risk of a Middle East or East Asia with three, four, or more nuclear actors?

Three Scenarios for Counterproliferation

Despite these reservations, the issue of armed force as a means of countering the proliferation of nuclear weapons has been moving to the forefront of policy debate.[12] The reality is that what shifted the Bush administration toward greater reliance upon military action is fear that nuclear weapons will fall into the hands of terrorists or their state-sponsors who cannot be checked by the same means that were used in the past.

Let us briefly consider three scenarios to understand the issues at stake. The first entails the spread of nuclear weapons to nations that are deterrable due to rational leaders who will calculate national interest and the risks of nuclear war. Certainly, if there are a growing number of nuclear weapons nations, the Nonproliferation Treaty will be in tatters, and an expanded list of nuclear powers does increase the risk of nuclear war. Yet the proliferation of nuclear weapons to countries such as Brazil or Egypt will not require a change from existing containment and deterrence strategies. Although not a future to be desired, it is one to which we ought to be able to adapt. Still, it would be best if this scenario were avoided. That is best done, however, not through threats of armed force, but measures that guarantee a nation's security without having to join the nuclear club, as well as offers to provide safe and reasonably cheap sources of enriched uranium for nuclear energy. In sum, this first scenario is not a persuasive case for expanding the *casus belli* to include counterproliferation.

A second scenario envisions the spread of nuclear weapons to nations that have a history of sponsorship or cooperation with international terrorism. Here the risk of nuclear attack appears to increase dramatically, should terrorists get access to the weapons. Yet we can ask if any leader would want to see such devastating weapons in the hands of people who would then be unaccountable for their use. Terrorists could turn around and use the weapons to blackmail the government that transferred them, demanding safe havens, greater involvement in governance, more financial support, even a transfer of power. Furthermore, the so-called "rogue states" are already under intense scrutiny and will have to presume they will be held accountable for any use of nuclear weapons. Finally, the science of reading the signature of nuclear weapons is already under development. This will make the risk of cooperation with terrorists much higher for a state. If a nation's leadership knows that retaliation for a nuclear attack would be aimed at the regime that provided the weapons, then we are very close to the first scenario of classical deterrence. It seems that this second scenario is at best a possible, though not entirely convincing, case for expanding just cause to include counterproliferation.

The final scenario entails the risk of terrorists obtaining nuclear weapons directly after theft of enriched uranium or plutonium. Presumably, the delivery of a weapon would be done not by missile but conventional transportation. It is difficult to see what difference the Bush doctrine of preventive force, or the duty to prevent, makes here. It is far better to secure and monitor all existing nuclear weapons as well as the storage of highly enriched uranium and plutonium. To achieve that goal, the emphasis ought to be on international cooperation in oversight of nuclear fuel through diplomacy; use of economic incentives to prevent the creation of a black market of nuclear materials or resources; employment of intrusive monitoring procedures; and improved protection of nuclear sites, both military and civilian. As for armed intervention, in this scenario it is more likely that any force would be employed not by a conventional military operation of state versus state, but special forces working with local authorities to detect and destroy terrorist cells that seek nuclear capability. In brief, this third scenario is not a compelling argument for expanding just cause within existing just war theory.

It appears, therefore, the case for expanding just cause to include counterproliferation comes down to the second scenario, when nuclear weapons come into the hands of what are called "rogue states." The difficulty is that the proposed scenario does not take into account the historical realities of likely targets for such counterproliferation intervention. It appears simply impractical to think that a "duty to prevent" can be universally applied. More likely, such a declaratory policy will create a climate of anxiety and resentment that fuels behavior inimical to diplomacy and non-military resolutions. The threat of force, recent events indicate, becomes a reason for certain nations to pursue the nuclear option.

Far wiser would be an approach that addresses the motivations for why some nations aspire to be nuclear powers. Searching for non-military methods of restraining proliferation is not a fail-safe option but the track record continues to show it has greater promise than an untested and unpersuasive argument for a new policy that will be highly selective in enforcement.

Conclusion

Those who support humanitarian intervention in principle do not all agree on what conditions make it justifiable. So too in the case for intervention as counterproliferation there will be difficult questions of "who" and "how," even if the "why" is satisfactorily presented. Put simply, any duty to prevent will be context-dependent.

If the list of what is to count as just cause grows, it will be crucial to raise up other criteria of just war theory when weighing military action. Legitimate authority, last resort, proper intent, reasonable hope of success, and proportionality are all relevant *jus ad bellum* norms to be considered.

As the debate over humanitarian intervention has made clear, proper authority for intervention ought to be multilateral, if not through the U.N. Security Council then via some regional authorization. A loose "coalition of the willing" falls short of the kind of multilateral authorization envisioned.

Last resort requires that diplomacy and non-military coercive measures should be given sufficient chance to prevent the acquisition of nuclear weapons. Proper intent demands that whatever military action is taken should be aimed solely at the destruction of the infrastructure supporting a nuclear weapons program. Reasonable hope of success means that it is deemed probable that any planned military action will actually halt or significantly delay the acquisition of nuclear capability. Proportion requires that the good attained by such counterproliferation activity is greater than any harm that occurs in conjunction with the activity, that is, it does not lead to full-scale war that results in significant loss of life and regional instability.

Additionally, support for new forms of military intervention under a revised *jus ad bellum* should require that *jus in bello* criteria be carefully observed in planning and carrying out an intervention. Proportional and discriminate uses of force are all the more important when there is an expanded set of circumstances permitting armed intervention.

In the end, there may exist a marginal possibility for armed intervention to counter nuclear weapons in situations where there is clear evidence that a state has hostile and aggressive intentions, ties with terrorism are clear, and there is overwhelming evidence that nuclear weapons are being developed. I say this even as I remain unpersuaded that "rogue states" are immune from existing policies of deterrence.

When the bishops assembled at Vatican II, they declared that it was imperative to evaluate "war with an entirely new attitude."[13] It was nuclear weapons that led to the conciliar call for rethinking modern war. The presence of these weapons continues to shape just war thinking, but three additional topics are also influencing the re-evaluation of what is a just cause for armed force: humanitarian intervention, terrorism, and the risks of nuclear proliferation. Due to this triad, it remains to be seen if the reasoning about just cause will expand to include counterproliferation of nuclear weapons.

Notes

1. John Courtney Murray, "Remarks on the Moral Problem of War," *Theological Studies* 20 (1959): 45. Murray, a careful interpreter of Pius XII's teaching, notes the difficulty in using the imprecise word "aggression" but interprets the papal position to be that the use of the term is an acknowledgment that either side in a war may have some claim to "justice," the more commonly used word throughout the tradition. According to Murray, "the issue of 'justice' is proximately decided by 'aggression' " (see 45, n. 10).

2. For a review of some of the literature during the early 1990s when the case of humanitarian intervention was being debated, see Kenneth Himes, "The Morality of Humanitarian Intervention," *Theological Studies* 55 (1994): 82–105. A more recent essay is that of Terry Nardin, "The Moral Basis of Humanitarian Intervention," *Ethics and International Affairs* 16 (2002): 57–70.

3. "The international community as a whole has the moral obligation to intervene on behalf of those groups whose very survival is threatened or whose basic human rights are seriously violated. As members of the international community, States cannot remain indifferent; on the contrary, if all other available means should prove ineffective, it is 'legitimate and even obligatory to take concrete measures to disarm the aggressor.' " See *Compendium of the Social Doctrine of the Church* (Vatican City: Libreria Editrice Vaticana, 2004), no. 506, quoting John Paul II, "Message for the 2000 World Day of Peace," n. 11.

4. The expression Weapons of Mass Destruction (WMD) includes biological, chemical, and nuclear armaments. In this essay I focus on the single grave threat of nuclear weapons.

5. The policy is also affirmed in the National Strategy to Combat Weapons of Mass Destruction (September 2002). It was reaffirmed in the most recent version of the National Security Strategy of the United States of America (March 2006).

6. International Commission on Intervention and State Sovereignty, *The Responsibility to Protect* (Ottawa: International Development Research Centre, 2001).

7. Ibid., 69.

8. Lee Feinstein and Anne Marie Slaughter, "A Duty to Prevent," *Foreign Affairs* 83 (January–February, 2004): 137.

9. For additional analysis of this distinction see Kenneth Himes, "Intervention, Just War, and U.S. National Security," *Theological Studies* 65 (2004): 141–57, esp. 147–48.

10. See *Compendium of Catholic Social Doctrine,* no. 501: "Engaging in a preventive war without clear proof that the attack is imminent cannot fail to raise serious moral and juridical questions."

11. Maryann Cusimano Love, "Real Prevention: Alternatives to Force," *America* 188 (January 20–27, 2003): 12–14.

12. The European Union, in a largely unnoticed statement in 2005, announced a strategy of counterproliferation that included the last resort use of force in accord with the U.N. Charter. A few weeks later, the G-8 group of industrialized nations, which includes Russia and Japan, acknowledged that WMDs and state-supported terrorism are the greatest threat to national security and that force may be appropriate. Finally, former Secretary General Kofi Annan asked the Security Council to establish criteria for the use of U.N.-authorized force.

13. Vatican II, *Gaudium et spes,* no. 80.

Part Four
HIV/AIDS

14

AIDS, Africa, and the "Age of Miraculous Medicine"

Naming the Silences

EMMANUEL KATONGOLE

After I had started working on this essay, Raymond Downing, a medical missionary friend in Kenya, passed on to me an email that confirmed my suspicions about a drug-based approach to AIDS in general, President Bush's Emergency Plan for AIDS Relief (Pepfar) in particular. The email was an exchange between Fr. Michael Czerny, S.J., the Nairobi-based African Jesuit AIDS Network (AJAN) coordinator, and Fr. Michael Perry, a representative of Franciscan International,[1] who had attended a consultation meeting in Nairobi. In an email to Fr. Czerny following the consultation, Fr. Perry wrote:

> Thank you for the opportunity to meet with you and to learn of your work and that of others who are engaged in the battle against HIV/AIDS. I found your comments about access to ARVs (anti-retrovirals) "interesting." You seem to place great emphasis on the caring/receiving/supporting community as the essential and principal "therapeutic" strategy for those living with HIV or AIDS (PLWHA). You played down significantly the ARVs, as if you thought they were not truly necessary as part of a comprehensive, community-based approach to care for PLWHA.... I am not sure I fully appreciate your stance on the issue of access to essential medicines.

In his response, Fr. Czerny made it clear that he was not opposed to ARVs as such. "Making available ARV's is an urgent issue of international justice, and AJAN joins the ecumenical advocacy alliance in advocating for 'universal access to treatment' and supporting 'efforts to provide access to essential medicines, particularly anti-retroviral therapies.'" Fr. Czerny's concern instead had to do with the current fixation on ARVs, which threatens other approaches to AIDS.

Under international pressure, the single issue now seems to be how to implant and expand ARV programs. And this medical/clinical noise is much louder, and the results more dramatic and immediate, than those of slower, less fashionable, step-by-step efforts to address Africa's problems in a holistic fashion.

Reading this correspondence, particularly Fr. Czerny's remarks, helped me to see more clearly the spiritual and theological challenges of an ARV-based approach to AIDS. Moreover, his remarks about the "dramatic and immediate" promises of ARVs confirmed that ARVs are one aspect of a wider culture. Nowhere was this fact made more evident than in President Bush's 2003 State of the Union Address, announcing the President's Emergency Plan for AIDS Relief:

> Ladies and gentlemen, seldom has history offered a greater opportunity to do so much for so many. . . . There are whole countries in Africa where more than one-third of the adult population carries the infection. More than four million require immediate drug treatment. Yet across that continent, only 50,000 AIDS victims, only 50,000, are receiving the medicine they need. Many hospitals tell people, you've got AIDS, we can't help you. Go home and die. In an age of *miraculous medicines*, no person should have to hear these words" (emphasis added).

An "Age of Miraculous Medicine"

What Bush helps to name clearly is the now almost universal sense that we live in an "age of miraculous medicine." Said simply, this is an age and a culture of drugs. The primary way our age deals with issues of sickness and suffering is through medication. Given this culture, it is not surprising that Bush picked Randall Tobias (a former CEO of the pharmaceutical giant Eli Lilly), who "knows a great deal about lifesaving medicines," to become the global coordinator of Pepfar. The assumption of this drug culture explains why the bulk of Bush's $15 billion Pepfar money (55 percent) was earmarked for the provision of ARVs to people living with AIDS.

Perhaps even more importantly, President Bush's remarks help us to see the (over) confidence and great expectations that an age of miraculous medicine sets us up for — expectations of dramatic, "life-saving" results. "Slower, less fashionable, step-by-step efforts" not only now seem archaic; they are also dubbed "irresponsible." In the words of Wende Marshall, this culture establishes a "canon of what can be thought or what cannot be thought of in any other way"[2] in relation to HIV/AIDS in Africa. Placed within this context, Fr. Czerny's reservations about ARVs point to the "fate" of theology within the culture of miraculous medicine. Given the promises of miraculous medicine, Christian ethics is easily reduced to a form of advocacy (focusing on issues of equity, access, or distributive justice),[3] with the wider considerations of human flourishing edited out of view.

My worry is that a program like Pepfar will end up instituting deep silences about HIV/AIDS in Africa. This might sound surprising since Pepfar was in part a response to the call to "break the silence" — the theme of the 2000 XIII International Conference on HIV/AIDS held in Durban, South Africa. There were several silences then that presumably needed to be broken: the silence of individuals with AIDS deterred by stigma from getting proper treatment; the silence of African governments said to be ignoring or denying their AIDS epidemic; the silence of cultural norms and taboos that contributed to the abuse of women; the silence of the world in not taking the epidemic seriously. Pepfar was initiated to break the silence, showing that the West (America) took HIV/AIDS in Africa seriously. Ironically, the resulting noise of an age of miraculous medicine risks masking deeper and more serious silences.

To be more explicit, the story of HIV/AIDS in Africa is both about Africa and about God — two converging stories that a culture of miraculous medicine easily obscures. To put it bluntly, HIV/AIDS has revealed that there is something sickening about Africa. This is a story whose ugly truth needs to be named, embraced, and confronted. But there is also the story of God — a God who is at work drawing all creation into the full realization of God's Kingdom. This is the Good News of which the church is both a recipient and a witness. Within this story, AIDS might indeed be a unique moment, through which God is inviting us to live out new visions of healing and hope as part of the journey toward the final restoration of a sinful and broken people into God's New Creation.

That journey must now be sustained both in the wake of HIV/AIDS and under the shadow of an over-confident culture of miraculous medicine. Given the silences this culture imposes, the task of theology in our time is not only to name silences but also to point out forms of Christian praxis and communion that need to be nurtured within those silences if the church is to patiently become the good news of God's new creation in Africa in the wake of HIV/AIDS.

Naming the Silences

The Power of Modern Medicine — A New Wall of Separation

In an earlier essay,[4] I noted how the "discovery" that the origin of AIDS was in Africa was not an innocent scientific discovery, but one that simply refocused the Western gaze on Africa as a dark continent, home to deadly diseases and individuals with primitive, promiscuous, and uncontrollable sexual energies and practices. While ARVs are important, ARVs do not question or engage this ideological gaze on Africa or Africans. Instead, they foreground it with modern medicine as the new marker that surveys and patrols the difference between the West and Africa.[5] As Michel Foucault shows, the development of modern medicine, just like the development of the modern accounts of rationality, is built on a distinction between the "normal" and "pathological."[6] For Foucault, this distinction creates the very conditions in which it becomes possible to think of one as either normal or pathological. In the *Birth of the Clinic,* Foucault extends his analysis about rationality to the field of modern medicine and shows that modern medicine not only operates within the logic of this distinction, but also patrols the normal/pathological dichotomy through the surveillance of the medical expert.[7]

What Foucault helps to confirm is that modern medicine demands that the sick occupy a distinct space outside our normal/healthy way of living. That is perhaps why notions of shame, isolation, stigma, and even blame[8] underlie modern accounts of disease and sickness. The implications for the story of HIV/AIDS in Africa are obvious. Africa and Africans come under a renewed medical gaze with each new statistic showing the devastation of AIDS in Africa. Significantly, it is a seeing without being seen, which is the very essence of knowledge as power.

A mere humanitarian intervention does not call into question this divide between those who live in an age of miraculous medicine and those who can only be the beneficiaries of the former's humanitarian largess. In fact, just as within the practice of modern medicine contact with the patient is both occasional and sanitized (isolation units, gloves, etc.), contact between the West and Africa might easily be marked with the signs we have come to expect on a visit to a medical institution: "Danger: Highly Infectious."

That is why a deeper ethical and theological challenge to the advocacy for ARVs is needed: to question the distance that modern medicine now institutes and patrols between the West and the rest of us. What HIV/AIDS has exposed is not only the urgent need for treatment of the sick bodies of Africans, but the need for healing of the divide between Africa and the rest of the world.

While HIV/AIDS obviously has the power to widen that divide, a commitment to the Good News of God's new creation convinces Christians that HIV/AIDS can help heal the divide. To cease this moment, however, we need practices far stronger than pills, plastics, and prophylactics. We need a story — one that is not only more truthful than the lie of miraculous medicine, but also capable of creating what Czerny calls "caring/receiving/supporting communities" across the East-West/North-South divides. Such communities have the potential not only to call the dominant culture into question, but also to embody new communions that transcend our usual tribal, national, regional, or class enclaves. Such communion bears witness to God's reconciling work among us and to the emergence of God's new creation in our midst.

Christian theology and practice need to point to the power of Christ's cross. In talking about the mystery of the cross, the apostle Paul celebrates Christ's death and resurrection as what has broken down the wall of separation: "You who once were far away have been brought near through the blood of Christ" (Eph. 2:13). There is no doubt that HIV/AIDS has gifted Africa with a heavy cross of pain and suffering. However, in order to connect HIV/AIDS to the mystery of Christ's death and resurrection, we must allow HIV/AIDS to break down the walls of separation, so that we "who were once far away" may be brought together into beloved communities of care, support, and gift.

Beyond Biological Individualism

A culture of miraculous medicine is one that approaches issues of health and sickness through a predominantly technological or biomedical lens. To be sure, this mechanistic account of the human body accounts for a great deal of the "success" of modern medicine and the ever expanding industries of health. However, to the extent that within this model the object of disease (and therefore the target of medical intervention) is the individual (body), quite often the social aspects of disease are not taken into consideration.

Increasingly, medical researchers and epidemiologists are pointing to "biological individualism" as a blinder that keeps us from seeing the social inequalities in health as well as the social production of disease. In an essay in the *American Journal of Public Health*, Elizabeth Fee and Nancy Krieger rightly note:

> Ultimately, the biomedical model embodies an approach to analyzing disease that is fundamentally individualistic.... Profoundly ahistorical, it contains within itself a dichotomy between the biological individual and the social community, and then it ignores the latter.... Reflecting an ideological commitment to individualism, the only preventive actions seriously suggested are those that can be implemented by solo individuals. Little attention is accorded to situations in which negotiation is required between persons (or communities) with unequal power.... Intended or not, these attitudes implicitly accept social inequalities in health and fail to challenge the social production of disease.[9]

I find Fee and Krieger's observation to be not only extremely relevant, but also consonant with an African conception of health. Given the deep social anthropology that characterizes life and shapes personal identity in Africa, a person can be considered healthy only if she belongs to a healthy community. But the fact that a deep spiritual and religious conception of the universe generally characterizes life in Africa also means that health and sickness in Africa are never regarded as merely physical or biological. These are at once social, somatic, religious, and spiritual phenomena. It is this comprehensive background that explains both the constant quest for healing (as well-being) and the fact that healing could never be viewed as merely the curing of an *individual* beset by disease.

This holistic understanding of health is undermined by a fixation on ARVs and a "drug culture" approach to HIV/AIDS in Africa. Christian theology and ethics need to recover the positive aspects of African culture as a way to resist the biological individualism inherent within modern medicine. For what the African account of sickness and healing points to is akin to God's shalom. As Tammy Williams notes in a discussion not directly related to AIDS in Africa, but pertinent nevertheless:

> The Old Testament concept of shalom best captures the concept of health. It suggests the idea of completeness, soundness, well-being, and prosperity, and includes every aspect of life: personal, relational, and national. Because shalom entails living in covenant relationship with God and others, holiness and righteousness are inherent in it.[10]

Christian theology and ethics must give visible accounts of this holistic sense of well-being or flourishing. Doing so will not only reconnect discussions about HIV/AIDS in Africa with the story of God; it will also reinvigorate discussions about the meaning and value of human life, friendship, marriage, sexuality, fidelity, and chastity within the church and its vision for God's new creation. Engaging these questions beyond individual and societal survival requires theological practices that are committed to pointing "beyond" while also building communities in which healthy relationships between individuals and God are nurtured. Doing so will contribute to the recovery of the holistic roots of medicine.

Contagion and Miasma: The "Whole Story"

The story of HIV/AIDS in Africa is a complex one. There is, however, a sense in which we miss this complex picture if discussions focus only on *virus*, *viral* infection, *viral* loads, anti-retro*viral* cocktails, etc. Within a biomedical approach to disease, the challenge seems to be one of isolating the virus and then finding the relevant drugs to control, slow down, or kill it. What we may not realize is that this biomedical model reflects a recent development in the history of medicine.

Before the discovery of the germ theory of disease in the nineteenth century, there were two major theories to explain why people become sick —

miasma and contagion. According to miasma, *certain places* had diseases, caused by the surrounding, often filthy, atmosphere. According to the contagion theory, *certain people* carried diseases and could spread them to others by direct contact. The difference between these two theories led to different views and policies on how to contain the spread of disease. Miasma followers argued that the most effective way to prevent disease was to clean up the places (for example, the swamps) carrying the diseases. Contagionists said that to prevent disease from spreading, the people with it needed to be quarantined. Interestingly, before the discovery of bacteria and parasites as the cause of infectious diseases, both approaches were successful in containing the spread of disease.

When the French chemist Louis Pasteur discovered the existence of pathogenic organisms, the contagion theory received a decisive boost over miasma. There was now proof that all infectious diseases were caused by germs that grew in people and could be spread to other people. As science developed techniques (especially drugs) to prevent and kill germs, attention on the polluted environment decreased.[11]

I draw attention to the "triumph" of contagion over miasma in the development of modern medicine to help explain the huge success of the medical and pharmaceutical industry. This success, however, is attained at the price of significantly narrowing the medical focus from wider considerations of health into the narrow focus of "cure."

This irony was recently confirmed in the PBS *Frontline* documentary "The Age of AIDS." An official in the Bush administration was discussing some of the problems that Pepfar has encountered in distributing ARVs in Africa. The official mentioned several problems: the lack of road infrastructure to transport the drugs; the lack of electricity and refrigerators to store the drugs; people who do not carry watches to alert them to the time to take the drugs. Finally, he added, "in many places people do not have any clean water to take the drugs with."

The irony could not be more startling: the provision of miraculous medicines in a place that lacks such basic necessities as water. The story of HIV/AIDS in Africa is as much about the lack of water, nourishment, basic hygiene, and security as it is about a biological virus.

This is the story that Christian theology and ethics needs to uncover. Christian ethics must state the obvious truth that it is not simply the bodies of Africans that are sick. Something is sick and sickening about Africa's modern ways of living.[12] The HIV/AIDS pandemic manifests the distress of Africa's social, spiritual, and material relationships. Christian theology must commit itself to naming this "whole story" and, most importantly, probing its silences. To point to the whole story of Africa and embody signs of healing and hope within that complex story is the invitation and gift of the Gospel.

Theology and Pastoral Ministry
in the Wake of AIDS and Miraculous Medicine

What does all of this concretely mean in the face of HIV/AIDS in Africa? I believe the signs of the times call us to proclaim that HIV/AIDS is not simply about biological bodies and virus, but about a moment of grace in history when we can see that something is deeply wrong with Africa's modern ways of working, playing, and living. In light of this truth we begin to see that what we need are not simply miraculous drugs that "fix" the viruses in our bodies and allow us to return to the same way of life. What we need is an alternative and more promising social vision for modern Africa.

We must be very clear, however. It is not the world of medicine that institutes our unhealthy way of life. The point of this essay has been to show that an age of miraculous medicine might simply mask our deeper sickness. The unhealthy forms of working, playing, and living in modern Africa are embedded within cultural practices that encourage the abuse of women and multiple sex partners, view sex as male conquest, and make the discussion of sex a taboo topic. These practices are encouraged by the postmodern media in Africa, which disconnects sex from a lasting relationship and makes it mere entertainment.

What is more, our modern way of life is sustained by forms of Christianity that either encourage fatalism or deal in forms of prosperity gospel exploitation. Our unhealthy ways of working, playing, and living are formed and reaffirmed through modern social political processes and systems that exploit the poor, create dependency, and fuel endless warfare. Politics has become a game, a means of "eating" (politics of the belly) for a few elite. The majority of the population of Africa is reduced to a life of desperation, deflation, and mere survival. These are the systems that compromise the social, economic, and political immune system of Africans long before a biological virus attacks their bodies.

"Poverty" does not rightly name the disorders at the heart of Africa's modern way of life. Poverty describes a settled state of affairs. What HIV/AIDS reveals, however, is an ongoing process of malfunctioning that results in an endless disenfranchising. There is something deflating and thus sickening about Africa's major institutions and the way of life they institutionalize. This is the whole story of Africa.

To offset such a story takes much more than the "fix-it" mind-set of the biomedical model. Moreover, such a story can neither be uncovered nor confronted by the standard clichés of ethical recommendations: behavioral change, humanitarian assistance, abstinence, faithfulness, condom use, ARV provision, and medical research. This is not to say that such recommendations have no place in the effort to recover healthy forms of working, playing, and living in Africa. The point, rather, is that we need a new pastoral priority in the wake of HIV/AIDS.

The story of the Gospel shows that establishing God's reign is not a quick fix; it is a new world that comes slowly through the less fashionable, step-by-step efforts of journeys through the countryside — journeys where Jesus engages in activities of care, healing, and forgiveness while teaching us the truth about our lives (Luke 24:13–35). God's new creation comes through the patient work of building friendships and communities, through death and dying.

The call of the church is to be on this journey, through which she learns and seeks to embody not only the gifts of care, truth, and hope, but also the art of living, suffering, and dying well. That call is made more urgent in Africa in the wake of HIV/AIDS. We desperately need pastoral ministry directed toward building up the church. We must become a church that is at once a community of moral discourse, a community of healing, and a community of peaceable difference[13] in face of Africa's modern way of life. We must become a community that nurtures and sustains alternative visions and patterns of work, play, and life. Only within such a community can medicine become a true gift that contributes to the art of living, suffering, and dying.

Does this mean that ARVs or medicine is inimical to our task? Certainly not. But to end with the wisdom of Czerny:

> Forming and guiding vital communities are a prior and more demanding task than the relatively straightforward one of distributing medicines.... We need to do everything else that constitutes building the Kingdom of God — including prevention programs, care for orphans, developing small Christian communities, and teaching about our faith. Medical missionaries who have been fighting AIDS on the ground for nearly twenty years tell me, "Good pastoral work is the number one way of keeping the CD[14] count high and of defeating AIDS."

Notes

1. Franciscans International is a non-governmental organization (NGO) working on behalf of the poor for peace, justice, and the care of creation at the United Nations in New York and Geneva. See *www.franciscansinternational.org*.

2. Wende Marshall, "AIDS and Black Bodies: Towards Critical Humanist Interpretations of Epidemic" (unpublished), 16. A significantly modified version of the same essay has been published as "AIDS, Race and the Limits of Science," *Social Science and Medicine* 60, no. 11 (June 2005): 2515–25.

3. An unchastened account of distributive justice may be in one of two forms, calling either for the *charitable* distribution of discounted medical products or for the *unfettered* expansion of the medical market. See Amy Laura Hall, "Whose Progress? The Language of Global Health," *Journal of Medicine and Philosophy* 31 (2006): 1–20.

4. Emmanuel Katongole, "Christian Ethics and AIDS in Africa Today: Exploring the Limits of a Culture of Suspicion and Despair," *Missionalia* 29, no. 2 (2001): 144–60.

5. On modern medicine as the new language of modernity, see Hall, "Whose Progress?"

6. See Michel Foucault, *Madness and Civilization* (New York: Random House, 1967), esp. Preface.

7. See Michel Foucault, *The Birth of the Clinic* (New York: Vintage Books Edition, 1994), esp. 107–22.

8. Paul Farmer, *AIDS and Accusation: Haiti and the Geography of Blame* (Berkeley: University of California Press, 1993), cited in Marshall, "AIDS, Race and the Limits of Science," 2.

9. Elizabeth Fee and Nancy Krieger, "Understanding AIDS: Historical Interpretations and the Limits of Biomedical Individualism," *American Journal of Public Health* 83, no. 10 (1993): 1481.

10. See Tammy R. Williams, "Is There a Doctor in This House? Reflections on the Practice of Healing in African American Churches," in *Practicing Theology: Beliefs and Practices in Christian Life*, ed. Miroslav Volf and Dorothy Bass (Grand Rapids, Mich.: Eerdmans, 2002), 100.

11. My reconstruction of the history of modern medicine owes a great deal to Raymond Downing, *As They See It: The Development of the African AIDS Discourse* (London: Adonis and Abbey Publications, 2005), 64–65.

12. Ivan Illich said it best in his critique of modern medicine's fixation on drugs: "I believe it is time to state clearly that specific situations and circumstances are 'sickening' rather than people themselves are sick. The symptoms which modern medicine attempts to treat often have little to do with the condition of our bodies; they are, rather, signals pointing to the disorders and presumptions of modern ways of working, playing, and living." See his "Brave New Biocracy: Health Care from Womb to Tomb," *New Perspectives Quarterly* 11, no. 1 (Winter 1994): 10.

13. For this sense of the church as a community of moral discourse, a community of healing, and a community of peaceable difference in the world, see Allen Verhey, "The Spirit of God and the Spirit of Medicine: The Church, Globalization, and a Mission of Health Care," in *The Spirit and the Modern Authorities*, ed. Max L. Stackhouse and Don S. Browning (Harrisburg, Pa.: Trinity Press International, 2001), 107–38.

14. The CD count tells your doctor how strong your immune system is.

15

Ethics of HIV/AIDS Prevention

Paradigms of a New Discourse from an African Perspective

AGBONKHIANMEGHE E. OROBATOR

It seems unnecessary to indulge in an excursus on statistics of sero-prevalence in Africa. The gravity of the situation prompts many people to facilely equate HIV/AIDS with sub-Saharan Africa. On the "silver jubilee" of this pandemic, statistics continue to paint a frightening tableau of the havoc unleashed by this modern plague on the African continent. Relative to the carnage of this disease, proven successes in the form of a substantial increase in access to treatment and the stabilization or reversal of rates of infection remain marginal and — judging by recent UNAIDS figures — could easily unravel. This reversal, recorded in a handful of African HIV/AIDS flashpoints like Uganda, Senegal, and Zimbabwe, especially among young people, underscores the value of sustained and integrated HIV prevention programs in the face of a massive tragedy that continues to impede the socio-economic development of Africa.

Yet contemporary moral discourse falls short if it overlooks the fact that, far from simply being a hapless victim of a colossal tragedy, Africa has a valid contribution to make toward re-examining orthodox paradigms of sexual ethics and developing new principles of HIV prevention. It cannot be plausibly maintained that the matter has been resolved by a one-dimensional ethics of abstinence and fidelity *only* — certainly not for us in Africa, where native wisdom reminds us that, "A single finger cannot pick a louse from one's hair." Nowadays it is difficult to shake the conviction, even among some Catholic ethicists, that traditional norms evoked to establish an exclusivist approach to HIV prevention appear unduly inflexible and, therefore, could pose a hindrance to prevention efforts. This conviction functions like a "stigma"; oftentimes, it obscures the excellent HIV/AIDS ministry of the church in Africa.

Three significant developments indicate the futility of imposing any one line as *the* Catholic approach to HIV/AIDS prevention. First, the absence of consensus between "orthodox" ethicists and their more "tolerant" counterparts; second, the growing body of evidence-based research that suggests alternative approaches to HIV prevention; and third, the increasing number of senior ecclesiastics who openly question specific elements of the Catholic position on the ethics of HIV prevention.

The intensity of the AIDS pandemic in Africa focuses much of the current debate on the morality of condom use in the context of discordant couples, that is, when one partner is HIV positive; and in the context of at-risk and vulnerable groups, like commercial sex workers. Against the backdrop of longstanding principles of Catholic sexual ethics, which affirm that the transmission of life is central to conjugal sexual acts, another position has emerged that maintains the moral priority and imperative of protecting life within the context of sexual intercourse, whether conjugal or transactional.

In light of the above, a fourth significant development has opened up the possibility of reappraising Catholic resistance to the use of prophylactic devices like condoms. This development is indicated by the recent comprehensive Vatican-sanctioned study, under the auspices of the Pontifical Council for Health Care Ministry and the Congregation for the Doctrine of the Faith, on condom use in HIV prevention. The shroud of secrecy surrounding this "study" does not obscure the significance of this doctrinal appraisal of a device that has gained wide endorsement among medical and scientific experts as an important tool for HIV prevention.

This essay focuses on three interrelated themes: the meaning of life, the wisdom of proverbs, and the lessons of women. Set within an African context, the principal objective is to construct a useful framework or paradigm for the ethics of HIV/AIDS prevention, drawing upon the African conception of life, its font of practical wisdom discernible in the use of proverbs, and the vital role of African women. The approach adopted here prioritizes lived experience as a useful hermeneutical tool for conducting an effective discourse on the ethics of prevention. This will help avert the tendency for discourse to become a disincarnate disquisition over moral niceties. A clear need exists to stress the ineluctable fact that, in addition to the estimated 40 million people *infected* with HIV, millions more are directly or indirectly *affected* by HIV/AIDS — as spouses, children, orphans, parents, grandparents, and entire communities and nations. Simply put, the discourse on the morality of HIV prevention should be conducted primarily as a discourse about people rather than a polemic over prophylactic devices.

The Meaning of Life

As one African theologian has phrased it, African religion and its moral traditions turn on the "purpose or goal of human life."[1] From an African perspective, "life" symbolizes a *dense* and *expansive* reality. The density of life relates to its character as an all-encompassing moral category. Life constitutes the principle against which the value of individual actions, behavior, and choices are measured. Their ethical value is determined or evaluated by the measure in which they enhance or diminish the "power" or "force" of life.

The notion of expansiveness of life relates to the fact that life is not construed only as a reality constituted by the living; it also includes the ancestors and the yet-unborn. Furthermore, the category of life extends to and includes the natural universe. In this sense, therefore, from an African religio-cultural perspective, the moral imperative to protect human life also warrants the protection of sacred forests, trees, rivers, mountains, streams, and animals. This moral imperative, or duty, to protect the physical environment is founded on the vital link between the survival of human life and the environment. To protect the environment is to protect human life, since the survival of the latter ultimately depends on the survival of the former.

As a moral category, life is essentially fragile and vulnerable to myriad natural and man-made threats. HIV/AIDS, as a deadly disease, poses a serious threat to this moral tradition of abundant life or the principle of life as *the* foundational moral value. In this context of a holistic and integrated conception of life, the specific character or nature of the threat posed by HIV/AIDS, like any other serious illness, appears as a violation of the balance, harmony, and order essential to the preservation of life in its dense and expansive reality. Quite clearly, in a concrete manner, HIV/AIDS assaults this balance and harmony of the African moral universe, be it in the separation of spouses, parents, and children; the reversal of long-term economic and development fortunes in some African countries (for example, the loss of productive sectors of the economy, such as farm workers, teachers, and nurses); or the distortion of demographic configurations (for example, the sharp drop in life expectancy, to less than 40 years in countries like Zimbabwe and Swaziland).

In its communal or shared dimension, the notion of the density and expansiveness of life is expressed in the familiar saying in many parts of sub-Saharan Africa: "I am because we are." This affirmation generates an ethical principle that acknowledges that the threat to individual life undermines the fullness of the community's life. For, as we say in Africa, "The danger that threatens the hunting dog also threatens the hunter." Theoretically, every member of the community, whether that community is a social unit or a religious entity, is at risk of being infected or affected by HIV/AIDS. It is in the interest of the community (common good) to protect individual life, in which resides the collective destiny and hope for survival of its members. Stated differently, and applied to the purposes of HIV prevention, *principles of the ethics of prevention "are to be sought within the context of preserving human life and its 'power' or 'force.' "*[2]

Understood in this way, this principle has immediate consequences for the ethics of HIV prevention. Thus, it could be argued that, from this African perspective, the use of prophylactic devices in the time of AIDS could constitute a morally viable and ethically commendable *option for life considered in its totality.* Not that the end justifies the means, but that this particular means offers a concrete possibility of enhancing the community's "life-force." There is a most important ethical issue here. If protecting, enhancing, and preserving the life-force in its density and expansiveness constitutes the primary objective of HIV prevention, the moral necessity to keep the sexual act open to the transmission of life ought not to foreclose the use of prophylactic devices *in specific instances* where this intended transmission of life may pose a threat to the lives of the partners and their unborn child. The position indicated here recognizes the possibility of a compatibility of purposes between transmission of life and the prevention of the transmission of HIV in order to protect life.

The Wisdom of Proverbs

"Words," wrote Chinua Achebe in his African literary classic *Things Fall Apart,* "are like yam.... And proverbs are the palm oil with which they are eaten." Successive generations and different schools of African philosophical thought have recognized the validity of proverbs as a dynamic source of African native wisdom. Only rarely, though, has this recognition translated into systematic integration of proverbs as a tool for constructing an appropriate moral discourse from an African perspective. Without being merely quaint expressions, African proverbs, rich in variety and diversity, offer salutary elements of ethical principles in the time of a crisis such as disease or illness.

What moral principle does an African reflect upon to make choices in the time of crisis, especially one like HIV/AIDS, which carries the threat of personal death and communal annihilation? My observation in eastern and western Africa suggests that in a situation of crisis, in addition to other sources, an African looks to proverbial sayings for collectively sanctioned warrants, justifications, and precedents to inform his or her reflection, options, and actions. Ugandans, for example, are familiar with the proverb, "The goat grazes where it is tethered," which contextualizes the message of fidelity to one's partner, a.k.a. "zero grazing," and serves as one of the central components of the country's HIV prevention program. Perhaps some would cite other proverbs: "You do not care what means you adopt to neutralize your enemy." From this, one might adduce the following principle: keeping in view the criterion of respect for and preservation of life — assuming the complexity and multiplicity of factors associated with HIV/AIDS — the community ought to defend human life with all available means, as long as these contribute to the fuller growth of the life of the community.

Within this category of moral thinking, exclusivity of means appears ethically untenable, while complementarity of means appears as virtue. For, as an African proverb affirms, "If one thing stands, another stands beside it." Or, "When many spider threads unite, they can tie a lion."

Assuming this logic of complementarity of means, one may not overlook the fact that proverbs lend themselves to multiple interpretations; they may also contradict one another. This raises two cautionary notes: first, one may not use them exclusively; second, the particular meaning that one derives from a proverb is subject to debate in order to arrive at a consensus on its shared meaning. This imperative of debate and consensus conforms to the procedure for establishing principles of morality via a dynamic communicative discourse known as "palaver." The key point to retain here is that there exists within this framework an action-oriented moral discourse that proffers new possibilities for enriching the ethics of HIV prevention from an African perspective.

The Lessons of Women

Prevailing patterns of ecclesial organization, the tenets of orthodox ecclesiology, and the exercise of ecclesiastical leadership combine to reinforce the gospel-based gender bias of "not counting women and children." A close observation of the experiences of women in Africa in the time of AIDS leads to the conclusion that the face of HIV/AIDS — like the one of poverty — is predominantly feminine. However, this face is Janus-like: one side traces a profile of women as prime victims of the AIDS pandemic; the other highlights the commitment of women as primary agents in the frontline of care for "people living with HIV/AIDS" and their resolute quest for a more humane ethical response to the challenges of HIV/AIDS.

Twenty-five years after the outbreak of the deadly HIV/AIDS disease, a general consensus now exists across various disciplines that sero-prevalence embodies an incontrovertible gender quotient. This quotient is commonly accounted for by resorting to a variety of statistical categories, such as the number of women infected by HIV. Absolute numbers may present in bare form the scale of sero-prevalence; but they also can mask or blunt the poignancy of the gender inequality that underlies and aggravates the disproportionate vulnerability of women to HIV infection and AIDS-related deaths. The gender quotient in HIV/AIDS operates as a combination of risk factors manifested at several levels. These gender-based risk factors are *biological/physiological* (compared to men, women are more likely to be infected with HIV during sexual intercourse, especially in cases of sexual violence; they also face the risk of mother-to-child transmission of HIV), *social* (women are more likely to be infected at a relatively younger age, oftentimes due to a pattern of social relationship where older men target young women and teenage girls for sex), *economic* (lack of adequate means

of livelihood and survival renders some women vulnerable to prostitution),
political (lack of empowerment of women and the concomitant inability to
negotiate "safe sex" with partners, spouses, or clients, especially in the case
of commercial sex workers and minors), *cultural* (harmful culture-related
practices, such as sexual post-mortuary cleansing, wife inheritance, and female genital mutilation), and *religious* (inability to renegotiate the terms of
marital relationships where one partner, oftentimes the woman, faces the
real threat of HIV infection).

Notwithstanding the hindrance imposed by these factors, African women's
creative commitment and approaches to HIV/AIDS information, education,
and communication — born of their experience and burden of providing
primary care for people living with HIV/AIDS (for example, spouses and
orphans) — serve as a counterwitness to the self-righteous condemnation
of PLWHA and the harmful politics of stigma and discrimination. Leaving
aside the reductionist assumption that women's response to HIV/AIDS is the
social corollary of their maternal instinct, a more useful and valid analytical
focus for understanding the role of women in HIV/AIDS lies in the solutions
they adopt at the time of crisis. As a general principle, in the time of AIDS,
women's radical and non-risk-averse engagement in combating HIV/AIDS
offers critical lessons for constructing and evaluating the ethics of prevention.
Essentially, they teach that, as a community of faith, we need to risk shedding
burdensome and outmoded interpretations and applications of traditional
moral principles in the time of crisis in favor of active and compassionate
solidarity with those infected and affected by AIDS. The concomitant principle can be formulated as follows: *in the time of crisis the community called
church acts in solidarity with the most affected, which solidarity entails the
risk of sacrificing attachments to traditional norms for the sake of promoting,
protecting, and preserving life.*

The position indicated here evokes aspects of Catholic social teaching, in
particular the notion of solidarity (and compassion), which, as John Paul II
has argued, "is not a feeling of vague compassion or shallow distress at the
misfortunes of so many people, both near and far. On the contrary, it is *a
firm and persevering determination* to commit oneself to the *common good;*
that is to say to the good of all and of each individual, because we are *all
really responsible for all.*"[3]

Concluding Remarks

To conclude this essay on the ethics of HIV/AIDS prevention, it may be
useful to make three salient observations.

First, to the extent that the position advanced in this essay is credible and
practical, we should expect Catholic sexual ethics to (a) risk sacrificing some
of its disincarnate moral fixations for a context-based approach in view of
a radical and preferential solidarity with millions of Africans infected and

affected by AIDS; (b) refocus attention on the protection and preservation of human life construed in its communitarian dimension, and (c) adopt a dialogical and consensus-building (or palaver) stance vis-à-vis concrete realities of life as a fundamental precondition for its teaching on methods of HIV prevention.

Second, this approach does not prescribe a particular course of action. Rather, it argues for a less polemical framework or paradigm for understanding the ethics of HIV prevention. It should create a more conducive and understanding pastoral space for the discussion of controversial issues, like the use of condoms. The ongoing comprehensive review by the Vatican of condom use in HIV prevention may yet facilitate the emergence of a less polemical discourse on the ethics of HIV prevention.

However, it is important to stress that condoms are not the solution to the problem of HIV/AIDS. While they offer an effective, albeit temporary, means for controlling HIV transmission, they do not address the root causes of the disease. As a complex disease, HIV/AIDS exposes inherent deficiencies and lapses in global, continental, regional, and national patterns of socio-economic and political organization. To speak of HIV/AIDS is to implicate a multiplicity of socio-economic and political ills, such as illiteracy, poverty, inadequate or nonexistent healthcare and treatment delivery systems and facilities, gender discrimination, sexual gender-based violence, human rights abuses, and multiple forms of injustice. These ills are not treated by massive distributions of condoms to impoverished African countries — the preferred strategy of many international agencies and non-governmental organizations. The AIDS pandemic delineates a complex reality of which the discourse on the methods of prevention represents one facet. To reduce the problem of HIV/AIDS to only the condom debate amounts to an oversimplification of a complex picture and a grave injustice to millions of people living with AIDS and millions who have already succumbed to this deadly disease.

Third, my position does not prejudice the tradition of Catholic sexual ethics; it is intended to facilitate an open and compassionate reappropriation — in the time of AIDS — of traditional principles of "lesser evil," "double effect," "cooperation," and "tolerance" — principles with a distinguished, if somewhat anguished, history in Catholic moral theology.

The agonizing reality of HIV/AIDS, especially in Africa, points to the need for an "ABC" of moral discourse, comprising: *abstinence* from entrenched positions, *being critically faithful* to longstanding categories of morality, and *consistent and correct use* of African moral traditions of abundant life. The ethics of HIV prevention should neither be so inflexibly attached to orthodox positions as to ignore contemporary realities of life, nor so excessively indifferent to tradition as to offer no meaningful reference point for reflection, action, and judgment. It is a delicate and precarious balance: there are no shortcuts to the top of a palm tree.

Notes

1. Laurenti Magesa, *African Religion: The Moral Traditions of Abundant Life* (Maryknoll, N.Y.: Orbis Books, 1997), 31.
2. Ibid., 31–32.
3. John Paul II, *Sollicitudo rei socialis* (December 30, 1987), 38.

Recommended Readings

African Jesuit AIDS Network. *AIDS and the Church in Africa*. Nairobi: Paulines Publications Africa, 2005.
Bujo, Bénézet. *African Theology in Its Social Context*. Maryknoll, N.Y.: Orbis Books, 1992.
———. *The Ethical Dimension of Community: The African Model and the Dialogue between North and South*. Nairobi: Paulines Publications Africa, 1997.
———. *Foundations of an African Ethic: Beyond the Universal Claims of Western Morality*. Nairobi: Paulines Publications Africa, 2003.
Catholic Bishops of Africa and Madagascar. *Speak Out on HIV & AIDS: Our Prayer Is Always Full of Hope*. Nairobi: Paulines Publications Africa, 2004.
Healey, Joseph, and Donald Sybertz. *Towards an African Narrative Theology*. Nairobi: Paulines Publications Africa, 1996.
John Paul II. *Sollicitudo Rei Socialis* (On Social Concern), encyclical letter, December 30, 1987.
Keenan, James F., ed. *Catholic Ethicists on HIV/AIDS Prevention*. New York and London: Continuum, 2000.
Kelly, Kevin T. *New Directions in Sexual Ethics: Moral Theology and the Challenge of AIDS*. London and Washington: Geoffrey Chapman, 1998.
Magesa, Laurenti. *African Religion: The Moral Traditions of Abundant Life*. Maryknoll, N.Y.: Orbis Books, 1997.
Orobator, Agbonkhianmeghe E. *From Crisis to Kairos: The Mission of the Church in the Time of HIV/AIDS, Refugees and Poverty*. Nairobi: Paulines Publications Africa, 2005.
Paterson, Gillian. *Women in the Time of AIDS*. Maryknoll, N.Y.: Orbis Books, 1996.
Shorter, Aylward, and Edwin Onyancha. *The Church and AIDS in Africa: A Case Study: Nairobi City*. Nairobi: St. Paul Publications/Daughters of St. Paul, 1998.
Symposium of Episcopal Conferences of Africa and Madagascar (SECAM). "The Church in Africa in the Face of the HIV/AIDS Pandemic: 'Our Prayer Is Always Full of Hope.' " Message issued by SECAM, Dakar, Senegal, October 7, 2003.
Webb, Douglas. *HIV and AIDS in Africa*. London: Pluto Press, 1997.
World Council of Churches. *Facing AIDS: The Challenge, the Churches' Response*. Geneva: WCC Publications, 1997.

16

HIV/AIDS in Africa

An Urgent Task for an Inculturated Theological Ethics

PAUL CHUMMAR

No African nation currently owns a nuclear or atomic "weapon of mass destruction," yet a different potent weapon, "a virus of mass destruction," is accelerating in Africa. The greater the knowledge about the aggressive nature of HIV/AIDS, the more the world is perplexed and frightened. Having failed in its piecemeal approach in the fight against the pandemic, UNAIDS is now proposing a "comprehensive approach." I would like to suggest three main steps to this approach in the African context: (1) HIV/AIDS as an ethical issue; (2) HIV/AIDS as a theological ethical issue; and (3) HIV/AIDS as a crucial and urgent task for an inculturated theological ethics.

HIV/AIDS: An Ethical Issue

AIDS is defined as "Acquired Immune Deficiency Syndrome," a description intrinsically related to human actions. "You don't get AIDS, but you acquire AIDS," says the slogan. In 95 percent of the cases in sub-Saharan Africa this fatal disease is "acquired," either through one's own action or through the actions of another person. Therefore 95 percent of the cases of HIV/AIDS in Africa have an ethical dimension because HIV/AIDS results from unethical ways of acting that obstruct the fullness of life. Ethics is the rational, practical, and normative discipline that deals with the different aspects of human actions and activities. Ethics, which brings natural morality to the level of science through critical thinking, analysis, and scrutiny, now has the task of identifying the root sources of this fatal infection. From this perspective HIV/AIDS relates to three main applied ethical areas: the socio-political, the socio-sexual, and the medical, each of which is highly relevant in the African context.

The Socio-political Context

The core reason for the spread of the AIDS pandemic in Africa is poverty. Africa's current political and economic situation exacerbates the inequality between rich and poor. People are increasingly divided by extremes of wealth and poverty. The need to survive and to feed their children drives some women and men to offer their bodies for sexual activities, indifferent to whether they die of AIDS or hunger. Sex remains the last resort for survival. Those engaged in casual labor, working in distant cities, are not financially able to return home every weekend. In such situations men often find sexual gratification with casual sexual workers who are much cheaper than commercial sex workers. On their home visits they infect their partners.

In this context the inadequacy of many governments is apparent. Huge international debts and corrupt politicians frequently deprive African countries of the financial resources required to counter the spread of infection or care adequately for the infected and the affected. Often faith communities and NGOs are the sole providers of services for AIDS sufferers.

The Socio-sexual Context

Traditional African society gives women and girls less status than men and boys. Sexual violence is tacitly accepted and fuels the infection rate. Gender inequality and subordinate roles that marginalize women and prevent their self-sustenance and self-empowerment result in economic powerlessness, feminized poverty, and feminized illiteracy. Women are limited in making free and independent decisions, even in sexual matters. For example, they often don't have the ability to say no to sexual activity with an infected husband, or, as in the case of widow inheritance, with other persons. Superstitions, such as the belief that sexual intercourse with virgins and young girls cures AIDS, are not condemned but silently tolerated. Some men see women solely as objects of sexual gratification and as child-bearers, and, despite infection, often compel them to bear children, whom they see as future breadwinners and care-givers. In refugee camps women and girls are sexually exploited by the armed forces and camp officials on whom they are very often dependent. In some cultures (such as the Maasai) visitors of the same tribe are customarily offered sexual contacts and coitus with wives as a gesture of friendliness and respect. The culturally accepted practice of polygamy is another serious root of infection.

Zealous Western missionaries to Africa abolished the traditional moral African customs that upheld the ethical matrix. They did so partly because they failed to understand the real anthropological, social, and cultural meanings of these customs. For example initiation, one of the most important rites of passage from childhood to adulthood, was abolished. Initiation is traditionally preceded by a number of social and sexual ethical instructions that prepare a young person ethically for adulthood. The elders of the family pass on wisdom relating to how to live responsibly as an adult and as a partner in married life, as well as how to behave in matters of sexuality and procreation, in parenthood, family, and community. This transmission of ethical principles, linking one generation to the next in the context of initiation, is now largely broken, leaving a moral vacuum. The growing curiosity for sexual knowledge and practice is then satisfied mainly through the media or through peers without moral context.

The replacement of traditional marriage customs by foreign Christian marriage customs has further undermined the ethical system. The African traditional understanding of marriage and its rites encompasses a life-long, binding character supported by the bride and groom's families and their communities. Moreover, premarital rites and rituals are a means of preparation for marriage and procreation, marriage's greatest goal. Unlike Western marriage customs, African marriage is a progressive reality that does not come into existence at the marriage ceremony. It is a gradual, maturing process of the man and woman into an intimate relationship, developed through a process of negotiations, visiting, and gift-giving first by each family, and later ratified by each community. In this lengthy process of growing together into partnership and inseparable unity, procreation plays a most important role. Therefore, even before the solemn marriage in the community, which may take place years later, couples have to prove their capability of bringing forth children as security for themselves, their families, and their properties. The whole community then acts as support for the couple.

Christian doctrine, in which the legality of marriage is first ratified through the sacrament of marriage, challenges the traditional custom in which a partnership develops by creating a family and whereby marriage is a crowning event. Church law even condemns as concubines those African Christians who live in this progressive reality of partnership without church marriage, excluding them from the sacramental community and degrading them to second-class Christians.[1] However the African traditional marriage custom could, theoretically, be equated with religious and priestly formation in which both the candidate and the receiver institution, such as the diocese or religious community, mutually discern the candidate's suitability during the so-called formation period. Is it not feasible for the sacrament of marriage to be thought of in terms similar to the sacrament of ordination, celebrated sacramentally after years of preparation?

The African marriage celebration between the extended families and the communities incurs huge expense. The combination of the financial burden of African marriage customs and of Christian marriage regulations has increasingly discouraged people from marriage but rather encourages them to live as partners without family and community support, causing unstable relationships and changing partners. Thus the abolition of African traditional marriage customs and delayed marriages can often lead to unethical sexual contact and also incur the risk of HIV infection.

In Africa colonialism, slavery, illiteracy, and exploitation each have generated pressure to remove the moral "oughts" from life. Globalization has brought Western contraceptives capable of controlling the biological consequences of pregnancy. It has also brought sex stimulants, including pornographic materials, television programs, and chemicals to enhance sexual vitality. The innate nature of sexual activity as an expression of love, intimacy, and partnership between two legitimate partners is degraded to a form of consumerism. As traditions are abandoned, the healthy transmission of moral values to the younger generation has been disrupted and many find themselves in a "moral vacuum." A mixture of traditional and modern sexual practices under the maxim "Enjoy your life!" causes discordance in partnerships, promiscuous behavior, and premarital and extramarital sexual relationships, increasing the possibility of infection and assaulting the innate right to exercise human sexuality in its proper context.

The Medical-Ethical Context

African anthropology understands the human in terms of a *homo patiens:* health (or illness) is closely related to a person's community and to the Creator of life. The holistic healing process reintegrates the person with the community — with the living, with ancestors, with forthcoming generations, and with the Creator. Illnesses are understood as natural and unnatural. In many African minds an epidemic occurs through supernatural forces when humans break taboos and moral values. Many believe that HIV/AIDS is unnatural illness and an ethical issue, since the illness is the consequence of breaking ethical codes.

In Africa care of the sick, including bearing its financial implications, is traditionally a community responsibility, beginning with family members and extending to friends and the community at large. Such solidarity provides the most effective support for the patient and avoids isolation. However the stigmatization of HIV/AIDS has increased the tendency to isolate HIV/AIDS patients and to abandon them to the anonymity of hospitals or elsewhere. Since there is no comprehensive health-care insurance system for all, and since the political resources are inadequate to provide antiretroviral drugs (ARVs) for the infected, the ethical responsibility of caring for the sick according to the UN's Universal Declaration of Human Rights (1948) is still an unfulfilled obligation of the global community.

HIV/AIDS: A Theological-Ethical Issue

It is ironic that at the same time Christianity is growing rapidly in Africa, the highest infection rates of HIV/AIDS are in the so-called Christian countries. While the Catholic Church shoulders about 26 percent of the care of AIDS patients and education for prevention worldwide, in the church as a whole there is no real acceptance or understanding of the reality of AIDS within the church community. People infected and affected by the virus are often frowned on by pious Christians and by the clergy, and often regarded as bad people. However HIV/AIDS is about persons and their lives and deaths, and thus it confronts us as a theological-ethical issue. The church is a community of weak and strong, healthy and ill, holy and sinful, in which God manifests God's presence and activity in all people, including those infected by HIV. This theological truth has not, however, been understood or accepted at a deep level. The provocative but powerful expression "the body of Christ has AIDS" does not resonate well in the church.

It is said that the global village no longer has a church at its center. Moral appeals of the Catholic Church such as: "Don't use condoms, be faithful" are well intended, but they do not provide normative principles for morally good behavior, nor do they evoke compassionate attitudes toward the infected or those still unable to eradicate the virus from the continent. Although churches in Africa are always overcrowded on days of obligation, what is said in church is not necessarily accepted. For example, if the good Catholic is HIV infected, on Sundays the priest tells him: "Don't use condoms!" Then during the week the government-run health care center tells him: "Use condoms!" People are confused. African Christians walk with one foot in African religion and culture and the other in the church and Western culture.[2]

The way theological ethics is taught in Africa contributes to this moral confusion. Even institutions specializing in developing an inculturated theology largely teach Western moral theology as if it were a universal theological ethics. This is a form of theological colonialism. Many theologians have silently withdrawn from the development of an inculturated theology. Although a good number of native theologians contribute to the development of African theology, its application is sparse.[3] Courses on the theological ethical aspects of HIV/AIDS are optional for students, including theology students. AIDS is a "disease of bad people." Theological ethicists must urgently rise to the challenge of confronting the reality of AIDS in all its complexity.

HIV/AIDS: An Urgent Task for an Inculturated Theological Ethics

Some African thinkers and scientists maintain that HIV/AIDS is a Western creation whose purpose is to destroy Africans and that in the short-term the promotion of condoms and ARVs makes good business sense. "A stick in your neighbor's house can never kill a snake in your house" states an African proverb.[4] African problems can only be addressed by African means. *An African ethical problem can never be solved by imported Western solutions or by a material solution, but needs an African ethical solution out of its own innate culture, its anthropological understanding, and its moral values.* Africa has its own ethical theories that have been known and practiced for thousands of years. It is insulting and absurd to say that "Africans don't have any morality; we have to teach it to them!" Before missionaries

brought Christianity to this continent, God was here, as was a sound morality. Africa is the cradle of human life, and the church and its theologians,
confronted with a fatal pandemic, must be reminded of the inherent and
rich moral principles of this continent, principles that are so familiar to its
peoples. What is taught must be plausible and acceptable to Africans so
it can be totally integrated into their lives. Western ethical principles can
play a complementary role if there are gaps so that both together enrich the
universal church. An African dimension would contribute substantially to a
universal theological ethics.

HIV/AIDS is often acquired because of a lack of proper knowledge or
moral discernment in Africa. Ordinary people must be taught to differenti-
ate between actions in their moral education. Theological ethics has a serious
obligation to state norms and give clear directions for a fulfilled and holistic life to the peoples of different cultures and anthropological settings. The
primary aim of theological ethics is to liberate human persons from everything that will destroy their lives, and it is critical now in this time of AIDS.
The methodology of Jesus Christ, how he taught his contemporaries, how
he lessened their pains and cured them, indicates norms and principles for
a life in fullness, based on the cultural and anthropological understandings
of every people. The church and its theology will be seen as the touchstone
only insofar as it does or does not act in accordance with Jesus of Nazareth,
for "by their fruits you will know them" (Matt. 7:16).

Theological ethics is the only bridge among the theological disciplines
that connects the world of today with the Christian message and mission.
Its fundamental objective is to enable persons to build up their morally good
behavior. Christian ethics has freed itself from former ways of communicating through narrow, fearful, and dictatorial moral principles and has moved
to a system of personal and autonomous morality that helps the individual
person and his or her development. Today ethical principles are compatible with the modern sciences and disciplines and they need no longer be
relegated to the church and confessional. Indeed, theological ethics must be
capable of communicating sound ethical principles, but also of discussing
the burning problems of our time openly and sincerely.

Africa has many hopeful resources in the fight against the AIDS pandemic. Among these are (1) the congruence between African and Christian
anthropological and fundamental moral understandings — for example, the
principle of life as the greatest gift of God, respect for life, love for life and
procreation, and an understanding of the place of the person in the chain
of past ancestors and the lives that are to come; (2) the deep religious sense
and the rich expressions of interiority that are essential for fostering moral
values and principles; (3) the great human resource of young and energetic
people who are capable of education, knowledge, and the development and
contextualization of African values in a modern world; (4) a strong sense
of solidarity, family and community life, and care for the sick and dying;

(5) an ever-growing political awareness and political sense that is capable of changing the social and economic reasons for the spread of HIV/AIDS; and (6) a greater thirst for the recognition and promotion of human rights, freedom, and equality.

Traditional African ethical and theological understanding has much in common with fundamental Christian anthropology and can thus provide basic norms and differentiated principles for an inculturated theological ethic. These include "the principle of life" as the greatest gift from God; "the principle of liberation," which serves to free people from every kind of suffering and slavery; "the principle of inclusion," which seeks liberation for both the oppressed and the oppressor so that a holistic salvation can take place; and "the principle of faith and moral relevance" by which universal characteristics in line with the church's teaching are established.

Conclusion

Such an African fundamental theological ethic based in Christian anthropological, cultural, philosophical, and moral principles provides the foundation for further ethical considerations. The goal of an inculturated theological ethics is to help Africans form an *African consciousness* and to have an African *ars vivendi* derived from their own culture, sound traditions, and practices for the prevention of HIV and the care of those infected. In facing the reality of death due to AIDS, theological ethics has to develop a new version of *ars moriendi* that affirms the dignity of the person even at death. This task of deriving new forms of African educational methods for theological ethics would help to eradicate the infectious behavior of humans from the continent, in other words, to help people to live healthy, fully human, and fully Christian lives. It will be a long and vast undertaking. Africa needs programmatic theologians to develop a moral theological pattern for Africa.

An African proverb states that "the best time to plant a tree was twenty years ago; the next best time is today." That "today" requires that steps are now taken to develop an inculturated theological ethic. It is a crucial and urgent challenge that lies before the church and especially before African theological ethicists.

Notes

With immense gratitude I dedicate this belatedly to my respected Doktorvater, Philipp Schmitz, S.J. (Frankfurt am Main and Rome), for his seventieth birthday.

1. Two remarks. First, it is amazing to see how more and more Western Christians are imitating the African custom of "progressive reality" of partnership and marriage by living together and begetting children before they finally undertake the sacramental ceremony of marriage. Second, African theology students with a cultural understanding of the progressive reality of marriage suffer severe internal conflicts

due to the fact that the traditional custom is still prevalent on the continent but conflicts with prevailing church law. Moreover, in their ministry they have to teach and implement church laws against their own cultural traditions.

2. See Musimbi Kanyoro, "Engendered Communal Theology: African Women's Contribution to Theology in the 21st Century," in *Talitha cum! Theologies of African Women,* ed. N. J. Njoroge and M. W. Dube (Pietermaritzburg: Cluster Publications, 2001), 158–80.

3. It is seen that theologians from former French-speaking countries have contributed comparatively more in the field of inculturated theology than others. A good description of African theologians and their theological contributions is given in Bénézet Bujo and Juvénal Ilunga Muya, eds., *African Theology in the 21st Century: The Contributions of the Pioneers,* vols. 1 and 2 (Nairobi: Pauline Publications of Africa, 2003 and 2006).

4. A Ganda proverb, from discussions in the seminar: "HIV/AIDS: An Ethical Task for the Church in Africa" at the Catholic University of Eastern Africa, Nairobi, Kenya (November 2005).

17

Who Sinned?
AIDS-Related Stigma and the Church

GILLIAN PATERSON

Service Provider or Moral Arbiter?

Churches have been influential in the discourse on AIDS. On the one hand Catholics, in particular, have been at the forefront of practical responses to the epidemic. On the other hand, churches have been blamed for sabotaging these same efforts by their judgmental attitudes, endorsement of patriarchy, and cultures of denial. Their difficulties in talking about sex and sexuality have often led to the silencing of truthful sex education; and the combined role of service provider and moral arbiter may — when the two roles conflict — put health-care workers in the (painful) position of having to choose which should take priority.

Anti-Christian (especially anti-Catholic) polemic is common and may be venomous. At international AIDS conferences, applause has greeted speakers who describe the church as "rigid," "fossilized," "judgmental," "patriarchal," or "exclusive." On the other hand, the religious right continues to turn a blind eye to vulnerable groups it would prefer not to exist, namely, the commercial sex workers, the injecting drug users, and the men who have sex with men.

Hence in 2000, African church leaders meeting in Nairobi endorsed, unanimously, a statement that admitted:

> Our tendency to exclude others, our interpretation of the scriptures, and our theology of sin have all combined to promote the stigmatization, exclusion, and suffering of people with HIV or AIDS.... For the churches, the most powerful contribution we can make to combating HIV transmission is the eradication of stigma and discrimination.[1]

Is Stigma Eradication Possible?

Six years later, the rhetoric of "stigma eradication" has become familiar. Whether eradication is possible is another matter. Stigmatization has to do with social "othering," a term used in feminist or post-colonial discourses to describe the boosting of the institutional or individual ego through the distancing of that which threatens to undermine it. This dynamic, I would suggest, is endemic to institutional identity. For how is there to be "identity" without a degree of othering? How can we say "we *are* like *this*" without simultaneously saying "we *are not* like *that*"?

Liberals talk a lot today about solidarity with the Other and the need to celebrate diversity, but this can be mere self-congratulatory fantasy unless such diversity is expressed in actual models of community. Otherwise, it becomes another luxury item for the postmodern consumer, to be enjoyed and photographed before retreating into a safe haven of the like-minded. For Catholics reflecting on stigma, how then can the "solidarity" that is so central to our teaching become a solidarity of *inclusion* rather than of *exclusion*?

First, exclusionary othering often stems from fear. If there is a well-founded fear of infection, then it is appropriate to apply proportionate measures to protect oneself and others. But when ignorance or disinformation leads to inappropriate othering, and when it goes unchallenged by the institution responsible for it, then that is systemic stigmatization. We find it hard to address this issue, though, mainly because in order to do so we have to talk about sex, sexuality, and sexual behavior, using terms which, in church circles, tend to be uttered in hushed tones or not at all. This means one often encounters a staggering level of misinformation, even among highly educated people. In Nairobi, I talked to a newly ordained Augustinian. "I just don't know what words to use to say these things," he said, "and especially in church."[2]

Stigma is deeply embedded in the value system of the community, one of its functions being to maintain that system. Thus we may be sincere in our condemnation of AIDS-related stigma but hesitate to do what it takes to reduce it. Nevertheless, it is not always clear whose truth we mean. Anthropologist Mary Douglas describes what happens to institutions when "the norms of behavior are contradictory" because "the social structure is cushioned by fictions of one kind or another."[3] For example, the "official" sexual code of the church is either abstinence or fidelity within a monogamous relationship. Fear of stigmatization may prevent me from disobeying that teaching, and if I fail it may prevent me from admitting it. But where HIV is widespread in the church (in Britain it may be teenage pregnancies or sexually transmitted infections) then the "real code" (which actually prevails in people's non-Sunday lives) is manifestly at odds with the "official" one, and generally most people know it.

A Case Study

"Gabriela" comes from Latin America and "Joshua" from an African country where adult HIV prevalence is more than 25 percent.[4] Both of them are living with HIV and both are on antiretrovirals. Joshua is a priest in the Anglican Church; Gabriela is a Catholic. Both are members of campaigning groups: Gabriela of an international community of women with HIV or AIDS, Joshua of an African network of clergy and others with HIV or AIDS. Joshua's bishop, whom we will call "Bishop Michael," has been energetic and thoughtful in combating HIV in his own diocese and province.

After two years of secrecy about his HIV status, Joshua could bear it no longer. He told the local bishop, who was shocked at first, but then sympathetic, and finally offered ways of raising the cash for antiretroviral treatment. In return, Joshua must promise to keep his HIV status a secret in the parish. For to allow someone living openly with HIV to celebrate the sacraments, somebody known to "carry the marks of sin upon his body," would be to condone the sin and undermine church teaching on sexual morality. Also, the bishop has long suspected Joshua to be homosexual, and if that is the case then he should keep quiet about that too.

At the time, Joshua was so relieved and so grateful that he agreed to this deal. For some months he did as he had promised. But one of the reasons why he had decided to disclose his HIV status was that he had hoped that by "coming out," as an HIV-positive priest, he would help to break the silence that surrounded AIDS in his church, and also that his experience would help others who were living with HIV or afraid of testing positive. Looking back, he is staggered both by the two-facedness of the bishop's response and by his uncritical acceptance of the Christian community's moralistic attitudes toward gay sexuality and people with AIDS.

Gabriela became infected with HIV when she was a student.

"I was so immoral then," she says, "and I was so ignorant." She thought her parents would throw her out when she told them, but instead, after the first shock, "they hugged me and said I would always be their daughter."

A year later she told her parish.

"That was the hardest thing I've ever done," she says. "I stood up at the end of Mass and said I knew I'd sinned against God, and I'd hurt my family and friends, and I asked to be forgiven. Most people were great, but some walked out and haven't spoken to my family since. But that was the thing that made it possible for me to go on belonging to my church."

After a joint session on AIDS at a recent conference, Gabriela and Joshua left together.

"Gabriela," says Joshua, "you *must not* say all that stuff about sin. It reinforces stigma and it encourages hypocrisy. You've done nothing other people haven't done: it's just that you were unlucky."

"But I *did* sin," says Gabriela. "I *have* hurt people, and I *am* sorry. I can't live without my family and my church. HIV put me outside, and this is what I needed to do to get back in. And now I feel loved and forgiven, and I do want to live a better life."

"But all you really did was to have sex," says Joshua. "You're letting us all down by suggesting the church has a right to exclude you for that. That way, things will never change. You've done nothing you need to be forgiven for.... "

Ethical and Ecclesiological Challenges

Of the various ethical and ecclesiological questions raised by this story, I want initially to draw attention to two.

First, in connecting AIDS-related stigma with sinfulness, what are we really saying is the sin? Is it (a) the means by which HIV transmission is assumed to have occurred in the first place, such as sex, or intravenous drug use? Or is it (b) the stigmatization of those who, for whatever reason, have been infected? Is it (a) adultery or is it (b) the religious or societal response to adultery? Is it (a) homosexuality or (b) the outlawing of homosexuals? Is it (a) the use of banned substances or (b) the judgmental attitudes directed toward those who use them?

Options "a" privilege institutional stability, constructing the sinner as one who breaks with communal taboos and thus contaminates the whole community, an impression confirmed by the language of pollution used in the bishop's comment that Joshua "carries the marks of sin upon his body," and also the ritual "cleansing" process that Gabriela went through before she could rejoin the community. Options "b" privilege the individual who has strayed from the institution's stated norms. These options are unassailable from the human rights standpoint. They suggest, though, that there is no connection between the matter of membership of Christian community and an individual's public adherence to its moral norms, a view that many members dismiss as unrealistic, relativist, and dictated by political correctness.

Second, after the "official code" has been broken, what ethical principles are raised by the process of negotiating reentry to one's church community in a situation where the "real code" is manifestly at odds with the "official code"? For both Joshua and Gabriela, continuing to belong to their churches was crucially important. In the event, they took different routes to achieve this. Gabriela accepted the assumptions of the "official code" and the language of sin with which it is supported and did what she felt she had to do in order to reintegrate into the community. Joshua, in the end, refused to play the official "game" required for reentry. His hope now, he says, is that he will find it possible to confront the church with its inconsistencies, judgmentalism, inability to cope with sex and sexuality, and hypocrisy of much of its moral teaching.

The bishop, though, is in trouble. He is a kind and compassionate man, with liberal leanings and a record of active support for AIDS work in his diocese. Furthermore, he fully appreciates the advantages of having an openly

HIV-positive priest among his clergy. But he is also the shepherd of an impoverished and struggling diocese, whose many problems include family breakdown and disintegrating social mores, often associated with rising levels of violence, rape, and crime. It is not HIV *as a disease* he has a problem with, he says; it is the morality or otherwise of the circumstances in which the virus was acquired. He is afraid of being seen to be condoning promiscuity or infidelity. This epidemic, catastrophic as it may be, is, after all, an incident in the long history of Christian mission. What if "his" church slides into anything-goes morality that invalidates longstanding moral teaching? Is there not a danger that too broad an inclusiveness will shatter the cultural or ethical foundations of the church and render it morally meaningless? Privately, the bishop is thoroughly exasperated with Joshua, who be believes to be arrogant and naïve, asking,"Why can't the young man be properly grateful, admit that he has sinned, and apologize?"

Breaking the Silence

Exclusionary othering *stems from* fear, but it can also *lead to* fear; and fear breeds silence, separation, and the othering of discourses that do not coincide with our own. In our globalized society, where instant communication theoretically reduces the strangeness of the Other, such fragmentation may be concealed behind the illusion that the human family is becoming more inclusive. In fact, the tower of Babel is with us and among us, the dominant voices are winning, and the Babel-system itself doing its work of promoting fragmentation and mutual incomprehension. In reality, as John Paul II, put it, the world itself is facing a crisis of belonging, and "the more globalized the market becomes, the more we must counterbalance it with a culture of solidarity that gives priority to the needs of the most vulnerable."[5]

In Paul Ricoeur's theory of discourse we find a tool for analyzing the various voices that are heard in Babel.[6] In the case study, our bishop speaks from a *discourse of authority* and institutional maintenance and in fear that the truth will undermine the church's historic mission. Joshua speaks from a *discourse of progressive activism* that distrusts institutions and whose main interest is to help the church support people in their communities who are living with HIV or AIDS, and to challenge the hypocrisy, denial, and judgmentalism that conflict with those aims. He thinks Gabriela has capitulated. But in fact Gabriela's challenge to the church ("I have sinned but I still want to belong") proves just as empowered and radical as his own, because it subverts the discourse of authority (which is generally opposed to change) in order to move the community to a greater acceptance of the presence of "the other" in their own ranks and, by implication, in society at large.

In his contribution to this collection, Emmanuel Katongole says:

Given the silences this culture imposes, the task of theology in our time is not only to name silences but also to point out forms of Christian praxis and communion that need to be nurtured within those silences if the church is to patiently become the good news of God's new creation...in the wake of HIV/AIDS.

One challenge of Katongole's "tasks of theology" is to find a space, between Babel and silences, where such a dialogue can take place. A part of this task must lie in the process of uncovering, truthfully and compassionately, the genuine discourses (as opposed to the false ones) that exist in that space, of honoring genuine discourses even if we do not share them, and of throwing a non-judgmental light on the theological priorities of each. Another is to ask the question: Are our renewed praxis and communion to embody the idea of morality or the idea of grace? A third aspect of the task is to identify the orientation of the discussants themselves. Is it redemption-centered (focusing on the sinfulness of creation and its need for redemption) or is it creation-centered (focusing on the basic goodness of creation and the need to engage with that)?[7]

Where the focus is on sin, it has been slammed, rightly, by anti-stigma lobbies in the churches. But to deny the reality of sin is as dangerous a strategy as overemphasizing it, implying as it does a denial of the need for the church to be a communion where sinners (which means all of us) may be welcomed and forgiven rather than judged and ostracized. This places those who hold authority in the church in an extraordinarily difficult position, both as human individuals and as institutional leaders. Bishop Michael's predicament suggests why ordination was seen by the desert fathers as something to be shunned. Rowan Williams tells the story of Theodore of Pherme, who was made a deacon but constantly fled from exercising his ministry:

Time after time, the old men brought him back to Scetis, saying, "Do not abandon your role as a deacon." Abba Theodore said to them, "Let me pray to God that he may tell me for sure whether I should function as a deacon in the liturgy...." A pillar of fire appeared to him, stretching from earth to heaven, and a voice said, "If you can become like this pillar of fire, go and be a deacon." So he decided against it. He went to church, and the brothers bowed to him and said, "If you don't want to be a deacon, at least administer the chalice." But he refused and said, "If you do not leave me alone I shall leave here for good." So they left him in peace.[8]

So now I come to my third question, or group of questions, namely, how do we identify these "most vulnerable"?[9] Are they individuals living and dying with HIV or AIDS? Are they the orphaned children? Are they the silent-fearful or silent-ignorant ones who may die or kill others if nobody tells them the truth? Are they "the little flock" that needs a safe place to belong and some rules to limp along with in a world that is often hostile and confusing? Or are they our leaders themselves, carrying the unenviable (perhaps unachievable) task of deciding what contemporary Christians, individually and in communion, should do or be, and called upon constantly to be the prophetic voice of the non-stigmatizing church at this time? For them I have a message. When all is done and all true discourses come to rest in the being of the great I AM: on that day, we shall know that prophesy never had to do with silence; prophesy, in the end, has to do with truth.

Notes

1. World Council of Churches, *The Ecumenical Response to HIV/AIDS in Africa: Plan of Action* (Geneva: World Council of Churches, 2001), 2.

2. Gillian Paterson, *AIDS and the African Churches: Exploring the Challenges* (London: Christian Aid, 2001), 25.

3. Mary Douglas, *Purity and Danger: An Analysis of the Concepts of Pollution and Taboo* (New York: Routledge, 1966), 144, 159.

4. This is a true story but identities have been concealed.

5. John Paul II, *Homily for the Workers' Jubilee*, 2001.

6. Paul Ricoeur, *From Text to Action: Essays in Hermeneutics* (Evanston, Ill.: Northwestern University Press, 1991).

7. I refer here to the idea of basic theological orientations described by Steven Bevans in his *Models of Contextual Theology* (Maryknoll, N.Y.: Orbis Books, 2002).

8. Theodore of Pherme 25; see Isaac of the Cells 1 and Peter of Dios 1, quoted in Rowan Williams, *Silence and Honey Cakes: The Wisdom of the Desert* (Oxford: Lion Books, 2003), 64–65.

9. John Paul II, *Homily for the Workers' Jubilee*, 2001.

18

Religion in the AIDS Crisis: Irrelevance, Adversary, or Ally?

The Case of the Catholic Church

BERTRAND LEBOUCHÉ,

JEAN-FRANÇOIS MALHERBE,

CHRISTIAN TREPO, AND RAYMOND LEMIEUX

When we investigate the connections between the Catholic Church and the AIDS epidemic, we find ourselves confronted by a paradox. It is a fact that more than 25 percent of the care provided to those who live with HIV/AIDS is provided by Catholic organizations.[1] How then do we explain another fact, namely, that statements by the church are ignored or dismissed?[2]

This perspective leads us to formulate the hypothesis that will guide our suggestions, namely, that a perception of the HIV/AIDS epidemic in terms of a strictly biomedical paradigm or by means of an excessively rigorist moral approach does not allow us to comprehend the experience of those who are confronted by AIDS and who thereby become "foreigners" (so to speak). The new faces of the epidemic, which are increasingly linked to social inequalities and to phenomena of exclusion, summon the church to get involved by proposing, on the basis of its theological reflection, an anthropology that is both critical and welcoming, so that those affected by HIV/AIDS may be enabled to reconstruct themselves as acting subjects.

An Epidemic with a Social Co-Transmission

Abandoning a Biological and Rigorist Paradigm

The first public medical and religious statements that were made about HIV/AIDS focused on individual responsibility and neglected the ancillary socio-economic factors. Thus, the biomedical world came to regard condoms as a sufficient solution to prevent AIDS, while the officials of the Catholic Church came to promote abstinence and fidelity within marriage. Each of these two reactions fails to see the whole picture.

The Social Dimensions of HIV/AIDS

Epidemiological researches into HIV/AIDS show how social inequalities and structural violence in numerous human relationships predispose human bodies to infection, and thus promote this epidemic.[3] AIDS then exacerbates the poverty, the social inequalities and structural violence, which in turn favors the spread of the epidemic. We have a vicious circle here. This epidemic reveals the social inequalities with regard to health[4] that entail differences in the risk of exposure to HIV/AIDS and unequal access to care, screening, and preventive measures. These differences make a profound impact on people's health. In the United States, for example, although the African American population represents only 12 percent of the U.S. population as a whole, it represents more than 50 percent of all new cases of infection by HIV.[5] If we may employ an expression drawn from the church's social teaching, we may say that this illness has a "preferential option for the poor"[6] and for the "foreigners" in our societies.

Among the new faces of the epidemic, women pose a fundamental challenge. For more than twenty years, this has been the only infectious disease that affects women to such an extent, they account for half of the forty million cases of infection throughout the world. In sub-Saharan Africa, they account for 60 percent of the new cases of infection. Women are, in fact, vulnerable on two fronts:[7] there is a biological vulnerability, leading to a greater susceptibility to sexually transmitted infections (including HIV),[8] and a social vulnerability thanks to inequalities, poverty, sexual and cultural norms, a lack of education, the violence to which they are subjected,[9] precocious marriage, and economic dependence, which includes exploitation by "sugar daddies."[10]

It follows that, if we are to fight effectively against this epidemic, we must bear in mind this double vulnerability — both biomedical and social.

Theological Instruments for the Construction of an Anthropology Both Critical and Welcoming

The persons affected by HIV/AIDS confront us with a question: How are they to be integrated into the definition of what it means to be human, despite this specific experience? They address this question above all to our societies and to the world religions.

We turn to those theologies that have their starting point in the concrete situation of human persons and are motivated primarily by indignation at the conditions that so many of our contemporaries must face. Theology must propose a critical anthropology that is open to a broader definition of the human being and that includes these persons in the definition of what it is to be human. What might such an anthropology look like?

Taking into Account the Context of Specific Persons

In his *Summa theologiae*,[11] Thomas Aquinas reflects on the Aristotelian approach to the good by means of the natural law, the native capacity of the human intelligence to recognize what is good for the human person (Ia-IIae, q. 94, a. 4). Thomas's theology does justice to the human person: while it accompanies the moral agent who strives to find the path to the good, it does not fall into the trap of relativism. The more specifically one draws closer to the good, the greater is the possibility of error in determining the concrete choices to be taken in conformity with the natural law (Ia-IIae, q. 94, a. 5 and 6).

"Laws ought to be imposed upon human beings only in keeping with *the condition of these persons.* . . . Imperfect persons are permitted many things that one must not tolerate in the virtuous" (Ia-IIae, q. 96 [the power of human law], a. 2, reply).

When he speaks of acting "in keeping with the condition of these persons," Thomas is insisting on the importance of the context in which these "imperfect" ones live. The law is applied in a gradual manner, in accordance with the situation of individual persons with regard to their social and emotional conditionings, their poverty, etc. Otherwise, as Thomas says, quoting the Book of Proverbs (30:33), "Pressing the nose too hard produces blood" (Ia-IIae, q. 96, a. 2, s. 2).

In a very specific manner, therefore, prevention must be adapted to the contexts of the persons who are at risk. One might justifiably ask whether the blanket application of the principles of abstinence and fidelity within marriage, or the use of condoms as solutions to the AIDS epidemic, without taking account of the specific contexts, does not entail the risk that the weakest will fall, or that they will be excluded from the Good News. The application of such principles must be accompanied and mediated by a third level of discourse, namely, that of the good that is a genuine possibility for these persons here and now.

Thanks to distributive justice, this notion of capacity recalls the modern idea of *empowerment*,[12] which has been employed very extensively in the AIDS epidemic. It has the merit of not reducing people to their vulnerabilities. Rather, it asks how far it is possible to help them to regain control over their own lives and improve the lives of those around them.

An Anthropology of Graduality

Aristotle and Thomas propose a gradual approach to the good, which takes account both of the context of the persons involved and of their moral or social imperfection (Ia-IIae, q. 96, a. 2, s. 2 and 3) and does not depend directly on the will of the agents. This graduality is a very interesting concept in the context of the discussion of antiretroviral treatments, which have a considerable biomedical effect: they ameliorate the state of health and allow a return to the non-symptomatic stage, even in countries in the southern hemisphere where sanitary conditions remain very unfavorable.[13] Their social effect is likewise undeniable: they reintegrate the person into life and into community (resumption of work, preservation of the family cell, etc.). Studies have also shown that persons who receive good treatment do not "go off the rails" in their sexual behavior. Besides this, AIDS is no longer synonymous with death but with medical care, and this encourages the acquaintances of those infected to come for screening. Dr. Paul Farmer has shown that a person who receives treatment is less stigmatized and, because of his or her experiences, can play a vital role in prevention by encouraging others to receive treatment.[14] Thomas's idea is that morality should be made desirable. A major challenge in the struggle against the AIDS epidemic, especially vis-à-vis those who are "imperfect," is how to show people that it is good for them to avoid contracting HIV.

A Preferential Option for Women

In the church's social teaching, the preferential option for the poor, which is rooted in the biblical teaching of the prophets and Christ, takes account of the obligation of solidarity with the poor; but at the same time, it obliges us to get actively involved in the fight against a dehumanizing poverty. The inequalities and the violence to which women are subjected contribute inexorably to the spread of HIV infection and make the efforts at prevention worthless. This epidemic shows us that our primary task is to establish a preferential option for women and children. This option can be translated into action on several levels.

First, a liberation from the social, political, economic, and cultural factors that make women more vulnerable to infection. This may mean taking action to help them recover the full exercise of their rights, their empowerment, and their health.

Second, a personal liberation of the women who are carriers of HIV by means of high-quality care and treatment free of charge. These treatments must envisage the reduction in the transmission of HIV from mother to child[15] and the prevention of new infections. Access to treatment itself contributes to improving social conditions and can thus help attenuate the social inequalities with regard to health.

Third, forms of prevention where women take the initiative must be made available by supplying them with microbicides.[16]

Fourth, these women must be considered as experts. When they have been treated, they can become agents in treatment and prevention for their community and look after orphans. In considering the expertise of these vulnerable women, the challenge is to envisage how it might be possible to integrate them as normative figures into the normative societal praxis.

We should note that this preferential option is not determined by the responsibility of the person, but by her vulnerability.[17] Besides this, it is possible to establish "inegalitarian" preferences[18] in providing access to treatment and care, to the benefit of the most vulnerable persons; in this way, one can do something to reduce the long waiting lists that have accumulated. In Haiti, Paul Farmer has developed his organization Partners in Health on the basis of the preferential option for the poor and of the community dimension of care.[19]

Opening Up a Space Where Subjects Can Be Reconstructed

After twenty-five years of the epidemic, prejudices, ignorance, and sheer stupidity are still so strong that many women choose to hide their seropositive status, since openness all too often results in rejection, discrimination, and stigmatization. In more general terms, our societies, dominated by the demands of the market, practice a selection process that tends to marginalize the weakest and make them invisible in order to celebrate the success of those who perform best; those bodies that do not conform to the norm simply disappear from sight. Those who are weakest are made even more fragile, and this makes them particularly vulnerable (*inter alia*) to HIV. In this way, the HIV epidemic makes the bodies of women and children disappear as "social bodies."

How might we as theologians imagine a place or places where these persons could reappear? The theologian William T. Cavanaugh argues that we must promote the emergence of spaces for those who have no space, where they can reconstruct themselves as subjects by means of their vulnerabilities. As Michel de Certeau explains, these are "spaces of praxis."[20] Cavanaugh refers to the Eucharist, which makes death present, above all by means of the anamnesis of the death of Christ, incorporating those who receive communion into a body that is marked by death and by suffering.[21]

The Eucharist,[22] which constitutes the Body of Christ, is the model of these spaces where the center is everywhere, even at the margins, since Christ is the center of his Body with each and every person. To open out the Body of Christ means to open up spaces where human beings can reconstruct themselves. Whereas our societies are mostly tempted to establish frontiers between the sick and those who are well, and to make the sick or dying bodies vanish from sight, the Body of Christ abolishes the frontiers, especially those between the healthy and the suffering (1 Cor. 12:26). In the countries of the southern hemisphere, eight hundred thousand mothers transmit HIV to their children each year, while less than one hundred children are affected annually in Europe or North America. This says something about the choices made by our societies with regard to the availability of medical care. Ultimately, this praxis entails the *disappearance* of the bodies of these children and the *appearance* of conditions favorable to the future development of this epidemic. Societal inequalities in health are stigmata on individual bodies and on the body of society as a whole. This means, then, that we must recreate spaces with an anthropological structure modeled on the Body of Christ, where those bodies that do not conform to the norms may reappear and reconstruct themselves. They must receive access to good care, and the transmission of HIV must be prevented. To make them reappear, especially by caring for them, bears witness to the inestimable value of the human person, and makes the act of caring a genuinely political act. This theology of the Eucharist thus opens the door to a political anthropology of medical care and of committed involvement in the struggle against the HIV/AIDS pandemic. To give care means not only improving the biological parameters: it permits a real return to life and a return to the community. And this amelioration transcends the individual dimension.

Overcoming the stigmatization that prevents people from openness about their seropositive status is one way of helping the bodies of persons with HIV to reappear. In the case of migrant populations, who are particularly vulnerable, this means enabling them to defend their rights and their expectations in the public sphere, and this ought surely to mean helping them to maintain practices that protect them against infection for the whole of their lives. When they are given control over care and prevention, there is a good chance that this will help them to make personal choices and assume individual responsibility. And when a person is capable of assuming appropriate responsibility, this will be manifested in knowledge of one's seropositive status, protection of one's sexual partners, prevention of contamination by another strain of HIV if one is already infected, ensuring one turns up regularly for treatment, and so on.

Anti-AIDS medicines not only act against the infectious vulnerabilities of the organism: they likewise help diminish social vulnerabilities. In this process of the reappearance of the body, attention is paid not only to pathology, but also to the concrete life of the patient, who can re-establish a social framework. When the individual takes charge of his life, this has repercussions on both societal groups and the continuity of a society. Joia Mukherjee and Paul Farmer have shown how a person in Haiti who receives treatment is less stigmatized and can become a vital actor and an expert on prevention, encouraging others to seek treatment, precisely because of what he or she is going through.[23] In this respect, anti-AIDS treatment is essential for all who require it, since it helps create the space where one can be reconstructed as a subject in one's own life.

The Eucharist sketches the outlines of a world that is expanding toward the kingdom, where all persons — even those on the margins — find themselves at the center and can constitute themselves as subjects. The Eucharist seeks to reintegrate the "foreigners" in our societies, who are particularly vulnerable to infection, and it can thus open the door to an anthropology of welcome.

Eschatological Spaces

Christian eschatology is an eschatology menaced by death, which never loses its power to obscure the promises, and this is why it can certainly go hand in hand with an existence that is highly vulnerable and precarious — as in the case of a serious illness. Instead of fleeing from this precariousness, Christian eschatology attains its full stature by entering into it: it is through love for those who are least of all, and through solidarity with them, that Christian eschatology becomes the guarantor of their hope. The critical and creative eschatology that the theologian Johann Baptist Metz has developed[24] enters directly into the stories of the vulnerabilities of people today and tries to identify the specific conditions that will bring them salvation in our societies.

The church must, therefore, rediscover its prophetic role and choose "a critical and liberating position when confronted with social conditions,"[25] which can open the door to a political anthropology and recall the fact that human persons cannot be reduced to the concepts that they may employ about themselves. Firmly anchored in hope, this anthropology always looks to a future — that of the kingdom — where every person will become a human subject. In an illness that is as symbolic as HIV/AIDS and that affects the human dimension so deeply, this anthropology can ward off the risk of a normative totalitarianism in biomedicine, society, and religion. The church's task is to recall unceasingly that the human person is always greater than that which he or she does. One role of theology (as we have said above) is to remind us that human persons cannot be reduced to the concepts that they choose to employ about themselves. Our societies are becoming increasingly aware of the importance of health, but there is a danger that the social norm may simply be adopted by biomedicine, so that public health will be transformed into a huge normative enterprise — with the consequence that our societies will have room only for "normal" individuals, that is, those without any kind of psychological or physical uncertainty. Biomedicine must not refuse these subjects the possibility of life. It must remain a force capable of creating places even for those often regarded as deviants and the uncertain persons in our societies. This is the path that the church must take, because it is in the risk of fraternal love — and not in "normalization" — that the Christian hope triumphs over death.[26]

Conclusion

If this critical anthropology is put into practice, we will be able to identify those points where carers, charities, and politicians must exercise ethical vigilance in their fight against the epidemic. The development of new treatments and methods of prevention requires both a very complex scientific technology and integration into research of the voices of vulnerable persons. The effectiveness of new treatments depends on a genuine collaboration with the populations for whom these medicines are designed. Through her words, the church can become a privileged ally in the fight against HIV.

This anthropology has theological consequences too. Let us mention one of these, on the level of ecclesiology. Opening up welcoming spaces to be used by those who are sick means constituting a church that comes into existence not *for* them, but rather *with* them, a church where God reveals himself through the history of their suffering. This allows us to glimpse an ecclesiology that finds its starting point in the conquered; an ecclesiology that is open to the fragility of each individual and exercises solidarity with regard to this fragility. It is in fragility, not in power, that solidarity is born. Far from paralyzing the action of the believer, this solidarity propels us to action in order that the struggle against the injustices that dominate the world everywhere may never cease.[27] The community comes into existence for the sake of this fragility, and it seeks to establish solidarities beyond its own present limits in order to establish renewed places where human persons may recognize one another. And thus, despite itself, this pandemic will bring a deeper humanity and solidarity into our world. And the church, which has been engaged through its actions in the struggle against this pandemic for a long time, will also have a word that people will hear.

— English translation by Brian McNeil

Notes

1. Cardinal Javier Lozano Barragán, president of the Pontifical Council for the Pastoral Care of Health Care Workers in the Vatican, Message for World AIDS Day, December 1, 2003: "Una parola di amore e di speranza per le famiglie e per le persone colpite dal terribile male," published November 30, 2003.

2. Patricia Miller, "The Lesser Evil: The Catholic Church and the AIDS Epidemic," *Conscience* (Fall 2001); *www.catholicsforchoice.org/conscience/archived/Lesser%20Evil.htm.*

3. Paul E. Farmer, Bruce Nizeye, Sarah Stulac, and Salmaan Keshavjee, "Structural Violence and Clinical Medicine," *PLoS Medicine* 3, no. 10 (2006): e449.

4. Annette Leclerc, ed., with Didier Fassin, Hélène Grandjean, Monique Kaminski, Thierry Lang, *Inégalités sociales de santé* (Paris: La Découverte/INSERM, 2000).

5. "Conspiracy Theory of HIV/AIDS," *The Lancet* 365 (2005): 448.

6. Pope John Paul II used this concept in his encyclical *Sollicitudo Rei Socialis* (1987): "Here I would like to indicate one of them: the option or love of preference for the poor. This is an option, or a special form of primacy in the exercise of Christian charity, to which the whole tradition of the Church bears witness. It affects the life of each Christian inasmuch as he or she seeks to imitate the life of Christ, but it applies equally to our social responsibilities and hence to our manner of living, and to the logical decisions to be made concerning the ownership and use of goods" (42).

7. The Gender and Development Group [Poverty Reduction and Economic Management (PREM)], *Integrating Gender Issues into HIV/AIDS Programs* (Washington, D.C.: World Bank, 2004), cited by Thomas C. Quinn and Julie Overbaugh, "HIV/AIDS in Women: An Expanding Epidemic," *Science* 308 (2005): 1582–83.

8. This is due to the hormonal modifications in the microbial ecology of the vagina; besides this, since women are receptive in the act of intercourse, they have more contact with the potentially dangerous genital secretions.

9. Quinn and Overbaugh, "HIV/AIDS in Women."

10. UNAIDS, The Global Coalition on Women and AIDS, 2004; see online *http://womenandaids.unaids.org.*

11. Fathers of the English Dominican Province, trans., *The Summa theologica,* 2nd rev. ed. in 22 vols. (London: Burns, Oates & Washbourne, 1912–36), reprinted in 5 vols. (Westminster, Md.: Christian Classics, 1981); *www.newadvent.org/summa.*

12. Meaning the action of a person, a group, or a team, that allows those who take part to develop their autonomy and their responsibility vis-à-vis both their own persons and their environment.

13. Louise C. Ivers, David Kendrick, Karen Doucette, "Efficacy of Antiretroviral therapy programs in resource-poor settings: a meta-analysis of the published literature," *Clinical Infectious Diseases* 41 (2005): 217–24.

14. Arachu Castro and Paul Farmer, "Understanding and Addressing AIDS-Related Stigma: From Anthropological Theory to Clinical Practice in Haiti," *American Journal of Public Health* 95, no. 1 (2005): 53–59.

15. Quinn and Overbaugh, "HIV/AIDS in Women."

16. The name "microbicide" is given to every substance capable of significantly reducing the transmission of sexually transmitted diseases, including HIV, when it is applied in the vagina or the rectum. Microbicides can take the form of a jelly, a cream, a suppository, a pellet, a sponge, or a vaginal ring. Microbicides may be one of the most promising forms of prevention, since such products could be safe and effective, cheap, easy to get hold of, and widely accepted: UNAIDS, *Microbicides for HIV Protection*, UNAIDS Technical Update (Geneva: UNAIDS, 1998).

17. This is particularly important in the case of sex workers, prisoners, and drug users.

18. In the field of biomedical ethics, see Pierre Boitte and Bruno Cadoré, "L'allocation des ressources en santé: du 'mauvais argument des contraintes' à une politique de santé," a paper presented at the European Ethics Network Third Annual Meeting, Barcelona, September 14–15, 1998.

19. Paul E. Farmer, "Medicine and Social Justice: Insights from Liberation Theology," *America* 173 (1995): 14.

20. Michel de Certeau, *L'invention du quotidien* 1: *Arts de faire* (1980), new edition, ed. Luce Giard (Paris: Gallimard, Folio essais, 1990), 173.

21. William T. Cavanaugh, "Dying for the Eucharist or Being Killed by It? Romero's Challenge to First-World Christians," *Theology Today* 58, no. 2 (July 2001): 177.

22. William T. Cavanaugh, *Theopolitical Imagination: Discovering the Liturgy as a Political Act in an Age of Global Consumerism* (Edinburgh: T&T Clark, 2002), 113.

23. Joia Mukherjee and Paul E. Farmer, *Access to Antiretroviral Treatment and Care: Experience of the HIV Equity Initiative, Cange, Haiti: Case Study* (Geneva: World Health Organization, 2003).

24. French translation: *Pour une théologie du monde*, Cogitatio Fidei 57 (Paris: Cerf, 1970), 110.

25. Ibid., 134.

26. Ibid., 111.

27. Ibid., 101.

Part Five

Bioethics and Social Justice

19

The Contribution of Theology
to Bioethical Discussion

JOSÉ ROQUE JUNGES

The origin of bioethics is intimately linked to Christian theology. Most of the early authors and writings come from the field of theology. The consolidation of bioethics as an independent domain with its own epistemological rules obliged the theologians to make explicit the role and specific contribution of theology in discussing the challenges confronted by bioethics. The question is this: In a plural and public forum, do theologians simply defend the confessional positions of their church in a dogmatic way, or do they reflect rationally, based on faith with an open mind, endeavoring to build a consistent anthropology inspired by Christianity on which to build their position?

Ecclesiastical Theology, Public Theology, and Bioethics

Theologian Jürgen Moltmann draws a distinction between doing theology within a particular church (ecclesiastical theology), which is confessional, and doing theology for the public space of the university and society (public theology), which is pluralistic in its positions.[1] The first of these is directed inward to the church and is therefore focused on the ecclesial communion, for the confirmation of the members of the confessional church in their faith and the formation of ministers and others who serve its mission.

The second takes place in the public space and is concerned with a relevant and pertinent presence of Christian faith in secular society, proclaiming the reign of God in an already post-Christian cultural context.

The first is more concerned with the coherency of the lives of the faithful on the path of following Christ, and the second with the public relevance of the Christian message for a secularized society. Ecclesiastical theology is more concerned with helping the faithful to understand and put into practice what they profess in faith, while public theology aims to justify and argue in support of the pertinence of the Christian message in responding to the challenges of today's world.

These two facets of theology are necessary and complementary. They respond to different specificities due to the present cultural context that is no longer that of Christendom, without separating ecclesial communion (coherency) from apostolic mission (communication), but rather holding them in a mutually enriching tension. However they are both ecclesial because although their purposes and concerns are different, the social location from which they do theology, both ecclesiastical and public, is the ecclesial community.

The church is a historical figure of the reign of God proclaimed by Jesus of Nazareth, not its full realization. For this reason the reign of God opens a broader horizon of hope and future for all humanity. Today, reducing the reign of God to its ecclesial expression often makes it harder to open up and gain access to the newness of the gospel. In this sense, theology cannot be reduced to its function as a service to the "ecclesial communion"; it must also assume the function of proclaiming the reign of God to the world.

In this function, public theology relates to the political, cultural, economic, scientific, and ecological spheres of life in society. Thus public theology participates in the *res publica* of society from a critical and prophetic perspective, because it sees realities in the prospective of the coming reign of God. It tries to speak a public language accessible to the whole social collectivity, without losing the integrity of the Christian message.

"The *parrhesia* of faith must be matched by the boldness of reason," said John Paul II in *Fides et Ratio* (48); that is, the courageous affirmation of faith must be matched by a bold and creative effort to make it understood in our time. For this reason, theology cannot forget its ecclesial roots, on the one hand, but, on the other, neither can it submit to formulations that are outdated and incomprehensible to today's mentality, forgetting the hierarchy of the truths of faith. This demands ethical creativity rooted in a hermeneutical rereading of its tradition based on contemporary situations.[2]

Public theology is the most appropriate perspective in which the Christian faith can contribute to the social forum of bioethical discussion, because it attempts to express itself in a language understandable to the collectivity and participate in the public debate of society with a critical and prophetic focus. This debate is characterized by interdisciplinarity, pluralism, secularism, and the criterion of argumentation. Theologians must be able to move within these discursive conditions with openness and critical intelligence. They must also identify their specific contribution in the field of bioethics. Here it is important to distinguish between two necessary types of bioethical knowledge.

Casuistic and Hermeneutical Bioethics

Bioethics has two facets with different, mutually complementary methodologies.[3] The first is seen in hospital bioethics committees and in committees on the ethics of research with human subjects. Their purpose is to pronounce judgments of moral evaluation on clinical or investigative cases that entail ethical challenges and conflicts based on the consideration of risks, harms, and benefits. These committees are forums of discussion that profess a consensual procedural ethic, characterized by secularism, pluralism, and multi- and inter-disciplinarity. Their primary ethical concern is with procedures. The committees profess a casuistic bioethics.

But although a healthy casuistry is important and necessary, bioethics cannot be reduced to the solution of cases. A second stream is needed, called hermeneutical bioethics. Many of today's ethical challenges respond to implicit cultural dynamics, which must be interpreted in order to gauge the problem. Without this cultural hermeneutic we remain at the surface of the problems and reach solutions that merely respond to demands artificially created by the technologies. All case solutions are based on anthropological presuppositions and depend on underlying moral conceptions that need to be clarified. The hermeneutical effort focuses on basic issues that cannot be set aside without falling into a simple, accommodationist pragmatism. That is the role of hermeneutical bioethics.

These two facets of bioethics express and respond to two dimensions of human action itself. First and foremost, actions have a dimension that could be called pragmatic, because they arise out of immediate and contextualized needs. To respond to these needs one must have a *phronetic* (prudential) sensitivity or practical wisdom, which allows the application of principles and norms to a concrete situation in order to decide whether or not a particular solution is morally or juridically acceptable. Here the question is whether or not a particular action can be taken in response to a felt need. Casuistry takes on this pragmatic dimension of the action.

Of course human activity not only has a pragmatic dimension but also a symbolic expressivity, pointing to underlying meanings and long-range consequences that are not immediately clear. Human action builds meanings based on cultural reference points and transmits a message of values that are often not conscious but need to be clarified. This is the expressivity, or the symbolic dimension, of an action. The more deeply these reference points are involved, the more necessary it is to consider the expressivity of the action. Hermeneutics contributes the symbolic dimension of an action.

The Theologian's Contribution
to Bioethical Discussion in Society

Although theological ethicists play an important part in the casuistry developed in the committees, their more specific contribution is at the level of hermeneutical bioethics. Their role is not so much to assist in the pragmatic solution of concrete cases, but to focus on the symbolic expressivity of the actions discussed in bioethics. Their expertise is mainly to interpret the meanings and underlying message transmitted and expressed by the solution that has been proposed and subjected to ethical analysis.

Thus, hermeneutical bioethics is the particular interface for public theology, because it enables the Christian faith to pose critical questions in the public discussion of new biotechnological challenges, based on an analysis of the cultural reference points that affect the underlying mentality, and of the anthropological consequences that the proposed solutions may entail.

Without the ethical courage to question the cultural dynamics that affect many decisions and without the reflective expertise to develop a critical hermeneutic, the public discussion will remain enclosed in a purely accommodationist pragmatism, manipulated by lobbies that respond to short-range interests. These cannot guide decision-making when reference points are in play that affect what is specifically human. In such a case, the conditions are not present for an authentic ethic of discourse on the use of biotechnologies, guided by an argumentative and critical dialogue and by the search for a consensus that permits the preservation of human identity and the natural environment. Assuming the perspective of hermeneutical bioethics, theology has the expertise to help create an environment of argumentative and critical dialogue in the public forum on the ethical challenges from biotechnology.

This is not a matter of imposing practical solutions, let alone moral ones, because that is not the task of hermeneutical bioethics; it is rather to develop the ethical reflection that establishes a critical distance in the face of the dynamics that affect the actions demanded by biotechnologies. The goal is to encourage deep and critical thinking.

However, the role often conferred on bioethics in the face of biotechnology can be compared metaphorically to the task of a chaplain in the royal court: to find moral arguments justifying the actions of the king, soothe his conscience, and minimize the harmful effects of his acts. Such a role deprives bioethics of its critical vision of scientific progress and limits it to reducing any adverse effects of biotechnology by suggesting guidelines for application. Bioethics must refuse to become a mere chaplain in the royal court of science. That would be a passive role that does not do justice to the critical specificity of ethical reflection. Theology reminds bioethics of that specificity.

The Moral Argument on "Playing God" in Relationship to Biotechnology

An ostensibly theological argument is often invoked in the bioethical debate, that the scientists are "playing God" when they "push forward" with certain biotechnological innovations.[4] In the background is an assumption that some spheres of reality belong only to God and cannot be invaded by human beings. Basically, the argument aims to define limits that cannot be overstepped. But it is not really about playing God because it refers to scientific knowledge and to power over nature.

Scientific knowledge has been in a hegemonic position ever since the Enlightenment. Humanity has come of age and no longer needs the "god" hypothesis to resolve its problems. Science is not allowed to fill in the unknown with God, because science works *etsi Deus non daretur,* that is, as if God were not a given. Thus there is no room for a "god of the gaps." That argument was invoked whenever human beings felt powerless to explain a phenomenon, but it has been losing ground as the boundaries of scientific power and knowledge expanded; thus God also seemed to be losing ground.

So the warning against "playing God" is not a principle, but a point of view. It aims to remind human beings of their fallibility and finitude. It sets itself against the narcissistic desire for omnipotence that characterizes the culture that gives rise to biotechnologies. In English, the word "playing" has a variety of meanings: playing for fun, playing the game, playing music, playing a theatrical role. They must be held together in order to understand the argument about playing God. The problem is not that we are pretending to be God as a child would; it is that we are not playing the game, the music, the role as God would.

The problem is not in wanting to take God's place in creation, because God and human beings are not competing for space; it is in not being present, not intervening in nature in the way God has done and continues to do in creation, respecting the logic of life. It is not about taking the place of an absent God, let alone trying to be God, but playing the role as if God were a given, *etsi Deus daretur,* because we must look at God to see how to act as God would. We must ask, "Who is this God that we are invited to imitate when we intervene in nature."

This leads us to rethink the common affirmation of God's omnipotence, as E. Babut has shown so well.[5] That understanding shows through in the argument about "playing God." Since in contemporary culture God is no longer a presupposition in explaining nature, human beings consider themselves omnipotent like God.

What we say of God as omnipotent was often anthropomorphically derived from the image of the emperor as *pantocreator,* that is, all-powerful; now human beings say it of themselves as having dominion over nature. In order to question that human omnipotence as the image of divine omnipotence, we must come back to the God revealed in Jesus of Nazareth. That is, when we speak of God, the accent belongs not on omnipotence but on love.

In making all creatures, especially human beings, God in love self-limited his power. Jesus was the revelation of that self-limitation. To see it we must try to understand creation and incarnation as intimately related. Creation follows God's laws, and God does not intervene to annul them. Human beings, created free, are able to set themselves over against God. The *kenosis* of God's incarnation is present in the dynamic of creation. If God is love, he can create only in a self-limiting way. It is a limitation that God self-imposes for the sake of love. So yes, God is all-powerful, but in love. This is the God who is revealed in Jesus of Nazareth. Love always leads to self-limitation, and God is total love. Human beings need to learn loving self-limitation, if they want to "play" God by intervening in the rhythms of life.

Theological criticism cannot use the argument of divine omnipotence to challenge human omnipotence, as it is manifested in many biotechnological interventions, because that is the source of the problem; rather we must proclaim the kenotic love of God as it is manifested in creation and revealed in Jesus of Nazareth, who is the Christ in whom and through whom all things were created. This critique can help to challenge the narcissistic tendency toward human omnipotence that is present in the ideology underlying many biotechnologies. Thus we can learn from this God — who limits himself in love and in creating allows the creatures to develop at their own pace — how human beings should intervene in life: learning to limit ourselves, respecting the logic of life.

— *English translation by Margaret D. Wilde*

Notes

1. Jürgen Moltmann, *Dio nel Progretto del Mondo Moderno: Contributi per una Rilevanza Pubblica dessa Teologia* (Brescia: Queriniana, 1999).

2. M.-J. Thiel, "Le défi d'une ethique systematique pour la théologie," *Revue des Sciences Religieuses* 74 (2000): 92–113.

3. José Roque Junges, "Bioética como casuística e como hermenêutica," *Revista Brasileira de Bioética* 1 (2005): 28–44.

4. A. Verhey, " 'Playing God' and Invoking a Perspective," *Journal of Medicine and Philosophy* 20 (1995): 347–64.

5. E. Babut, *O Deus poderosamente Fraco da Bíblia* (São Paulo: Loyola, 2001).

20

Multinational Biomedical Research in Impoverished Communities

Toward a Theory of Global Social Justice

JORGE JOSÉ FERRER

Posing the Problem

By "multinational research" we mean research projects in biomedicine, epidemiology, or the social sciences that involve the participation of researchers, subjects, and institutions from diverse countries. We are particularly concerned with the problems that arise when scientists and institutions from the economically developed countries carry out research in developing countries.[1]

According to Ruth Macklin, four problems have been identified with regard to such multinational research. The first two represent classic issues: the vulnerability of citizens of poor countries due to low levels of education and their unfamiliarity with scientific vocabulary, and the cultural differences that make communication difficult between the researchers and their experimental subjects. Two others have been recently added, and have received more attention in the past ten years: whether the research subjects in poor countries should receive the same level of medical care and therapy that they would be given if the experiment were being conducted in a rich country, and what obligations, if any, the researchers and their sponsors have toward the subjects and their communities once the research is completed. Rather than analyzing these problems in detail, we shall focus here on what we consider their least common denominator from the perspective of ethical analysis: justice in a global context.[2] This approach needs to be justified because, as Macklin and Darrell Moellendorf point out, not everyone accepts the application of the principle of distributive justice in ethical analysis at the international level.[3] For some, the problems of justice require a type of linkage not seen in international relations. We shall return to this point later in justifying the application of obligations of justice at the international or, rather, the global level.

Paradigmatic Cases

We begin this reflection by presenting two of the cases, which, as Macklin points out, have given rise to the current debate.[4]

The Search for Alternatives to Regimen ACTG 076

In 1994, the *New England Journal of Medicine* published the results of a study known as ACTG 076.[5] Regimen 076 consists of the oral administration of AZT to women carrying HIV during their pregnancy, intravenous administration during the delivery, and subsequent administration to the newborn babies. This study established that the regimen could reduce vertical transmission of HIV by two-thirds. In the United States and Western Europe, the application of regimen 076 has become the standard treatment for seropositive pregnant women.

In the developing countries, where 90 percent of HIV carriers lived, regimen 076 was prohibitively expensive. Its cost at the time was calculated at a minimum of $800 per woman treated, while the average per capita health expenditure budgeted in the countries of sub-Saharan Africa (where the majority of HIV cases were located) was not more than $10. The $800 includes only the cost of the medication, without counting the costs of transportation and administration.

In its September 18, 1997, issue, the *New England Journal of Medicine* reported that eighteen studies were being carried out in a search of more economical therapies than regimen 076. Two of these studies were taking place in the United States and sixteen in poor countries. In the U.S. studies, all the subjects had full access to AZT or other antiretroviral medications. The situation was different for the experiment subjects in the developing countries. In fifteen of the sixteen studies carried out in those countries, at least some of the subjects did not have access to any antiretroviral medication. In other words, there was a control group that received only placebos.

The debate touched off by this information can be summarized as follows: Critics of the studies held that the use of placebos was unjustified. After the success of regimen 076, the null hypothesis, traditionally required to justify the use of placebos in the case of potentially mortal illnesses, could no longer be invoked. Defenders of the experiments argued that the subjects in any case would not have received the validated treatment, since it was not available in their countries. Participation in the study did not make their situation worse, but it did allow for definitive answers on the effectiveness and safety of the experimental treatment. This position implied that the poverty of these countries authorized the application of an ethical double standard. From our viewpoint, a comparison study would have been more appropriate from an ethical viewpoint. And in fact, studies of this type were carried out as part of these experiments.[6]

The Surfaxin Case

Another famous case is the study of the drug Surfaxin, which was never carried out.[7] In 2001, the Public Health Research Group, the same organization that had sounded the alert in the case of the studies to find alternatives to regimen 076, discovered that a similar study was being prepared in several Latin American countries — Mexico, Ecuador, Bolivia, and Peru — to seek an alternative to treatment with Surfaxin. Surfaxin is a surfactant for the treatment of a common ailment of premature babies — respiratory distress syndrome.

The pharmaceutical corporation that was sponsoring the study, Discovery Laboratories, was actually preparing two different studies. The first, to be carried out in Western Europe, would compare the experimental drug with four regimens approved for the treatment of that respiratory syndrome. The second study, to be carried out in Latin America, included a placebo group. It is known that this second study would be considered ethically unacceptable in the United States or Western Europe. The host countries were to receive some important benefits in exchange for authorization of the study. Discovery made a commitment to improve and modernize the neonatal intensive care units in those countries. As a result, all the children participating as subjects would receive better medical attention than they would have had if the study had not taken place.

One might argue in favor of the experiment more or less as follows: Carrying out the clinical trial guaranteed that 50 percent of the children would receive the treatment, which they would not otherwise have received; and 100 percent would receive improved neonatal care, which they also would not have received. Discovery would benefit from the study, but so also would the host countries and the research subjects.

The objections to this study are similar to those raised in the previous example: Is it legitimate to use placebos when we know that there are effective treatments, and when the subjects may suffer important harm? But this case is different in one significant aspect. Alternatives to AZT or other treatments were being sought mainly for impoverished populations, which could not afford the more costly treatment. In the case of Surfaxin, there is no reason to think that the medication would be especially indicated or especially appropriate for countries with limited health resources. Thus the exploitation is more easily flagged in this case. The experiments were not carried out. The alert was sounded before the protocols were implemented.

Reasons for Such Studies and Why They Are Problematic

These are not the only cases, of course. Biomedical experimentation with human subjects, especially clinical trials, in developing countries is important. It seems to be one of the models of outsourcing that are increasingly thriving in the world of business (which includes biomedical research). The pharmaceutical corporations derive many benefits from clinical trials in developing countries: an abundance of subjects, ill and lacking medical care; lower research costs; and, in general, less stringent regulation for the protection of research subjects than in the developed countries. This last factor allows studies to be performed that would not be possible in the first world, as well as reducing the time and costs required.[8] The time and cost reductions are not in themselves unworthy objectives. They are, however, if the studies are not responsive to the health needs of the impoverished community, or if the community does not benefit from its participation.

Models for the Moral Justification
of Multinational Research

Different solutions have been proposed to ensure ethical quality in multinational research. Three alternatives are presented here. Although they all have valid aspects, we consider the first two to be inadequate. The third, although it needs further development, correctly articulates the problem and the way to a solution.

The Model of Reasonable Access

The Council of International Organizations of Medical Science requires in its *International Ethical Guidelines for Biomedical Research with Human Beings*, guideline no. 10, that any research to be conducted in developing countries or other vulnerable communities should meet the following criteria: (1) responsiveness to the health needs of the participating population; and (2) access to the results of the research for the subjects and their communities once the research is finished. This model, which we shall call *reasonable access*, leaves several questions without a satisfactory answer. Are the researchers and their sponsors obligated to distribute the fruits of the research free of charge or at reduced prices? Does this obligation refer only to the subjects who participated in the study, or to all those community members who need it? What happens if the protocol is unsuccessful, or if new knowledge is generated with no immediate clinical application?[9] Not all research projects are successful clinical trials, with clinical applications immediately relevant to the community. Please note that we are not suggesting that the criterion of access to the fruits of the research should be discarded. We would simply argue that this criterion alone is insufficient.

The Model of Equitable Benefits

In its May–June 2004 issue, the *Hastings Center Report* published an article signed by participants in the 2001 Conference on Ethical Aspects of Research in Developing Countries.[10] The authors propose to substitute the criterion of *fair benefits* for that of reasonable access. The requirements of the new standard are summarized in three principles: *equitable benefits, collaborative association,* and *transparency.* The benefits for the subjects and their communities can be classified in three groups: (1) for the participants, while the study is in progress; (2) for the whole community, during the course of the study; (3) for the participants and the community, after the end of the study. The affected population itself must decide what benefits it wishes to receive as equitable compensation for the research subjects and for the rest of the community. Transparency would have to be guaranteed by some international organization, such as the World Health Organization (WHO), which can advise the host community on the benefits that other communities have received in comparable circumstances.

This model is right on some important points. The benefits would not be limited to successful clinical trials, and it seeks ways to assure the transparency of the negotiation through the assistance of international organizations. On the other hand, the model is very advantageous for the multinational companies, which would not be obligated to make the results of successful experiments accessible to the communities, unless a clause to that effect were included in their negotiation with the specific community. It also does not prevent the companies from conducting research that does not respond to the needs of the communities, as long as negotiation has taken place. It is a free-market, free-contract model, too optimistic about the poor communities' opportunity to negotiate on an equal basis with, for example, the giant multinational pharmaceutical companies, even with the good offices of the WHO.

The Human Development Model

Alex J. London has proposed a third model, which he calls the "human development approach."[11] London suggests that the discussion on justice in international biomedical research has left out the broader issues of social justice and the relationship between justice and health.[12] In his view, both the model of reasonable access and that of equitable benefits are *minimalist approaches.* London maintains that multinational research in poor countries and communities is justified if: (1) it responds to the health needs of the host population; and (2) it helps to expand the basic capacities of those communities to serve the fundamental interests of their members. It is unacceptable to take the status quo of the community as an ethical reference point, without questioning it. Those who justify the double standard use as a criterion, for example, the level of access to medication that the members of a community or nation currently possess. This position does not meet the requirements of justice: to contribute to the development of the community, leaving it in a better situation than it was in when the researchers approached it to conduct the study. Minimalist approaches are not concerned with the *true requirements of justice.*

Of the three, London's approach is the most compatible with the theological vision of social justice in the Catholic tradition. Marciano Vidal notes in *Moral de actitudes* that in the history of morality, justice has often been used as an ethical attitude at the service of the established order, justifying and supporting structural injustices. Vidal affirms a need to recover an understanding of justice as prior to the established order and thus possessing the critical capacity to question it from a higher perspective. The appropriate category for an adequate formulation of this idea is social justice.[13] Vidal adopts the definition of justice given by Julián Marías: "That which corrects or rectifies a social situation involving a prior injustice which, if maintained, would invalidate just conduct, individual acts of justice."[14] This understanding of justice applies well to the case we are discussing. The situations of poverty and marginalization found in the countries we call poor or developing are, in large part although not exclusively, a consequence of political and economic colonialism.

Although we can find in the theological tradition other categories that could be useful and should be included in a broader reflection (solidarity, social charity, preferential option for the poor, etc.), we have chosen the principle of justice as the central ethical concept for analyzing biomedical research in developing countries. The next step is to justify the concept of global social justice.

Global Social Justice

Like Vidal, we have adopted Julián Marías's definition of social justice in order to apply it at the global level. Such an application is a use of the concept that Marías expressly rejects since "inequality in the world is not a synonym of injustice. It is not possible . . . for everyone to live at the same level as the countries that have a high level. . . . The countries that for centuries have struggled to dominate nature, to order themselves socially, to live according to intelligent and efficient principles, have a right to the prosperity they have achieved, and there is not the least injustice in that."[15] Clearly the author is still anchored to the idea of self-sufficiency in nation-states, before the age of globalization. He does not consider that the wealth of some may be linked to the poverty of others. That vision is not acceptable in a time of globalization, when we are all part of a single economy and a single global social fabric. As Diego Gracia observes, "economic globalization has profound political effects, because it relativizes the role of the fundamental political figure of modernity, the nation-state."[16]

The new economy and today's communication media link us all together in a way never before seen in human history. This is why Anton van Niekerk argues that, in modern society, we are our brothers' keepers in a very real way. He points out that our understanding of society is transformed day by day — we might also say broadened — by the advanced means of communication and transport, the blurring of traditional economic and even political boundaries, and a growing international awareness in almost everyone.[17] These new global relationships make way for what Allen Buchanan calls *global basic structures,* a notion he defines as: "A set of economic and political institutions that have profound and enduring effects on the distribution of burdens and benefits among peoples and individuals around the world."[18]

We contend that this *global basic structure* is a sufficient basis on which to establish obligations of global justice, just as the traditional basic structure of the state has done at the national level. Indeed, we have already accepted the validity of requirements of justice in international commercial contracts and, at least since Nuremberg, we establish international tribunals to judge offenses that are considered crimes against humanity. If we accept the existence of obligations of international or global justice in those areas, how can we deny a principle of social justice at the global level? Is it perhaps because we think it might harm the interests of the large global corporations, the most powerful forces at the international level? But as van Niekerk argues, if not altruism, enlightened self-interest should show the importance of attending to issues of global justice in an interdependent world. The urgent need for a perspective of global responsibility is very clear in the health field. We need only contemplate the danger of global epidemics, like AIDS. Outside the health field, we might say the same about the danger posed by the focal points of grievous economic inequality, which lead to social and political instability in diverse regions and eventually threaten us all. Citizens of the United States, for example, have ample reason to be concerned about the conflict between the Shia and Sunnis in Iraq.

The requirements of global social justice are especially urgent in the biomedical field. Access to adequate nutrition, hygiene, and quality medical care, both preventive and curative, is essential for the flourishing of people and communities. If the disparities created by economic inequality are painful anywhere, they are especially so in the area of health. Anton van Niekerk offers the following statistics, which, despite the limitations and imprecision that affect all statistical data in this field, can give us an idea of the chasm that separates the poor from the rich in the health field: While life expectancy in the developed countries is around eighty years, there are regions in Africa where it is barely older than forty because of the impact of AIDS; the United States, with 5 percent of the world population, spends more than a trillion dollars on health care (U.S. $1.2 trillion) per year, about half the total global expenditure on health. In general terms, per capita expenditures on health in the developed countries range from U.S. $2,000 to $4,200, while in some African countries it is less than $10; a 90–10 split is commonly referred to in biomedical research, indicating that 90 percent of expenditures on biomedical research are for efforts to cure 10 percent of the diseases, those suffered by inhabitants of the rich countries; of the 1,233 new medications produced between 1975 and 1997, only 13 percent were for the treatment of the tropical diseases that are so prevalent on the African continent.[19]

The situation of extreme poverty for many people in developing countries is due in part to the internal situations in those countries. Many of them have corrupt governments and privileged elites who monopolize power and wealth. But it is also beyond doubt that colonialism and other forms of exploitation have retarded their development and helped to exacerbate ancestral problems, such as ethnic struggles. For this reason the principle of global social justice imposes on us certain obligations of rectification. Moreover, in the new global society, the problem of the poor countries becomes everyone's problem as members of one humanity, one economy, and one basic global structure. Globalization is here to stay. Like all meaningful social change, it forces us to rethink our moral concepts that no longer fit.

What does the principle of global justice mean for biomedical research in developing countries? In the first place, it is not enough to avoid exploitation. As London points out, biomedical research with impoverished communities must respond to their needs and contribute to their development. We cannot resign ourselves to the social oblivion into which the impoverished peoples have fallen. Contributing to the human promotion of the impoverished communities, in biomedical research and other areas, is an imperative of social justice. In a world where we are all linked to one another, the poverty of some — far from justifying their treatment as second-class citizens — imposes additional obligations aimed at guaranteeing them an equitable level of opportunities for integral development. Thus, it is essential to guarantee the right to needed health services. This means that doing research with impoverished populations is a duty, but it also means that such research must be clearly at the service of their own human promotion.

In order to guarantee the protection of the interests of impoverished communities when they participate as subjects in multinational biomedical research, there must be participation by international bodies that can help them, as we saw in the statement cited earlier from the 2001 Conference on Ethical Aspects of Research in Developing Countries. This assistance need not be limited to the WHO. Other bodies can and should play an important part, including the churches and theology itself. We Christians are called to serious involvement in the struggle for global social justice, in the biomedical field among others. It is part of our calling to the service of the faith, and of the justice that that faith requires.[20]

—English translation by Margaret D. Wilde

Notes

1. Ruth Macklin, "Research, multinational" in *Encyclopedia of Bioethics,* vol. 4, ed. S. G. Post (New York: Macmillan Reference USA, 2004), 2347.

2. There is an increasingly broad literature on this issue. The terminology is not uniform. Some authors use the term "global justice" or "global bioethics," while others prefer to speak of "cosmopolitan justice," using the ancient Stoic term. See, for example, Anton A. van Niekerk, "Principles of Global Distributive Justice and the HIV/AIDS Pandemic," in *Ethics and AIDS in Africa,* ed. Anton A. van Niekerk and Loretta M. Kopelman (Walnut Creek, Calif.: Left Coast Press, 2005), 84–110; Amartya K. Sen, Piero Fassino, and Sebastiano Maffettone, *Giustizia blobale* (Milan: Saggiatore, 2006); Darrell Moellendorf, *Cosmopolitan Justice* (Boulder, Colo.: Westview Press, 2002).

3. Ruth Macklin, *Double Standards in Medical Research in Developing Countries* (New York: Cambridge University Press, 2004), 69. See also Moellendorf, *Cosmopolitan Justice,* 30–67.

4. Macklin, *Double Standards in Medical Research in Developing Countries,* 13–18; Sonia Shah, *The Body Hunters* (New York and London: The New Press, 2006).

5. The articles that started the debate were Marcia Angell, "The Ethics of Research in the Third World," *New England Journal of Medicine* 337, no. 12 (1997): 847–49; and Peter Lurie and Sidney Wolfe, "Unethical Trials of Interventions to Reduce Perinatal Transmission of the Human Immunodeficiency Virus in Developing Countries," *New England Journal of Medicine* 337, no. 12 (1997): 853–55. For an overview of the issue see Macklin, *Double Standards in Medical Research in Developing Countries,* 14–17, and Shah, *The Body Hunters,* 77–99.

6. Marc Lallemant et al., "A Trial of Shortened Zidovudine Regimens to Prevent Mother-to-Child Transmission of Human Immunodeficiency Virus Type I," *New England Journal of Medicine* 343, no. 14 (2000): 982–91; Marc Lallemant et al., "Single-Dose Perinatal Nevipariine plus Standard Zidovudine to Prevent Mother-to-Child Transmission," *New England Journal of Medicine* 351, no. 3 (2004): 217–28.

7. Macklin, *Double Standards in Medical Research in Developing Countries,* 17–18.

8. Ibid., 7; Shah, *The Body Hunters,* 7–10.

9. These concerns are based on those presented in the work cited in the following note.

10. Participants in the 2001 Conference on Ethical Aspects of Research in Developing Countries, "Moral Standards for Research in Developing Countries: From Reasonable Availability to Fair Benefits," *Hastings Center Report* 34, no. 3 (2004): 17–27.

11. Alex J. London, "Justice and the Human Development Approach," *Hastings Center Report* 35, no. 1 (2005): 24–37.

12. On the relationship between poverty and health, see Norman Daniels, Bruce Kennedy, and Ichiro Kawachi, eds., *Is Inequality Bad for Our Health?* (Boston: Beacon Press, 2000).

13. Marciano Vidal, *Moral de actitudes,* vol. 3 (Madrid: Perpetuo Socorro, 1988), 112–13.

14. Julián Marías, *La justicia social y otras justicias* (Madrid: Espasa-Calpe, 1979), 16.

15. Ibid., 27.

16. Diego Gracia, "El Sentido de la Globalización," in *Bioética: Un diálogo plural,* ed. Jorge José Ferrer and Julio Luis Martínez (Madrid: Universidad Pontificia Comillas, 2002).

17. Van Niekerk, "Principles of Global Distributive Justice and the HIV/AIDS Pandemic," 92.

18. Allen Buchanan, "Rawls' *Law of Peoples:* Rules for a Vanished Westphalian World," *Ethics* 110, no. 4 (2000): 705; quoted by van Niekerk, "Principles of Global Distributive Justice and the HIV/AIDS Pandemic," 96.

19. Van Niekerk, "Principles of Global Distributive Justice and the HIV/AIDS Pandemic," 91.

20. This is consistent with what Lisa Cahill has called "participatory bioethics"; see her *Theological Bioethics* (Washington, D.C.: Georgetown University Press, 2005).

Embryo Adoption

Expanding the Terms of the Debate

DARLENE FOZARD WEAVER

In the United States alone there are currently some four hundred thousand "excess" cryopreserved (frozen) embryos — embryos created for in-vitro fertilization which the genetic parents no longer need or desire for that purpose. Some of these embryos are donated to genetically unrelated recipients in a growing practice known technically as heterologous embryo transfer (HET) and more colloquially as embryo adoption.[1] Although the practice remains relatively infrequent, the number of embryo adoptions is growing, thanks in part to publicity surrounding the 1996 destruction of thousands of excess embryos in Great Britain, which prompted some Catholic women to volunteer to gestate cryopreserved embryos, and thanks in part to a 2001 program initiated by the U.S. Department of Health and Human Services to promote public awareness of embryo adoption. Moral theologians debate the moral status of embryo adoption and the appropriateness of calling it "adoption" at all.[2] I argue that the terms of these debates are narrowly circumscribed and that an adequate moral analysis of embryo adoption requires expanding them.

Embryo Adoption in Roman Catholic Ethics

Embryo adoption presses the logic of traditional Catholic sexual ethics. On the one hand, this ethics operates on a particular account of human sexuality as involving unitive and procreative dimensions that may never intentionally be separated and that are licitly realized only in the context of a conjugal love that is open to the possibility of generating life. At its best, official Catholic sexual ethics looks not to the sexual act per se, but to the moral and spiritual significance of human psychosomatic constitution and the good of marriage as a relationship suited to human flourishing. This moral anthropology rules out the creation of human embryos *in vitro* and assumes that licit human procreation involves the unity of genetic and gestational parenthood, and, ideally, social parenthood. As we will see, some argue that embryo adoption

199

is wrong because it does not comport with human psychosomatic dignity as is properly expressed in faithful conjugal love. On the other hand, Catholic sexual ethics insists that human life begins at conception, and hence that human embryos, whether *in utero* or *in vitro,* are irreducibly valuable and enjoy a right to life. Moreover, Catholic moral tradition affirms the goodness of adoption as a response to the unfortunate disruption of genetic and social parenthood. Embryo adoption does not involve the creation of human embryos but is instead a response to already existing embryos, the likely fate of which, apart from adoption, is destruction. Thus, embryo adoption offers the prospect of life to cryopreserved embryos, albeit through a process that separates genetic and gestational parenthood.

To date, Roman Catholic ethical debates about embryo adoption center on three issues.

First, moral theologians argue about whether Catholic teaching against assisted reproductive technology applies to embryo adoption. While *Donum vitae* (*DV*) makes claims that do bear on embryo adoption, nothing it says necessarily excludes embryo adoption as a morally permissible human practice. Some opponents point to a particular passage in *Donum vitae,* which states that spare embryos "are exposed to an absurd fate, with no possibility of their being offered safe means of survival which can be licitly pursued."[3] However, the context for this claim concerns conducting research on spare embryos, which means its applicability to embryo adoption needs to be shown.[4] Briefly, opponents argue that embryo adoption falls under the Magisterium's prohibition of artificial reproductive technology because it necessarily involves taking an embryo that exists *in vitro* and transferring it into the uterus of a woman. Advocates of embryo adoption counter that this position turns on the question whether embryo transfer as such is morally licit, irrespective of the presence or absence of genetic ties between the embryo and the would-be gestational mother. Were we one day to be able technologically to treat an ectopic pregnancy by removing the embryo from the fallopian tube and transferring it to the mother's uterus, surely this would be morally permissible; therefore, goes the counterargument, embryo transfer as such is not morally wrong.[5]

It is important to note that not all HET is embryo adoption; one could, for example, have a genetically unrelated embryo transferred into one's womb, gestate it, give birth, and then surrender the child for traditional adoption. It does not follow that moral evaluation of embryo adoption should rest on moral evaluation of HET as such, because there is no such thing as HET "as such," but rather particular and morally different sorts of HET. Since the exegetical dispute itself and the arguments centered around embryo transfer "as such" treat embryo adoption primarily as the act of embryo transfer, they fail to appreciate this fact. They also forsake many riches in Catholic moral tradition's treatment of sexuality, marriage, and family. In any case, the Pontifical Academy for Life recently acknowledged embryo adoption as a matter of genuine debate.[6] In short, we should not rush to judgment on the basis on one questionable interpretation of a particular passage in *Donum vitae;* at the same time, we may and should engage *Donum vitae* and all relevant teachings and resources in Catholic moral tradition to inform and direct our assessment of embryo adoption.

The second issue debated among moral theologians treating embryo adoption concerns whether the practice necessarily involves cooperation with the evil of *in vitro* fertilization. Opponents of embryo adoption express concern about scandal, participation in quality control practices regarding embryo selection, and worry that embryo adoption may encourage the creation of more excess embryos. Proponents contend that embryo adoption provides a witness to the dignity of already existing embryonic life; other matters that may involve cooperation with evil pose practical ethical issues to be addressed in how we might conduct embryo adoption and do not settle the question of embryo adoption's inherent moral status.[7] While the available arguments consider the relation of embryo adoption to the "infertility industry," here too they stop short of comprehensive assessment of embryo adoption. They fail to analyze the gendered, economic, and cultural attitudes at play; neglect relevant models of adoption; and ignore the experiences of embryo adopters and adoptees. I will address these forms of neglect more fully in the following section.

The third and by far most prominent line of argument concerns embryo adoption in relation to marriage. Some argue that embryo adoption violates the sacredness of marriage and of the human body. *Donum vitae* insists "the fidelity of the spouses in the unity of marriage involves reciprocal respect of their right to become a father and a mother only through each other."[8] When a child is conceived through conjugal relations, the intimate union of mother and child extends and embodies the marital union of husband and wife. In heterologous embryo transfer, the woman becomes pregnant apart from the "marriage act" and isolates the husband from the gestational bond she comes to share with the fetus.[9] For this reason, HET is "akin to adultery."[10] Proponents of embryo adoption respond by distinguishing conception from pregnancy or the *coming to be* of a child within a woman from *having an embryo* placed in her womb.[11] The latter involves not conception, but "a particular form of nurturing an existing life up until birth."[12] Moreover, "in having an orphaned embryo implanted in her womb with the commitment to raise the child if it survives to birth [a woman] is consenting to become a mother through adoption. In adopting the orphan embryo she is offering a uniquely important, intimate, and necessary form of nurturing."[13] In what follows, I indicate how narrow and limited this line of argument is and suggest issues and resources that ought to inform future ethical inquiry into embryo adoption.

Critique

Already we have noted some limitations to ongoing Catholic arguments for and against embryo adoption. More specifically, I argue that these arguments narrowly frame the debate in terms of the inherent rightness or wrongness of the act of transferring genetically unrelated embryos into the uterus of a (married) woman. Embryo adoption is thereby treated in a reductive fashion. I make three particular claims in this regard.

First, analyses of embryo adoption to date mistakenly try to identify the object of HET to the neglect of salient normative frameworks such as the vocation of parenthood, the common good, (theological) accounts of adoption, and so forth. This approach is methodologically problematic insofar as it reduces the human practice of embryo adoption to the specific act of HET. Arguments against embryo adoption in particular endeavor definitively to identify the object of HET as a prelude to morally evaluating it, as though we must strip down the act to its barest essence, then submit this ostensibly morally neutral description to ethical assessment. Moreover, those writing against embryo adoption then look for the object of *this* act by repairing to another, namely, the "marriage act." Moral analysis of embryo adoption devolves into disputes regarding conception versus pregnancy and attempts to establish the temporal and physiological boundaries of the "procreative act." Does it end with coitus? With fertilization? With birth?[14] Such disagreements, notwithstanding their engagement with a theology of the body or reflection on the gestational bond, are regrettably removed from any sustained reflection on the lived reality of marriage and parenthood, and removed even further from any sustained *theological* reflection on the world in which we live our sexuality, in which marriage and parenthood are created, fallen, yet redeemed human bonds. Altogether missing from the literature is any sense that marriage and parenthood are complexly embodied relations of joy and sorrow and ambivalence and surprise, in which God's faithful and reconciling love makes us God's own children and provides a living, subversive norm for marriage and parenthood.

Second, focusing on the moral permissibility of the act of HET isolates embryo adoption from its cultural, political, economic, and gendered context. Consequently, many aspects of the practice of embryo adoption and many facets of arguments about it uncritically rely on deeply problematic beliefs and values. Let us consider briefly some of the gendered dimensions of the arguments. Marital infidelity arguments, for example, construe male participation in procreation in a purely causative fashion. Mary Geach, for example, identifies the male's part in the marriage act as that of the impregnator; the woman's part is the "act of admission which is of a kind to make one pregnant," that is, "the giving up of the body to the impregnator."[15] Others treat gestational motherhood with a jealous anxiety that belies underlying worries about securing male paternity. Both the fetus in the womb and the clinician who "impregnates" a woman can appear as the adulterous third party.[16] Some texts express outright repugnance at the notion that one's wife would become pregnant with a child "not their own." A recent article on embryo adoption (designated as embryo "rescue," in this case) boils the entire practice down "to the question of a woman taking a child conceived by another man into her womb."[17] Notice there seems to be no woman who helped to conceive this child, nor any sense that the would-be adopters are acting together in welcoming a child who is genetically unrelated to them both. The problem is one of a woman voluntarily becoming pregnant with a child that is not her husband's. Rather than deconstruct the sexism and "biologism" at play in these arguments against embryo adoption, advocates reinforce the basic framing of the question around the act of HET.[18] By focusing on the distinctive form of nurturing that occurs in gestational motherhood (which is relevant and important though not sufficient) they reinforce the depiction of embryo adoption as the choice to become pregnant (versus the choice to adopt) and thus continue to treat it as an act a married woman performs rather than her and her husband's joint decision to adopt.

Arguments for and against the practice invoke the adoption paradigm without endeavoring to understand how one becomes a parent in adoption. As a consequence, opponents have the bad habit of saying any adoptive parent is not a real parent,[19] while proponents minimize the adoptive bond and fail to consider adoption as a positive expression of marital love and fecundity. Opponents and advocates of embryo adoption also neglect the Christian tradition's theological relativization of biological kinship. As a result, deeply embedded, historically contingent, culturally specific, and unquestionably problematic conceptions of sex, gender, marriage, and kinship function normatively without adequate critical examination. Both sides of the debate neglect the theological relevance of our universal status as adopted children of God, a status we receive as ones incorporated into the body of Christ. More examples are possible for illustrating how embryo adoption is isolated from its multiple and overlapping contexts; the focus on HET, for example, totally ignores the economic dimensions of embryo adoption. The point is that those debating embryo adoption need to be far more critical of the historical and cultural dimensions of their arguments and far more attentive to the medical, cultural, and economic factors that have given rise to and shape the practice of embryo adoption.

Third, the literature neglects the rights, responsibilities, and goods of various parties involved, or normatively subordinates them to the question of whether HET is intrinsically wrong. This normative subordination extracts moral evaluation of embryo adoption from due attention to those who are agents in the practice — the genetic parents, the would-be adoptive parents, the clinicians, adoption social workers, and attorneys involved; along with the families, friends, and, importantly, the ecclesial community who together help to construct, confirm, or counter the moral meaning of this practice. By extracting moral evaluation of embryo adoption from consideration of the agential and communal roles of various parties to the practice, the act of HET is allowed to stand for the whole human practice of embryo adoption, and the "marriage act" is allowed to function as the primary moral framework in which we evaluate the practice.

Not only do the arguments mistakenly separate the question of embryo adoption's intrinsic moral rightness or wrongness from the entirety of the practice; they also neglect, or they distance from the process, the parties relevant to embryo adoption. For example, the literature uniformly ignores the rights and responsibilities of the genetic parents of excess embryos and, moreover, treats all excess embryos as "orphaned" embryos. Yet in some practices of embryo adoption, the commissioning couples select adoptive parents and may enter into a relationship of "open" adoption, which includes contact with the adoptive parents and child. What may we say about the parental responsibility they exercise, and how would arguments for or against embryo adoption be strengthened or weakened were we to grapple with the fact that some embryos are effectively abandoned while others are not? The literature ignores the voices of embryo adopters and adoptees, despite the fact that the natural law methodology employed in embryo adoption debates prizes experience as a source of moral knowledge.[20] The literature also neglects the roles and responsibilities of physicians who offer embryo adoption.[21] While consideration of these responsibilities obviously bears on practical questions concerning how to undertake embryo adoption in morally fitting ways, they are also directly relevant to the intrinsic moral status of embryo adoption. Theological ethical accounts of the ends, limits, and integrity of medical practice and health care are needed. These might flesh out or challenge attention to the physician's role as "impregnator." They certainly bear on the fact that the legal custody and material fate of some abandoned embryos seems to rest with clinicians.[22]

The limited terms on which embryo adoption is currently evaluated court significant practical costs. Quite simply, embryo adoption is and will continue to be practiced irrespective of the official teaching the Magisterium finally promulgates. Advocates ought to play a role in shaping how embryo adoption is undertaken and opponents of embryo adoption ought to inform how alternatives to it, such as a respectful and dignified disposition of cryopreserved embryos, will occur. To forestall influencing how both embryo adoption and embryo disposition are done is to forfeit their moral promise and peril to cultural and economic forces and to forfeit opportunities to build substantive moral consensus about these and allied ethical issues.

Conclusion

Rather than narrowly circumscribe and assess embryo adoption as the discrete *act* of embryo transfer, embryo adoption is more properly examined as a *practice* that requires analysis from multiple moral vantage points. Embryo adoption involves a complex medical procedure that is simultaneously a profound human commitment to welcome and parent a child, the entirety of which is undertaken in a cultural, political, economic, and gendered context that situates and shapes our realization of human goods. The current focus on HET cannot do justice to the full reality of this practice, especially since those writing on embryo adoption have thus far failed to reflect (self-)critically on how those same contexts situate and shape moral reasoning in better and worse ways.

The focus on HET also fails to develop the potential of embryo adoption to illuminate and guide corrections to our moral theologies of sex, marriage, and family. The unique character of embryo adoption challenges us to think about, among other things, reproductive integrity, responsibility, and generosity; the public significance of pregnancy; increasing tendencies in medical and cultural attitudes toward genetic determinism; and the role of patriarchy and sexism in all these matters. Embryo adoption and the ethical arguments surrounding it also provide an important opportunity to examine our moral methodologies more generally. The literature exemplifies recent Catholic ethical wrangling over the so-called "object" of moral acts as well as the unfortunately non-theological character of much contemporary moral theology. Adequate consideration of embryo adoption requires dexterous and theologically robust attention to the interplay of intentional, bodily, interpersonal, and structural dimensions in this complex human practice. Such skillfully capacious forms of inquiry would enrich theological ethics more broadly and respond more fittingly to God, who comes to meet us and wills our good in all these dimensions.

Notes

I am grateful to James Keenan, S.J., for including me in the Theological Ethics in the World Church conference. I want to thank Sarah-Vaughan Brakman, William Werpehowski, Mary Jo Iozzio, and Todd Salzman for helpful feedback and conversation about this essay.

1. I argue here that the terms on which we morally evaluate embryo adoption need to be expanded. This claim also provides the conceptual rationale for a forthcoming collection of essays on embryo adoption. See Sarah-Vaughan Brakman and Darlene Fozard Weaver, eds., *The Ethics of Embryo Adoption and the Catholic Tradition* (New York: Springer Academic Press, 2007).

2. See *National Catholic Bioethics Quarterly* 5, no. 1 (Spring 2005), which is devoted to the topic of embryo adoption. See also John Berkman, "Gestating the Embryos of Others: Surrogacy? Adoption? Rescue?" *National Catholic Bioethics Quarterly* 3, no. 2 (Summer 2003): 309–29.

3. *Donum vitae*, I, 5. Another significant and frequently invoked passage from *Donum vitae* appears on p. 201.

4. For a consideration of embryo adoption in relation to *DV*, see John Berkman, "The Morality of Adopting Frozen Embryos in light of *Donum Vitae*," *Studia Moralia* 40 (2002): 115–41.

5. Ibid., 134–35.

6. Pontifical Academy for Life, *Final Communiqué on "The Dignity of Human Procreation and Reproductive Technologies: Anthropological and Ethical Aspects,"* February 2004; online at *www.vatican.va/roman_curia/pontifical_academies/acdlife/documents/rc_pont-acd_life_doc_20040316_x-gen-assembly-final_en.html*.

7. For discussions of embryo adoption and cooperation with IVF, see Mary Jo Iozzio, "It Is Time to Support Embryo Adoption," *National Catholic Bioethics Quarterly* 2, no. 4 (Winter 2002): 585–93, and Nicholas Tonti-Filippini, "The Embryo Rescue Debate," *National Catholic Bioethics Quarterly* 3, no. 1 (Spring 2003): 111–37.

8. *Donum vitae*, IIA I.

9. Tonti-Filippini, "The Embryo Rescue Debate," 122.

10. Ibid., 124.

11. Helen Watt, "Are There Any Circumstances in Which It Would Be Morally Admirable for a Woman to Seek to Have an Orphan Embryo Implanted in Her Womb? 2," in *Issues for a Catholic Bioethics,* ed. Luke Gormally (London: Linacre Center), 347–52.

12. Berkman, "The Morality of Adopting Frozen Embryos," 129.

13. Ibid.

14. See, for example, the exchange between John Berkman and Nicholas Tonti-Filippini in "Colloquy," *National Catholic Bioethics Quarterly* 3, no. 4 (Winter 2003): 657–64.

15. Mary Geach, "Are There Any Circumstances in Which It Would Be Morally Admirable for a Woman to Seek to Have an Orphan Embryo Implanted in Her Womb? 1," in *Issues for a Catholic Bioethics,* 341–46; the two quotations here appear, respectively, on 344 and 345.

16. Tonti-Filippini, "The Embryo Rescue Debate," esp. 126 and 128.

17. Steven A. Long, "An Argument for the Embryonic Intactness of Marriage," *The Thomist* 70 (2006): 267.

18. The term "biologism" comes from Elizabeth Bartholet, *Family Bonds: Adoption, Infertility, and the New World of Child Production* (Boston: Beacon Press, 1993).

19. Tonti-Filippini, "The Embryo Rescue Debate," 118. See also Rev. Tadeusz Pacholczyk, "On the Moral Objectionability of Frozen Embryo Adoption," presented at the Fellowship of Catholic Scholars Meeting, 2003, 7.

20. J. L. Davidson, "A Successful Embryo Adoption," *National Catholic Bioethics Quarterly* 1, no. 2 (Summer 2001): 229–33. See also John Berkman, "Adopting Embryos in America: A Case Study and an Ethical Analysis," *Scottish Journal of Theology* 55, no. 4 (November 2002): 438–60.

21. Tonti-Filippini, "The Embryo Rescue Debate," 125–27; briefly comments on the role of the clinician, but only in terms of his role as the one making the would-be adoptive mother pregnant.

22. John C. Mayoue, "Legal and Ethical Challenges of Embryonic Adoption," in *The Morality of Adoption: Social-Psychological, Theological, and Legal Perspectives,* ed. Timothy P. Jackson (Grand Rapids, Mich.: William B. Eerdmans, 2005), 262–82.

22

Nutrition and Hydration
in the Care of Terminally Ill Patients

Ethical and Theological Challenges

MARIE-JO THIEL

Are nutrition and hydration forms of general human care or medical treatment? If they are regarded as treatments, one can choose to stop them and thus provoke the death of the patient (cf. Terri Schiavo). There has been no debate in France comparable to that which has swept the United States since the 1970s and has grown in intensity since the cases of Karen Ann Quinlan and Nancy Cruzan. Nevertheless, a recent evolution in French legislation could soon lead to such a debate. The "Law concerning the Rights of the Sick and the End of Life" (still known as "Leonetti's law" for short)[1] tends to consider nutrition and hydration as treatments. However, a discourse that John Paul II gave in 2004, which received considerable media attention and was echoed by a number of bishops in connection with the Schiavo case, considers nutrition and hydration as forms of care that cannot be stopped. The pope affirmed: "The administering of water and nourishment, even by artificial means, is *always* a natural means of maintaining life, not a medical action."[2]

What position should we take on this question?

On the Ethical Level

In a general perspective — in other words, without entering into details or making all the distinctions between enteral and parental nutrition or between nutrition and hydration, or considering separately all the possible situations of the sick person (conscious or unconscious, in a waking coma, chronic vegetative states, dementia) — we may make at least three observations.

First, nourishment and hydration belong de facto to our physiological needs. Further, they are linked to orality and to the first affective and instinctive bonds to one's mother. Since they form part of the most archaic layers of the human personality, their meaning is determined both by one's personal experience and by the images and the culture of the milieu to which one belongs. To speak of "eating and drinking" often evokes not only food in its material quality, but also an experience of conviviality and pleasure, a feeling of being alive. For an infant, the oral pleasure of incorporation is the first pleasure linked to another person — although as yet, no distinction is made between the other and the infant's own self. This pleasure is linked to an instinct for self-preservation and profoundly defines what it is to be a human being: a human being *is* what he or she eats.[3] But what if he stops eating? We will be tempted to conclude that he "is" no longer "anything," and finally, that he has ceased to exist. For a mother, giving her infant nourishment means giving something of her own self; this is why she will soon feel guilty if the child refuses nourishment. *Mutatis mutandis*, is not the carer in the same situation? Will he not be tempted to believe that his care is poor if the sick person refuses his care or if he were to be deprived of it? And what about the patient's family, who are all the more closely involved once the medical corps makes them "responsible" for the patient's nutrition? It is true that the collective aspect implies very different dimensions; nevertheless, it is not improper to ask what this question means for a society as such.

It is thus unsurprising that cases like that of Terri Schiavo provoked passionate reactions. The churches too reacted, since they are very sensitive to the question of respect for life.[4] In Europe, the reaction by Cardinal Karl Lehmann is very evocative: "It is ethically impermissible to let someone just starve to death."[5]

This conjures up an image of the suffering caused by hunger and thirst — and more generally, an image of life and of the relationship to another person that we are absolutely obliged to take into account in the ethical praxis of clinical medicine: it would be inhuman to let someone die of hunger or thirst. But toward the end of a person's life the appetite is considerably modified and the sensation of hunger and thirst tends to disappear. Usually what the patient drinks and eats is enough for him. To administer large quantities or food rich in calories would risk bringing a person's condition into disequilibrium, even accelerating his or her death (especially in cases of cancer). Generally speaking, a dryness of the mucous membrane or the lips requires only a humidification of the room, the lips, and the mouth.

The most important point here is that these primary forms of care have nothing in common with the nutrition and hydration that involve the forced immobilization of a person who is tied to feeding tubes, drips, and nutrition pumps and often strapped to the bed to prevent him or her from tearing out these various technological devices providing nourishment. No doubt, as with every medical action, there may be reasons for doing all this. But such practices are far removed from the social conviviality of a meal and indeed from any kind of stable relationship to other persons. The same is true of the treatment of elderly people when the family is "non-existent" and the carers have no time: they "save time" by leaving a few "packets" and then are off at once. The sick person is left alone for days on end.

Every ethical discernment must take account of *both* what orality means to the various people involved *and* what a patient experiences when he or she is confronted with an environment that has absolutely nothing in common with the experience of one who sits at the head of the table at mealtimes.

A second observation we can make pertains to the status of artificial nutrition and hydration. If eating and drinking mean the satisfaction of physiological needs, we may then agree that actions such as caring for the patient's mouth, moistening his or her lips, and using a plastic beaker with "duck-shaped lips" to allow drinking are "artificial" measures that require the patient's consent, but that do not imply an invasive intrusion into his or her body. In this sense, they would come under the heading of the basic forms of care. Let us then conclude that they belong to the "ordinary" forms of care (to use the expression of John Paul II and of a long ecclesial tradition), that is, to what we call today "basic care."

When, however, there is an intrusion through the skin of the sick person — and I am inclined to reserve the expressions "artificial nutrition and hydration" for this situation — we are in the sphere of invasive techniques that require a medical indication and evaluation with regard to the opportunity of this medical action and its adaptation to the patient in question. This is a matter of medical responsibility. Obviously, nuances are called for here: a physiological solute supplied by a drip does not have the same invasive character as a gastrostomy. In both cases, however, we are crossing the barrier of the skin, that metaphor of the self[6] which contains both the identity of the subject and his or her biological intimacy, which is always very sensitive to every external intrusion (cf. all that affects the immune system, etc.). This is not surprising when we recall that the skin and brain have the same embryonic origin, and that ectodermic invaginations involve an entry from the exterior to the interior in view of privileged relationships (which are sometimes extremely sensitive), as well as limits and frontiers that aim both at containing the self and at opening up to exchanges with another person. This is how the subject is able to construct itself as such. Today, there is nothing anodyne about all this, since the psychological suffering entailed by the "liminal states" has supplanted the suffering caused by neuroses. Doubtless, every intrusion involves risk, pain, and embarrassment. But doctors must be aware that intrusions are even more difficult in these "liminal states" with all the cortège of discomfort that they bring.

Third, if artificial nutrition and hydration are treatments rather than basic forms of care, may one "simply" discontinue them by claiming that this therapy is merely prolonging life? The discourse that John Paul II held in 2004 appears to affirm this, for otherwise the pope would not claim that they are "normal forms of care" (that is, "not a medical action") and therefore may not be discontinued. The opposite conclusion could however also be correct, since the "unreasonable obstinacy," which is the definition of a therapy that merely prolongs life, depends on a medical diagnosis based on knowledge and reason. No medical treatment can be begun, modified, or discontinued without rational arguments. It is indeed precisely because a *medical* treatment is involved here that discernment becomes absolutely necessary — and this discernment must be verified and (perhaps) adjusted. This is not true in the case of the basic forms of care, which have a much more fluid status and are often left, at least in part, to the evaluation of the entourage of the patient (whether or not these persons are directly involved in care) or even to the sometimes unforeseeable feelings of this entourage, since the secondary effects of the basic forms of care are limited, and it is easy to put them into practice. At the same time, however, we should remember that the basic forms of care can sometimes be dependent on medical action and vice versa.

Finally, it would be immoral to deprive someone of a beneficent, proportional treatment that is adapted and available to deal with a serious pathology, especially when this pathology endangers life and the sick person gives his or her consent. But it would also be immoral — in keeping with the tradition of church teaching since the sixteenth century — to begin the artificial nutrition and hydration of a patient who is informed about this treatment but clearly does not want it, since these measures are disproportionate with regard to the expected benefits versus the sources of discomfort, harm, suffering, incomprehension, fear, or repugnance. It is not necessary to die with a full stomach. And a number of studies have shown that nutrition and hydration at the close of a person's life, or when a patient has advanced dementia, brings no benefit and actually prolongs the process of dying.

According to the formula of Francisco de Vitoria, "One is forbidden to terminate one's life, but one is not obliged to look for every means (even illicit means) to prolong it."[7]

On the Theological Level

Since the sixteenth century, the traditional teaching of the church has employed the concepts of "ordinary" and "extraordinary" to appeal to a notion of "proportionality" between risks and benefits, taking account of the individual, family, and community (see Francisco de Vitoria, Domingo Bañez, Domingo Soto, and Cardinal John de Lugo).[8] This is a teleological perspective, without however being consequentialist, since it takes into account not only the foreseeable proportionate or disproportionate consequences, but also the rules for right conduct. The Magisterium has frequently recalled this perspective: see especially the address of Pius XII to an international Congress of Anesthetists in 1957, the encyclical *Evangelium vitae* (no. 65)

of John Paul II in 1995, the *Declaration on Euthanasia* by the Congregation for the Doctrine of the Faith in 1980, the statement of the Pontifical
Council Cor Unum in 1981 about ethical questions relating to seriously ill
and dying persons, and paragraph number 2,278 of the *Catechism of the
Catholic Church*.

In an address delivered in March 2004, which doubtless does not possess
the authority of teaching addressed to the entire church[9] but has nevertheless
attracted considerable attention,[10] John Paul II seems to distance himself
from this teaching: "I should like to emphasize that the administering of
water and nourishment, even by artificial means, is *always* a *natural means*
of maintaining life, *not a medical action. As a general rule,* therefore, its
utilization must be considered both *ordinary* and *proportionate*."[11]

Ought this deontological position to be understood as a change to the
tradition? A number of points must be borne in mind here.

First, this position, which was not repeated in later teaching statements
by John Paul II, is not very clear. It both stands within the tradition and
distances itself from the tradition, and could therefore function as a "double
bind."[12] It affirms that the administering of nourishment, even by artificial
means, is "always a natural means," while at the same time stating that "its
utilization must be considered both ordinary and proportionate *as a general
rule*" — in other words, there is a place for discernment. This teaching was
subsequently relativized to some extent by the attitude of John Paul II at the
close of his own life, when he did not wish to benefit from medical assistance
of this kind. What then do we have here: a modification of the tradition, or
an appeal to doctors and carers, and even to families, who are often tempted
to hasten the end of the patient's life in a direct manner, without reflecting
on the questions involved?

Second, John Paul II affirms in the same text that artificial hydration/
nutrition is "morally obligatory." Is this insistence a response to some kind
of relativism? But if one insists too strongly on this point and wishes to
make it universally valid, does one not risk being counterproductive? If the
pope's words are taken literally, *every* intervention in the form of hydration/
nutrition is on the same level, whether artificial or not. And this makes it
too easy to move from the fact of hunger or thirst to a moral obligation,
namely, the need for a medical intervention. But one cannot move directly
from the "fact" of hunger or thirst to the effectuation of a gastrostomy
without *discernment*. Besides this, a fact never implies a moral obligation;
the obligation arises only within a recognized symbolic context. And if it
is in fact medically necessary to carry out a gastrostomy, for example, this
necessity is not yet an "obligation" on the acting subject, without which
he would be supplanted and reduced to the status of a thing, deprived of
his autonomy (and more generally, of his capacity for discernment), a state
of affairs that would be absolutely contrary to the spirit of this text or of
other writings of John Paul II. The pope's aim is always to ensure respect

for every human being. This however means that if his intention here is to insist, he is acting against his own intention. For as we all know, a bow that is overstretched will snap. The clinical situation is always an individual situation, and if one applies too many norms to it, one weakens the Christian foundations.

Third, we should remember that Christian teaching is not concerned with the usage of one or another technique or specific medical intervention, but with respect for the human person and for his or her dignity — and that is something very different. Salvation is not a matter of counting the number of years a person lives. The ultimate goal of human existence is not life here below, but the definitive encounter with God after death.

One can also argue by means of a negative, as does James F. Drane: "Stop and think about this. Can you imagine a large Catholic hospital with hundreds of beds filled with dying patients attached to this technology? Can you imagine the expense? Can you imagine the burden on patients and their families? Can you imagine the scandal? Any reasonable person looking at such a scene would surely ask: Are these people crazy? Do they believe in life after death?"[13]

Christian theology does not supply ready-made solutions, but it does represent a touchstone at the service of a prudential discernment that will take into account the sick person, his family, the carers, those closely involved, society, and the church — as well as factors such as the human, spiritual, financial, and social costs.[14] Christian theology, on the basis of its own body of knowledge and thanks to its structural link to reason,[15] reminds us that a correct discernment involves a *global* evaluation of the needs and desires of the patient, together with his or her entourage. Equally, it reminds us — as does the Kantian perspective — that it is the person, not the biological life, that is a goal per se, and that we may therefore never attach an absolute value to life, turning it into an idol by seeking to preserve it at all costs, without considering the goals that every human existence posits in its search for fulfillment: for a human life in which the spiritual dimension had become definitively obsolete would no longer have any meaning. As Pius XII rightly observed, "Life, health, and all temporal activity are subordinated to spiritual goals."[16] Reflecting on these words of the pope, O'Rourke emphasizes that if the spiritual potential is lacking, every treatment or care that aims to maintain the physiological functions will be in vain. The person does indeed remain a human being, but there is no ethical obligation to prolong the life of this particular human being.[17]

The key question will therefore always be: What *benefit* does the human person derive from the nutrients that are introduced into his or her body — not what biological assistance is given to prolong material life, but what *beneficium*; what good for *the unity of soul and body* of the person; what therapeutic, spiritual, direct, or indirect benefit is envisaged? There is no reason to prolong a tragic life that is dying interminably, or to fetter to a bed a biological life that is disintegrating at every point. Rather, doctors who have received an appropriate training — and have experience, sometimes with the aid of an ethical committee, as the Swiss guidelines state[18] — should adjust or else discontinue the treatment. In this way, all the actors can get involved in a care that gives the patient a relational closeness and a quality of comfort that are also capable of bearing witness to the care of Christ for every human being and to faith in eternal life.

— English translation by Brian McNeil

Notes

1. Law no. 2005–370 of April 22, 2005.
2. Address to a Congress of Catholic Doctors, March 20, 2004.
3. It is this aspect that explains the debate (especially in Europe) about genetically modified organisms: in some sense, to eat genetically modified organisms means being "modified" by these organisms.
4. Kevin Wildes, ed., *Birth, Suffering and Death* (Boston: Kluwer, 1992).
5. Quoted by Christian Rath, "Kirche widerspricht Ärzten bei Sterbehilfe," *Kölner Stadtanzeige* (April 2, 2005).
6. Didier Anzieu, *Le moi-peau* (Paris: Ed. Dunod, 1995).
7. Francisco de Vitoria, "De homicitio" n. 35 in *Obras de F. de Vitoria, Relecciones teológicas,* ed. T. Urdanoz (Madrid: Biblioteca de Autores Cristianos, 1960), 1127.
8. D. A. Cronin, "Conserving Human Life: Part I," in *Conserving Human Life,* ed. R. E. Smith (Braintree, Mass.: Pope John Center, 1989). This is a decisively important study of the historical position taken by ethical teaching on the situations at the end of human life. Jason T. Eberl traces this teaching back to Thomas Aquinas in Marie-Jo Thiel, ed., *Les rites de fin de vie* (Strasbourg: Premières Journées Internationales d'Ethique à, 2006).
9. John J. Paris, James F. Keenan, and Kenneth R. Himes, "Quaestio disputata: Did John Paul II's Allocution on Life-Sustaining Treatments Revise Tradition?" *Theological Studies* 67 (2006): 163–68.
10. Thomas A. Shannon and James J. Walter, "Reply to Professors Paris, Keenan, and Himes," *Theological Studies* 67 (2006): 169–74.
11. He continues: " ... and as such, morally obligatory, as long as it succeeds in attaining and demonstrating its proper goal, which consists in supplying nutrition to the patient and alleviating his sufferings. ... In reality, the only possible result of suspending nutrition and hydration is death of hunger or thirst. And this means, if they are suspended in a conscious and deliberate manner, that this action takes the form of a genuine euthanasia by omission."
12. In other words, the simultaneous presentation of a message and of its negation, for example: "If you love me, do not love me."
13. James F. Drane, *More Humane Medicine: A Liberal Catholic Bioethics* (Edinboro, Pa.: Edinboro University Press, 2003), 342.
14. The financial cost does not play the same role in Europe, where the medical system is paid by insurance, and in the United States, where the system is open.

In principle, cost should never be a radically determinative factor, but in the European system, the money spent on certain treatments is no longer available for other treatments.

15. Marie-Jo Thiel and Xavier Thévenot, *Pratiquer l'analyse éthique: Analyser un cas, étudier un texte* (Paris: Cerf, 1999).

16. Address of November 24, 1957.

17. K. O'Rourke, "Should Nutrition and Hydration Be Provided to Permanently Unconscious and Other Mentally Disabled Persons?" *Issues in Law and Medicine* 5 (1989): 181–96.

18. U. Körner et al., "Ethical and Legal Aspects of Enteral Nutrition," *Clinical Nutrition* 25 (2006): 196–202.

23

A Contextual Approach to the Practical Tradition of Hospital Care

CATHERINE FINO

In his description of the search for norms in our pluralist societies, the philosopher Jean-Marc Ferry makes a distinction between moral decisionism on the one hand and juridical functionalism on the other.[1]

Values are a matter of private conviction, whereas norms are a matter of public interest and are mostly linked to legislative procedures. In order to steer the difficult course between values and norms, especially in bioethics and medical ethics, I should like to propose the thesis that *the nature and structure of ethics are largely determined by the specificities of history and of communities.*

I base my remarks here on my doctoral research into *hospital care as a praxis of charity* in Québec from the seventeenth century to the beginning of the twentieth, studying the history of two hospitals that were administered and animated by religious women. When we look at the tradition of a praxis of hospital care, we can see what constitutes its ethical character and what the theological life means when it is put into practice. My topic here is the abandonment of euthanasia by the Native Americans of Québec-Sillery in New France in the seventeenth century. At the origin of this change of behavior was the encounter between these Native Americans and the missionaries, especially the Augustinian sisters, who welcomed them and cared for them in the first Hôtel-Dieu in Sillery between 1640 and 1644.

First Approach:
An Evocative Picture of Care for the Dying

The principal body of texts to which I refer consists of the *Relations des jésuites en Nouvelle-France*[2] and the *Annales de l'Hôtel-Dieu de Québec.*[3] The many services performed by the missionaries included the care of the sick and the dying, and this allows us to grasp the set of conditions that it made it possible for some Native Americans to abandon euthanasia.

The first condition is the establishment of a medico-social network that allowed individuals to face up to their responsibilities. The Native-American custom prescribed that the feeblest persons, who were not able to move from place to place during the hunting season, should be abandoned in the forest: the survival of the clan was at stake, hence the praxis of euthanasia.[4] The director of the Jesuit mission station, Father Le Jeune, succeeded in dissuading the Native Americans from practicing euthanasia by caring in the hospital for those who would have been a burden on the Native Americans. Where necessary, he did so for several winters on end. In his 1641 report, he writes:

> I am sending Adam to the hospital, this good old man, the oldest among the savages. I have rescued him from the death that the barbarians wanted to inflict on him with a rope, in order to rid themselves of a burden that costs them a great deal; I asked the Frenchmen who were going down to that district to give him a place in their boat. I have no doubt that the Mothers will receive him gladly; they have already fed him and looked after him there throughout the whole of winter last year. This good man has no other illness than that which he began to contract more than a hundred years ago.[5]

The second condition that made it possible to abandon euthanasia is the reintegration of the sick and the dying into the field of social relationships. Whereas Native American culture broke the "bond of humanity"[6] as soon as a sick or old person could no longer meet the demands of the group, the first baptized Native Americans recognized that faith in the resurrection restores the bond of humanity on the far side of death. Old and infirm persons could regain their dignity in the little autochthonous Christian community. Indeed, they could attain a status of honor, as in the case of Pierre Tregatin, whose compatriots acknowledged him as "captain or master of the prayers. In the councils, it was his task to speak of the things of God, to demonstrate what was expedient with regard to these matters, and to admonish those who publicly failed to do their duty, especially those who did not attend public prayers."[7]

The third condition is the offer of a meaning — other than mere submission to an inexorable destiny — that can help people to live their last moments. The nuns who cared for the sick noted how a young Native American woman who was near death ceased to be shuttered up within herself: "In her agony, she seemed no longer to have eyes or ears; but as soon as one spoke to her about God, she seemed to come back to herself, showing by signs that she took pleasure in hearing about Him who is now her delight."[8] In addition to the hope offered by the resurrection, the Jesuits and the Augustinian sisters transmit an "experience of dying" that is addressed to others, following the example of Christ. The report for 1640 tells how Lazare Petitkovchkaovat was converted, abandoning his plans for suicide when he heard the narrative of the passion:

> This big and powerful savage had been very proud and debauched; at the beginning of his time in hospital, he was still full of himself and wanted to have his life taken in order to deliver him from the torments which he suffered. But Father Pijard related some part of the story of the passion in the poor persons' room every day in Lent, and this wretched man was touched by this and piously accepted his duty.[9]

This story was written down by the Jesuits and was then made available to the Augustinian sisters in order that they could pass on the experience of a "good death" and reveal to the dying the unheard-of meaning that charity can give to the ordeal of dying.

During the brief time it took for the hospital to be established in Sillery, the positive response of the Native Americans to these various propositions confirms their relevance. To begin with, the missionaries looked after the old and the infirm on their own initiative, but once structures of medico-social aid were in place, the praxis of the autochthonous populations was increasingly modified: the weak were still abandoned, but the Native Americans said where they had left their compatriots, so that the missionaries could go and bring them help:

> The day after their departure, on my way from Québec to Sillery, I found a cabin containing twelve or thirteen sick persons, both elderly and children, whom the savages had recommended to me on the previous evening, asking me to bring them to the hospital. When they saw me passing by, they arose and followed me as best they could, and came to the hospital to spend their winter there, some in the room of the sick, and some in a cabin close by the hospital.[10]

The change in attitudes to the sick and the old is perceptible. When the Native American Chief Charles Meiaskouät came to visit the sick during his stay in Sillery, he appealed to the hope of resurrection in these words:

> You others…who are sick, do not regard the illness as something evil.…Rather, think in this way of God: he is the Father of us all, he made us, he loves us. It is for our good that he sends the sickness, he will bring us into heaven and will give us a life that never dies. This is how you are to think of God. Have courage, therefore, do not be sad, believe firmly: what you are enduring will soon be over, but your joy will last forever in heaven.[11]

Prescinding from the ambiguities of these words, which turn suffering into an instrument of purification, we should note the shift in the text to the use of the personal pronoun "us." This shows that the sick had been fully reintegrated into the Native American community, and the Native American chief visits them in order to emphasize that they have regained their human dignity. They are no longer subject to the requirement that their existence favor the survival of the clan. The chief bears witness that the hope of resurrection has given new dimensions to the clan, beyond the frontiers both of illness and of death.

There is an obvious and genuine analogy between this historical picture of hospital care and the modern experience of palliative care — with holistic concern for the person and for his or her family, attention to interpersonal and social networks, and the new value attached to the actual period of dying — and this analogy lends support to contemporary praxis. It is, however, not enough to note that these two experiences, within one and the same tradition, have similar traits; if we look in greater depth at the historical picture, we shall find that it helps us to take into account the theological experience of those involved and to analyze the conditions that made possible this specific experience of hospital care.

Second Approach:
The Subjective Conditions That Made Possible
a New Praxis of Hospital Care,
or the Theological Experience of the Subjects

The foundresses of the Hôtel-Dieu in Sillery were clearly outstanding women who had shown themselves capable of putting their own lives at risk in order to care for plague victims in France, and who then succeeded in adapting to extreme conditions of life in Canada in order to realize their project of religious life and hospital care. What is the source of such a strength of character, and what formation had these women received?

The Augustinian sisters had profited from the new appreciation of action, fully integrated into the construction of a holy (*dévote*) personality, which is characteristic of spirituality at the beginning of the seventeenth century. An analysis of their *Constitutions,*[12] and of the treatise on *Direction spirituelle,* written for the novices in the order,[13] allows us to identify some elements in the formation of these nursing nuns. The construction of the person who leads this life presupposes that she works on her own desire: the sister learns to love "Poverty, Contempt, and Pain," which are the "Companions of Jesus."[14] She thus acquires the suppleness of character that permits her to serve in a hospital and[15]

> to suffer joyfully every inconvenience caused by the poor sick persons, without displaying any impatience in her dealings with them, supporting with love and charity the troubles they may cause. With a gentle

and affectionate compassion, let us courageously overcome the disgust we feel when we are surrounded by the dirt of a hospital, quelling our own sensual nature which naturally abhors this holy practice which is so highly pleasing to Jesus Christ our Savior. These are the mortifications which we must embrace every day of our lives, achieving ever greater perfection therein until our death.

She can then dedicate everything she does, "without any reservation," to the realization of the charity of Christ in the work of hospital care. The sisters must "endeavor to practice" vis-à-vis the sick "a great gentleness and patience, because they recognize that the service they render them is inspired by religious devotion and by charity."[16] When we read the treatise on *Direction spirituelle*, it is clear that the practical instructions given to the novices have a meta-ethical character: the aim is to instill the right intention in them and to awaken their sense of responsibility when they care for the sick. For example, in a prayer of consecration before she begins work, the novice addresses Jesus, offering to him her visit to the sick "to honor and pay homage to the visits to the sick which you yourself made when you were on earth...where you gave life to the sick, and received with such great charity and mercy those who came to you." After this thanksgiving, which recalls the foundational action of Jesus, the novice places the work she is about to do in the hands of the Lord, so that it may be a realization of his mercy, asking that she may enter "into all the intentions that it may please you for me to have in this action, in order that I may do it according to your most holy will."[17] Imitation of Christ the servant takes on the dimension of a genuine participation in the charity of Christ at work in her and through her in her praxis of hospital care.

The novice must apply herself diligently to the task of making the care of the sick a *relational* activity: this care becomes personalized and takes on a new dimension thanks to the attention she pays to those whom Jesus calls "the least of those who are mine":[18]

> Let the hospital sister take great pains to see that the sick are given beds, food, and medicine with charity, according to what is available in the hospital; taking heed of those who are convalescing and of those who are the weakest, who need to eat more frequently. They should also take note of those who have no appetite for food and have thus eaten only a little at mealtimes, so that they can give these persons something extra.

The actions involved in caring for the sick always refer to the very source of salvation, namely, Jesus Christ. The Augustinian tradition attributes a quasi-sacramental role to the act of caring for others, since these acts are the symbolic "application"[19] of salvation to the person in preparation for the sacraments that proclaim and genuinely effect salvation. For the Native Americans who stayed in the hospital or the village of Sillery, the offer of a new vision of the world is linked to a restoration to health that enables these persons to assume new responsibilities (that is, to serve the sick and accompany the dying):[20]

> The savages, who did not know what it meant to visit the sick, learn the work of charity. We see some good women who are excellent carers in the hospital: they transport the sick, care for them, and relieve their suffering, and they are more skilled than we at serving them the corn stew that they eat.
>
> The sickness of their companion reached the point of no return, and his life was despaired of; since then, two of them did not move from his side, in order that they might be able to assist him. This charity of theirs is no ordinary charity: the things of God are winning more and more power over their hearts.[21]

This transformation of persons is required by their entry into the Christian community, which is not only a community of faith, but also a community of charitable praxis. Ultimately, the acts of charity performed by a stranger are interpreted as signs that the charity of Christ is present in this person, and confirm that he or she has attained a new moral identity. *Charity thus makes care for the sick a path along which people can acquire a moral identity and holiness, thus coming to salvation.* The shared experience of the "goodness" of the other person, which bears witness to a shared theological commitment, allowed both the Native Americans and the nursing nuns to have confidence in each other. They could thus transcend their cultural differences and lay the foundations of the community.

At the close of this second "approach," we note that there is a link between the kind of life a community leads and the nature of moral existence. The abandonment of euthanasia was not due to the acceptance of rational arguments, but to intimate convictions about life and death, on which religion sheds a light. In the last analysis, this means the recognition[22] in practice that the vulnerable persons in Native American society are worthy of being loved, welcomed, and cared for — and this recognition constructs a new societal bond and inaugurates a new ethical norm that is strongly linked to the values of the Christian community. The question is: Does this confirm the communitarian position, which affirms that the social, moral, and religious communities are coextensive, so that it would be impossible to imagine any contribution on the part of foreign cultures to the identity of our contemporary globalized and multicultural societies? This brings me to the third "approach" in my essay: the principle of recognition and of openness to the universal dimension.

Third Approach:
The Openness of a Contingent Form
to the Universal Dimension

Recognition of the other person, within the community of Sillery, broadens out to the recognition of the other foreigner, in Europe. In a later text, from 1664, the *Annales de l'Hôtel-Dieu* note that the Native Americans have experienced, in the case of their French benefactors, how the ability to practice solidarity in prayer unites people across the ocean that separates them:

> The Reverend Father Superior one day asked a group of Christian Huron women if they could love persons whom they had never seen, speaking of some ladies in France who had sent them presents. One of the Huron women replied in a very spiritual manner: "Why not, Father? We love God, whom we do not see. The persons of whom you speak love us too, even without having seen us, and without being obliged to do so by any external force. As for ourselves, we see the alms that they send us, and these remind us continuously of the obligation that we bear to them."[23]

The experience of faith and entry into the Christian community allowed them to recognize a universal dimension that is to be understood, not as the negation of particularities, but as a path that leads to mutual recognition on the part of the particularities. This inculturation of charity is not a servile reproduction of the European ethos to the detriment of Native American culture, since the values which they have assimilated generate an authentic, normative creativity in the Native Americans. By adopting the practice of prayer for their benefactresses, the Native Americans freed themselves from the perverse discourse of the missionaries (who instrumentalize their suffering in such a way that this benefits the salvation of their benefactors)[24] in order to make explicit the shared experience of hope and love.

What we see at work here is a *spiritual universal in context*.[25] It must be put into practice in order to detach it from the abstraction proper to a formal principle; it must take on a precise form, so that it can be recognized in its own truth. One example: in order to claim her right to have her daughter buried with dignity, like the Europeans, a Native American woman rejects the ambiguous discourse of the nursing nuns whose appeal to economic rationality actually devalues the Native American culture. They refuse to let this woman place her most precious objects alongside her deceased daughter:

> Her mother had her buried with all the solemnity possible to a savage, and placed in the grave the most precious objects she possessed: beaver skins, porcelain, and other articles which they esteem highly. When the nuns reproached her on the grounds of her poverty and that of

the savages, and said that such things were not useful to the dead in any way, she said: "Well, you too buried your religious sister" — this was Mother de Sainte Marie, who died two years ago — "with her beautiful habit and with all the honor that you could give her. If what I am doing was offensive to God, I would stop; but since God does not forbid it, I wish to honor the dead."[26]

The editor of the Jesuit reports acknowledges that this mother was acting correctly. Her conduct is typically Indian, but at the same time, she appeals to the *universal* recognition of the dignity of her daughter's body — something she had learned from the Augustinian sisters. It is by discovering the transcultural character of charity that the Native Americans grasp the universal character of the new social and religious rules, even though these bear the marks of the contingencies of the cultures in which they take on concrete forms. The appeal to a shared theological experience is the key to the unification of this multicultural community around a renewed expression of values. This makes the specific practices meaningful; at the same time, the differences enjoy a higher measure of respect, and this allows both the missionaries and the Native Americans to transcend, at least in part, the temptation to racism, and to find the path that leads to the universal dimension.

Conclusion

A system of norms and values can be linked by a theological experience. Both norms and values are determined by the particularities of the Christian society and the cultural society. This, however, does not confine us within the narrow borders of communitarianism, since the Christian community experiences openness to a universal — although this is a "universal in context."

— English translation by Brian McNeil

Notes

1. Jean-Marc Ferry, "De l'élection de valeurs à l'adoption de normes," in *La rationalité des valeurs,* ed. Sylvie Masure (Paris: Presses Universitaires de France, 1998), 153.

2. *Relations des jésuites, 1637–1741, contenant ce qui s'est passé de remarquable dans les missions des Pères de la Compagnie de Jésus dans la Nouvelle-France,* vol. 2 (Montreal: Éd. du Jour, 1972).

3. Albert Jamet, ed., *Les Annales de l'Hôtel-Dieu de Québec, 1636–1716, composée par les Révérendes Mères Jeanne-Françoise Juchereau de St. Ignace et Marie-Andrée Duplessis de Ste Hélène, Anciennes Religieuses de ce Monastère* (Hôtel-Dieu de Québec 1939), reprinted 1984.

4. A letter from a neophyte, giving thanks for the kindness of the Sisters, attests to the praxis of genuine euthanasia: "We are very happy that they have compassion

for the sick: for we do not have this custom at all. We abandon other members of our tribe, and sometimes we strangle the sick — this is how we used to behave. And that is why we are very happy that the women dressed in white have arrived here. Since they arrived, they have had compassion for us" (*Relations des jésuites* [1643], 16).

5. Ibid. (1641), 25.

6. This meant that looking after the sick was a counter-cultural practice in the eyes of the Native Americans, and a source of great admiration: "If the savages are capable of astonishment anywhere, it is here: for among them, no account is taken of the sick, especially if they are thought to be mortally ill. They are regarded among the Indians as people from another world, with whom one has no dealings and with whom one does not speak. But when they see the caresses and the care shown to their compatriots, they come to esteem very highly Him for whose sake they receive this great help, namely, Jesus Christ our Savior" (*Relations des jésuites, 1637–1741,* [1639], n. 2, 9).

7. Ibid. (1643), 41.

8. Ibid. (1641), 27.

9. Ibid. (1640), 40.

10. Ibid. (1643), 11.

11. Ibid., 45.

12. They brought their constitutions from France: *Les Constitutions des religieuses Hospitalières de l'Ordre de Saint Augustin dites Filles de la Miséricorde, establies à Dieppe,* 1631. Where the text is identical, my references are to the more easily accessible edition of 1666, namely, *Constitutions de la Congrégation des religieuses hospitalières de la Miséricorde de Jésus, de l'Hôtel-Dieu de Québec,* 1666. Both editions are in the archives of the Hôtel-Dieu in Québec.

13. *Direction spirituelle, Pour s'occuper saintement avec Dieu, toute la journée. Pour les Sœurs du Noviciat des Religieuses de la MISERICORDE de JESUS de l'Ordre de Saint Augustin* (St-Malo: Raoul de la Mare, 1641), 481. (Copy in the archives of the Hôtel-Dieu in Québec.)

14. *Constitutions HDQ* (1666), 64.

15. Ibid. (1666), 46.

16. Ibid. (1631), 252; (1666), 173.

17. *Direction spirituelle,* "Direction allant aux Pauvres," 73–74.

18. *Constitutions HDQ, 1666,* 164; my italics.

19. "The service which we render to the poor for the health of the body concerns the salvation of the soul; since we receive the sick in our house in order to help them in a holier manner to support their illness as Christians should, and to pass more happily from this world when God will please to ordain this. And this means that our office, properly speaking, is to collect the drops of the precious Blood of Jesus Christ and *to apply these* through our little labors for the salvation of souls — for that is why this Blood was shed" (*Constitutions HDQ* [1631], 223; [1666], 155–56), emphasis added.

20. *Relations des jésuites* (1642), 30. Another example: "A young widow, *named Charitée...* has had herself brought to the cabin near the hospital throughout the whole of winter, in order to be cared for; but she does not remain idle: *she herself does the work of a hospital sister* and gives every possible assistance to this poor band. She fetches wood and water, she cooks, she repairs the animal skins, she

makes shoes; if a Canadian stag is killed three or four leagues away, she takes her sledge and goes to fetch her burden across the snow" ([1643], 43), emphasis added.

21. Ibid. (1643), 44; emphasis added.

22. "I have come to see discussion as more than an arena for testing out arguments, or as a clash between opposing forces of logic. Rather, it is a milieu of recognition, where emotional experiences too are communicating with each other" (Ferry, "De l'élection," 180).

23. *Annales HDQ* (1664), 131.

24. Father Le Jeune writes the following very clumsy words to the Duchess of Aiguillon, the foundress of this work: "This great lady is already repaid for her alms. At the hour in which I am writing these lines, several savages have already prayed for her in her hospital, and some are already dead" (*Relations des jésuites* [1639], 10).

25. The paradoxical expression "spiritual universal" is suggested by Servais Pinckaers, "La loi nouvelle et la permanence des lois morales," in *Universalité et permanence des lois morales,* ed. S. Pinckaers and C. J. Pinto de Oliveira (Fribourg: Ed. Universitaires, and Paris: Cerf, 1986), 442–54. Pinckaers distinguishes between "the rational universality based on the natural law and the universality generated by the new Law, which can be called 'spiritual' because of the action of the Holy Spirit who brings it about" (448–49). This concept allows him to make explicit the relationship between theological experience and the question of universals in moral theology: "The spiritual universality thus confronts us with a characteristic paradox: it proceeds from faith in the unique person of Jesus and, as such, separates the believer from the unbeliever; but this faith contains an effective power to appeal to every human being, and indeed to every creature, and surpasses reason. Let us return to our initial question: 'Do universal laws or norms exist?' We can see in the new Law a confirmation of the existence of such laws, primarily because of the correspondence that we can discern between the spiritual universalism that animates the Church as a community open to all the peoples, and the universalism based on the natural law that supports the formation of human society" (450). The position that Servais Pinckaers goes on to maintain, on the incapacity of "reason alone" to grasp the universal, goes beyond this first formulation of the contribution made by the theological life to the ethical universal.

26. The death of Louyse's daughter (*Relations des jésuites* [1643] 42).

PART SIX

SEXUALITY AND MARRIAGE

24

The Fragility of Marriage

Concerning Methodology in Christian Ethics

PHILIPPE BORDEYNE

When one in three marriages ends in divorce and even one in two in urban areas, as is the case in Western countries, a question emerges on the agenda of church ethics: Is it still moral to propose Catholic marriage on a large scale? When so many couples remain highly unprepared for marriage in spite of pastoral efforts, is it ethical to expose them to the risk of failure?

These questions have been raised not so much on a theoretical basis as on a practical level. During the 1990s, most delegates of diocesan synods expressed doubts about the rightness of preparing couples to make commitments when those individuals lack knowledge of "the profound meaning of the sacrament of marriage" or even "the Christian vision of love, marriage, and family life." Also, in pastoral circles at all levels, much criticism continues to be raised against the principle that faith should be presumed when the candidates have received baptism, especially if this occurred in their early childhood. Can faith be considered as sufficient for receiving the sacrament of marriage when "the candidates intend to do what the church aims at?"

These questions deserve serious consideration. However, the manner in which they are expressed raises several premises that can be questioned from a theological, ethical point of view. First, the meaning of Christian marriage is disconnected from the historical experience of those who apply for this form of Christian life, who are committed in it, or even have failed in it. When they approach the church, those people consider themselves as believers, and they would not tolerate being denied the right to marry in church. However, the questions I have echoed reconstruct the meaning of marriage through non-historical procedures, like theological essays that are based on a philosophy of nature, a metaphysics of mutual giving, or a phenomenology of sexual intercourse. Second, the sacramental views that underlie those questions tend to separate the faith of the church from that of the candidates for marriage. Saying that faith is required to embrace validly the ethical choice of marriage develops too simple a relationship between faith and ethics. In brief, many observations that seem pastoral turn out to be governed by a doctrinal rationale.

In responding to the ethical challenge of durability, it is probably more helpful to have a glance at Christian practices within marriage instead of reasoning on an idealized image of marriage that would hopefully stem the divorce figures. Practices give access to the way people try to shape their own lives in a responsible way. In France, new practices prove families to be subject to fragility and inventiveness at the same time.

1. In the pastoral program of Christian initiation of adults, diversity in culture and ethos makes it difficult to initiate into the Christian vision of marriage. However, taking part in a wedding celebration at church can prove to be more effective than a long course in Catholic doctrine. When embracing the Christian faith requires one to quit former sexual or gender practices, catechumens learn more from the whole atmosphere of the celebration; with scripture readings that have been carefully chosen; with the mixture of fragility and confidence that arises from the exchange of consent; and with the palpable support of the assembly. They learn more because they do not learn from reason only. They also learn from emotions, which can produce new motions. The witnessing of a happy and responsible couple is more likely to foster the desire of becoming a disciple of Christ in marriage than would a list of laws that govern marriage.

2. Couples that have chosen marriage discover that they need to be maintained in the memory of their public vows. Whereas they develop a great amount of creativity to celebrate their marriage anniversary in private with some touch of positive craziness, they also seek community support as far as the public face of marriage is concerned. Some of them choose a mass or a special blessing on the anniversary day, especially when they reach a good number of years. But more often, they join their parish for a special covenant day, when all married people are invited to renew their vows in the context of the Sunday assembly. This appears to be a responsible attitude regarding the prevention of divorce. If Christian marriage is to criticize the dominant model of private romance in the long run, the public face of marriage needs to be regularly made visible long after the wedding day.

3. This is a good reason to offer couple counseling that is officially inspired by the gospel values: durability of marriage, forgiveness, hope, and trust in the saving grace of God. Whereas some couples prefer to refer to professionals regardless of religious commitment, others find it easier to face a crisis with the expressed support of faith and with the certitude that divorce will not be presented to them as the easiest way to solve the problem. As long as some actions prove to be helpful in the context of marriage fragility, the church would be irresponsible if it did not get involved.

4. The durability of marriage is also highly dependent upon the couple's ability to manage their vocation as parents. Courses in spiritual preparation for childbirth draw large numbers of the public. They do not mask the difficulty of becoming a mother or a father and remaining a spouse simultaneously, without dramatizing such difficulty. Some useful advice is given

to overcome it concretely, fostering imagination among young parents. The Second Vatican Council described families as domestic churches in connection with their mission of developing in their children a Christian faith. But parents need to acquire self-confidence. More and more parishes organize Sunday catechesis for families. Parents are welcomed with any questions they might have about faith, the Bible, or church teaching. Instead of being sent to learn religion while not knowing if their parents still believe in God (churchgoing is lower than 5 percent in France), children experience that their own parents are still searching for God and growing in faith. As children join their parents for evening prayer, mutual tenderness can be expressed before God. The community becomes more family-like and families become more church-like. Interpreting families as domestic churches is an opportunity for mutual conversion.

5. There are a growing number of groups where divorced and remarried people get community support to pursue their moral vocation after failure. Many divorced people lose confidence in the institution of marriage; the remaining hope that Christians publicly put into marriage when they have found another stable union should not be underestimated. Even if their situation remains irregular because of the respect due to sacramental marriage as a public institution, the gospel demands that support never be denied to those who experience failure. Christ expressed preferential love to them, saying he did not come for the healthy, but for the sick.

Ethical subjects are being shaped for marriage in a diversity of ethos, combined with the specific formative potential of Christian practices. In today's pluralism, pastoral life appears to be the major *locus theologicus* for ethics. It should not be primarily considered as a system of authoritative decisions. Theologically speaking, pastoral life is the concrete, historical space of interactivity between the living faith and today's cultures. In ordinary Christian practices, two elements are closely linked: the questions people develop about marriage and family life, often expressed as moral dilemmas, and the call to solve them with the support of church resources, which are both tiny and fantastic. Referring to pastoral life prevents theologians from building too rigid an opposition between faith and ethics, or between individual faith and community faith. Pastoral life embodies the creativity of faith when exposed to diverse and emerging cultural trends.

Theological ethics must recollect segments of tradition that tend to be underestimated in fostering pastoral imagination. Today, some young married couples would like the church to talk more about sex. They certainly do not call for a renewal of the kind of moral teaching that disappeared with the Second Vatican Council, of which they have no idea. They rather express the need for guidance in dealing with sexual hopes and difficulties. As sex is a matter of performance and money in a consumer society, many couples are over-frightened when they experience the weakening of mutual desire, sexual misunderstanding, or disturbing feelings toward a third person. The spiritual tradition might be helpful, for it is used to dealing with the discrepancy between emotions and reason. Francis de Sales believed in the primacy of sensitive love, but he linked it with intellectual love. When emotions are weak or disturbed, he taught how keeping an eye on the intellectual knowledge of love can slowly revive or redirect emotions. Given that the moral basis for marriage is the reasonable choice of the institution of mutual love and education of children, it requires some kind of initiation into the interactivity of sensitive and intellectual love. In such matters, families would highly benefit from sharing experience and practical knowledge.

25

"What God Has Joined Together"

The Specifically Christian Quality of Conjugal Love

ARISTIDE FUMAGALLI

The Liquefaction of Marriage

In contemporary Western societies, the bonds of love are subject to a process of increasing and rapid loosening. In particular, the civil and religious institution of marriage appears to be subject to a kind of liquefaction whereby love — to use a metaphor dear to Zygmunt Bauman — takes on a liquid appearance.[1]

The relationship of love is no longer crystallized in the premodern form of the patriarchal family or in the modern form of bourgeois marriage. Not only does it seem fragile and unstable, as we see in the consistent growth in the number of separations and divorces and in the diffusion of cohabitation either prior to marriage or as an alternative to marriage; it also appears to be shapeless and changeable. The primary factors that structure the relationship of love are sexual pleasure and emotional well-being, and this relationship takes on a variety of forms. It no longer has characteristic traits — not even those of sexual difference (since this is disputed by the homosexual culture) or of the personal procreation of children (since this is supplanted by the techniques of artificial fertilization). This means that the pattern of marriage as a link between two parents and two generations, meaning between a man and a woman and between these two persons as parents and their children, has disintegrated. It has been reassembled in a plurality of models.[2]

The evaluation of this process of liquefaction oscillates between two extremes, either an absolute condemnation or an unconditional approval. On the one hand, some speak of decadence when they judge the current transformation and demand the reestablishment of a strong institution of matrimony. On the other hand, some greet the weakening of traditional marriage as a sign of its unstoppable evolution toward more flexible and lighter forms of relationship.

I believe that neither of these positions gets it right from the specifically Christian perspective. The Christian evaluation of human institutions — and marriage is one of the most ancient and universal examples of such an institution — is not primarily interested in their durability or dissolution, but in their harmony with that love which is revealed in Christ and which he himself envisages as the criterion of every human relationship: "A new commandment I give to you, that you love one another; even as I have loved you, that you also love one another" (John 13:34). Christian love, that is, that love which has its identity in the manner in which Christ loved, claims the authority to judge all the ideologies of marriage, whether conservative or progressive, and to function as the decisive criterion for the evaluation of the quality of contemporary relationships of love.

Jesus's Commandment about Conjugal Love

The application of the new commandment of love to the specifically conjugal relationship can draw on the teaching of Jesus himself. The existence of a commandment of Jesus with regard to marriage is proved by the words of Paul to the married members of the community in Corinth. He refers explicitly to a commandment of the Lord, which is not to be confused with the directives that he issues as an apostle: "To the married I give charge, not I but the Lord, that the wife should not separate from her husband (but if she does, let her remain single or else be reconciled to her husband) — and that the husband should not divorce his wife" (1 Cor. 7:10f).

Five New Testament passages bear witness to the commandment of Jesus about marriage. In addition to 1 Corinthians 7:10f, we have Matthew 5:31–32 with its parallel at Luke 16:18, and Mark 10:2–10 with its parallel in Matthew 19:3–9.[3] In the last two texts, besides the words of Jesus about divorce, we also find a principle regarding marriage: "What therefore God has joined together, let no human being put asunder" (Mark 10:9).

The New Testament thus offers us two logia of Jesus, one about divorce and one about marriage, and exegetes have strongly emphasized the logion about divorce — perhaps giving rather too much support to the legalistic approach to marriage that leads the Pharisees to put Jesus to the text: "Is it lawful for a man to divorce his wife?" (Mk 10:2b). We must, however, give honor where honor is due: the exegetes have rightly underlined the decisive change of tonality that Jesus imposes on the debate when he raises it from the level of a legalistic interpretation of the right of repudiation granted by Moses to the fundamental principle of God's will for marriage. My impression, however, is that the exegetes have not dwelt much on this principle. Rather, they have turned their attention to the adaptations that this principle undergoes at the hands of Paul and the synoptic evangelists in view of their respective audiences. This is why innumerable hypotheses have been proposed about the interpretation of the so-called "Pauline privilege" or of the Matthean clause that stipulates that marriage is indissoluble "with the exception of *porneia*" — to mention only the two most famous questions. We may conclude that Jesus's words about divorce, which are objectively more numerous, have driven into the background his words about marriage, which are certainly more fundamental.

Without in the least denying the importance of a hermeneutic that pays attention to the way in which Jesus's words about divorce were applied in the praxis of the Christian communities, I choose here to concentrate on the matrimonial principle on which these words depend: "What God has joined together...."

What is it that God joins together in such a manner that no human being is permitted to separate it? This question would be better formulated as follows: *Who* are the persons whom God unites "in one flesh"? And we could then ask: *How, and by means of whom,* does God make "one flesh" out of the two? We could then anticipate in the form of a question the issue that we shall study: Is it possible to conceive of the indissoluble link of the *una caro* independently of the link to Christ? Is it possible for a Christian to define marriage as a relationship of love that prescinds from the love of Christ? These questions do not at all intend to cast doubt on the Catholic doctrine of marriage. All they wish to do is to avoid a situation in which one would appeal to this doctrine to defend a natural and cultural institution, namely, the institution of marriage, even where it actually contradicts the love of Christ.

The Christian Quality of Conjugal Love

In the Markan redaction of the debate about divorce, the matrimonial principle that we wish to study forms the climax of the entire passage. Let us present its salient aspects:

> And Pharisees came up and in order to test him asked, "Is it lawful for a man to divorce his wife?" He answered them, "What did Moses command you?" They said, "Moses allowed a man *to write a certificate of divorce and to put her away.*" But Jesus said to them, "For your hardness of heart he wrote you this commandment. But from the beginning of creation, *'God made them male and female'* (Gen. 1:27). *'For this reason a man shall leave his father and mother and the two shall become one flesh'* (Gen. 2:24). So they are no longer two but one flesh. What therefore God has joined together, let no human being put asunder."

The affirmation "What God has joined together..." completes the *restitutio principii* that Jesus announces in the course of the debate, when he uses the adversative *but:* "But from the beginning of creation...." The Pharisees with whom he is debating interpret the norm of Moses about repudiation

as a legitimate right ("Is it lawful...?") instead of an indulgent conces-
sion ("For your hardness of heart..."). And this shows how far they have
strayed from the original will of God.

However, the real strategic move by Jesus consists in detaching the attention from divorce and turning it toward marriage: for the two quotations
from scripture that he combines (Gen. 1:27 and 2:24) speak of marriage, not
of divorce. These two texts envisage marriage as the result of a transformation that leads male and female to become husband and wife in "one flesh."
The meaning of this phrase is not restricted to carnal union. It refers to "the
unity of two bodily beings in all the dimensions that the union of husband
and wife can assume."[4] The "one flesh" designates not only the physical
union of the couple, but the personal communion of the two. I should like
to emphasize that the decisive point that allows us to grasp the specifically
Christian quality of marriage is the relationship between the expression *una
caro* and the principle (which usually remains in the background in the
exposition of this text) "what God has joined together...."

The *communio personarum,* which finds emblematic expression in sexual
union, is attributed to the creative work of God, since he is the subject who
joins husband and wife in one flesh. This is confirmed by the exegetes, who
affirm that the expression "what God has joined together" "underlines the
fact that marriage is not merely an arbitrary human union, but the outcome
of divine action."[5]

The best interpretation of God's uniting action must recognize the christological nature of this action. When "from the beginning of creation, '*God
made them male and female,*'" his hands were already imprinting upon them
the form of Christ, since husband and wife — like everything else — were
created "through him" (that is, through Jesus). And since that which was
created "through him" also exists "for him" (Col. 1:16), husband and wife
are not united by God independently of Christ. What God joins together
is joined together through Christ and in Christ. Husband and wife become
una caro in Christ, just as two branches unite in the trunk of the vine onto
which they are both grafted (see also John 15:1–6).

We find the development of this thesis in Ephesians 5:31–32, where the
divine project of *una caro* is explicitly related to Christ: "'For this reason a
man *shall leave* his father and mother and *be joined* to his wife, and the two
shall become one flesh.' This mystery is a profound one, and I am saying
that it refers to Christ and the church." It is significant that three verbs in
the future tense are used to tell the story of the love between a man and
a woman. We seem to hear an echo in this passage of something that the
experience of innumerable couples teaches us, that is, that the communion
of love is not present all at once: rather, it is offered to the couple as a
future promise. Even more important is the use of a verb in the passive
mood (unlike the other two verbs) when the text says that the man "will
be joined" to his wife.[6] This seems to hint that their union will not be the

result of an endeavor on the part of the couple themselves, but will be a gift that is offered to the couple. We could also translate: "He *will be united* to his wife."

The meaning becomes clearer if we follow the Pauline theology and interpret human love in the light of the mystery of love that links Christ to the church. The church can be understood as the result of the universal loving attraction that Christ exercises from his cross: "I, when I am lifted up from the earth, will draw everyone to myself" (John 12:32). This attraction, reaching to the uttermost ends of the world, permeates every existential situation, including that of the love between a man and a woman. Accordingly, we may say that the union offered to a man and a woman is Christ's gift to them: through the Spirit, he unites them by drawing them to himself. Developing the interpretation shown in the texts themselves, we could understand the action of becoming "one flesh" not as the outcome of the immediate union between husband and wife, but as a consequence of that union which Christ accomplishes with each of them. The "one flesh" of the two is accomplished in the body of Christ. The body of Christ is the place wherein husband and wife become one.

Christian marriage is not the loving bond that a man and a woman establish by themselves, but the loving bond between a man and a woman generated by the love of Christ. What God indissolubly joins, so that "they are no longer two but one flesh" (Mark 10:8), is not simply a man and a woman, nor even a man and a woman who are in love, but a man and a woman who love one another in Christ. And this means that despite all the reality of their enduring weakness and sinfulness, they make the manner of Christ's love the inspiring criterion and the vital strength of their loving relationship.

What is the specific quality of Christ's love? The richest synthesis of this love is perhaps to be found in his own words: "Greater love has no one than this, to lay down one's life for one's friends" (John 15:13). Christian love is the gratuitous gift of one's life in order that others may have life to the full.

The gratuitous gift of Christ's life for the life of humankind is so superabundant that it may almost seem excessive. It can be summed up in the Johannine phrase "to the end": "When Jesus knew that his hour had come to depart out of this world to the Father, having loved his own who were in the world, he loved them to the end" (John 13:1). Like a diamond that reflects the light from its various facets, this love "to the end" shows us the entire spectrum of the colors of which it is composed. If we restrict ourselves to four essential aspects that are the most relevant to the essence of conjugal love, we may say that the love of Christ is *total,* to the point of the gift of his person, of his body and blood; *faithful,* to the point of offering himself even to the friend who betrays him; *indissoluble,* going even to the uttermost point of dying; and *fruitful,* leading to the effusion of the Spirit of life.

The Discernment of Conjugal Love

In order that the love of Christ — total, faithful, indissoluble, and fruitful — may permeate the story of the love of a man and a woman, it is necessary (as I noted above) that each of the two be like a branch grafted onto the vine, inserted into Christ. When may we say that a man and a woman are in Christ, so that they attain that communion for which they would yearn in vain without him — since they were created in him and for him? To answer this question, we must look at the criteria that permit an evaluation of the married couple's Christian faith. It would, of course, be arrogant to claim to measure the state of grace of a husband and wife; but we cannot rely (more or less ingenuously) on criteria that are quantifiable but are insufficiently in accordance with the gospel. Examples of such criteria are the socio-demographic indicators of the stability of a marriage, or the rules of canon law, which may in fact be too rigid to permit us to discern a reality of *faith* such as that which is implied when we speak of a *Christian* marriage.

But let us not pause to criticize in detail extrinsic or insufficient criteria; here, all I wish to do is to recall one fundamental point about discernment in keeping with the gospel. This is the dangerous distance between verbal affirmations and existential praxis: "Not every one who says to me, 'Lord, Lord!' shall enter the kingdom of heaven, but the one who does the will of my Father who is in heaven" (Matt. 7:21). If the love of Christ is to circulate like lymph in the life of a couple, it is not enough for them to declare that they believe. They must become intimate friends of Christ. A relationship of love does not live on the basis of proclamations, no matter how impassioned these may be, but on the basis of living contact, and the same applies *a fortiori* to our relationship with Christ. The genuineness of our insertion into Christ the vine is attested by our life, rather than by our thoughts or our affirmations. Accordingly, in order to evaluate its quality, one must look more at the quality of love in our life than at a formal correctness, whether civil or ecclesiastical.

One obvious reply would be that ecclesial praxis requires a normative application of the gospel principle with regard to the Christian quality of conjugal love. This is correct, but one cannot claim that a normative application possesses the same absoluteness as the principle laid down by Jesus. "The primary interest of the New Testament is not the elaboration of ordinances for the legal regulation of marriage.... This is exactly the line taken in Jesus' words about marriage. He does not proclaim a new law about marriage, but emphasizes the will of God with regard to marriage itself."[7]

The *manner* in which Christ loves is the principle that transcends matrimonial law — not only civil legislation, but church law too.[8] This can be clearly seen from the fact that when Jesus is put to the test with regard to the liceity of the permission given by the law of Moses to repudiate one's wife, he confounds the Pharisees by raising the question of indissolubility from the normative level to the foundational level: "But from the beginning it was not so" (Matt. 19:8). The meta-legal nature of this principle leaves undefined the normative regulations with regard to marriage, which are entrusted to the mediation of the Christian community — as we see, for example, in the famous Matthean exception that permits repudiation "in a case of *porneia*" (Matt. 19:9), and in Paul's prescription about the possibility of dissolving a marriage where only one partner is a believer (1 Cor. 7:12–16). On the other hand, the very meta-legal nature of the principle functions as a critical authority vis-à-vis every definition of matrimonial law.

The *manner* in which Christ loves is the key to understanding his logion: "What therefore God has joined together, let no human being put asunder." It judges not only the conjugal instability that ends in divorce, but also a matrimonial stability that is not the expression of the partners' reciprocal gift of life.

If the Christian quality of love were to become the criterion for evaluating the life of a couple, we might see the truth of the principle that Jesus repeatedly enunciated: "Many that are first will be last, and the last first" (Matt. 19:30). In the case of married couples, we might translate this as follows: "Many of the (so-called) regular marriages will turn out to be irregular, and the (so-called) irregular marriages will turn out to be regular." This hypothesis may sound far too provocative. But it is not my intention to cast suspicion on the usefulness of the church's canon law when we must decide whether a marriage that has been celebrated in church is to be accepted as valid or invalid. All I wish to do is to remove the possibility of judging these questions on the basis of a simple appeal to Jesus's words about "what God has joined together" *prescinding* from the Christian quality of a couple's love, that is, independently of the question of whether the husband and wife are sufficiently united to Christ to be able to life *as* he loved, each giving his or her own life for the life of the other partner.

Blessing and Sacrament of Love

In order for this principle of the Christian quality of love to be accepted, a deeper reflection is needed on the questions posed some years ago by the then prefect of the Congregation for the Doctrine of the Faith, Cardinal Ratzinger, namely, "whether non-believing Christians — baptized persons who have never believed, or who no longer believe in God — can truly enter a sacramental marriage.... Faith belongs to the essence of the sacrament; we need to clarify the juridical question about what evidence of 'non-faith' leads to the conclusion that a sacrament does not take place."[9]

The prudence appropriate to studying the delicate question of the sacramental validity of marriage certainly requires great caution, in order that a "smoldering wick" of the personal faith of the partners may not be quenched. At the same time, however, this task requires the courage to recognize that although a couple was married in church, the candle of faith was never lit, or that it has since gone out, and that this prevents God from drawing the two of them to himself in Christ so that, loving each other as he has loved, they may become indissolubly "one flesh."

The recognition that not all conjugal relationships are in Christ (and hence indissolubly joined by God) does not mean devaluing them in such a way that they would be emptied of all goodness and legitimacy. Rather, it means accepting seriously the tension that runs through the whole of salvation history between the blessing that God wishes to bestow on the couple, as attested by one chapter of sacred scripture — "God saw all that he had made, and behold, it was very good" (Gen. 1:31) — and the sacramentality of the love of a couple who love *as* he loved, as this is recognized by another chapter of the sacred text: "This mystery is a profound one, and I am saying that it refers to Christ and the church" (Eph. 5:32).

— English translation by Brian McNeil

Notes

1. Zygmunt Bauman, *Liquid Love: On the Frailty of Human Bonds* (Cambridge: Polity Press and Oxford: Blackwell Publishing, 2003).

2. Xavier Lacroix, "Conjugalité et parentalité: Un lien entre deux liens," *INTAMS Review* 11, no. 1 (2005): 18–27.

3. For the exegetical analysis of these texts, see the excellent study by C. Marucci, *Parole di Gesù sul divorzio: Ricerche scritturistiche previe ad un ripensamento teologico, canonistico e pastorale della dottrina cattolica dell'indissolubilità del matrimonio* (Brescia: Morcelliana, 1982).

4. Maurice Gilbert, "Une seule chair," *Nouvelle Revue de Théologie* (1978): 68–89. This exact reference is on p. 78.

5. Heinrich Baltensweiler, *Il matrimonio nel Nuovo Testamento: Ricerche esegetiche su matrimonio, celibato e divorzio* (Brescia: Paideia, 1981).

6. The act of leaving his parents is expressed by a future active (*kataleipsei*), the conjugal union by a future passive (*proskollêthêsetai*), and the formation of the *una caro* by a future middle (*esontai*).

7. Baltensweiler, *Il matrimonio nel Nuovo Testamento*, 296.

8. With admirable lucidity, the theologian Joseph Ratzinger indicated as long ago as 1969 the meta-legal nature of the *logion* of Jesus: "Since Jesus goes back beyond the level of the law to the origin, his word itself may not be regarded immediately and without further ado as a law; it cannot be detached from the sphere of faith and discipleship, and it can be meaningful only in connection with the new situation that is opened up by Jesus and is received in faith" (Joseph Ratzinger, "Zur Theologie der Ehe," in *Theologie der Ehe*, ed. Gerhard Krems and Reinhard Mumm [Regensburg: Friedrich Pustet and Göttingen: Vandenhoeck & Ruprecht, 1969], 81–115). This exact reference is on pp. 83–84.

9. Joseph Ratzinger, "Introduzione," in *Sulla pastorale dei divorziati risposati: Documenti, commenti e studi*, ed. Congregazione per la Dottrina della Fede (Vatican City: Libreria Editrice Vaticana, 1998), 27–28.

26

The Truly Human Sexual Act and Complementarity

Proposing a Reconstruction

TODD A. SALZMAN AND MICHAEL G. LAWLER

Two important and related terms, "truly human" and "complementarity,"[1] have recently been introduced into the discussion of sexual morality in the Catholic tradition.[2] In this essay, we first present and critique the types of complementarity that the Magisterium finds in a truly human sexual act. We then suggest that heterosexual or homosexual orientation as part of a person's sexual constitution requires adding orientation complementarity as an intrinsic dimension of sexual anthropology. This addition yields the conclusion that holistic complementarity — an integrated orientation, personal, and biological complementarity — is a more adequate foundational principle to define a truly human sexual act.

Biological and Personal Complementarity

In *Considerations Regarding Proposals to Give Legal Recognition to Unions between Homosexual Persons* (CRP), the Congregation for the Doctrine of the Faith (CDF) has recently sought to clarify the meaning of truly human sexual acts. It first states that homosexual unions lack "the conjugal dimension which represents the human and ordered form of sexuality," and then articulates the principle that "sexual relations are human when and insofar as they express and promote the mutual assistance of the sexes in marriage and are open to the transmission of new life."[3] This is the standard unitive-procreative principle that, in the twentieth century, became the foundational principle for all Catholic sexual teaching. According to this principle, truly human sexual acts are acts within marriage that are simultaneously unitive of the spouses and open to procreation, and only such acts are judged to be "truly human."[4] CRP uses the term "sexual complementarity" in relation to this principle, which includes parenting or the education of children and, on this foundation, defends heterosexual marriage and condemns homosexual unions. In the next section we present (in Table 1) and critique several types of sexual complementarity reflected in the *CRP* statement to advance the understanding of both this concept and its implications for the "truly human" sexual act.

Biological Complementarity: Heterogenital and Reproductive

Biological complementarity is divided into what we label "heterogenital complementarity" and "reproductive complementarity." The CDF describes heterogenital complementarity this way: "Men and women are equal as persons and complementary as male and female. Sexuality is something that pertains to the physical-biological realm."[5] Heterogenital complementarity pertains to the biologically functioning male and female genitals used in reproductive sexual acts.

Heterogenital complementarity is the foundation for reproductive complementarity and "therefore, in the Creator's plan, sexual complementarity and fruitfulness belong to the very nature of marriage."[6] Heterogenital and reproductive complementarity, however, are to be carefully distinguished. While the Magisterium teaches that a couple must complement each other heterogenitally, it also teaches that it is not necessary that they biologically reproduce.[7] In light of this teaching, Paul VI's statement that "each and every marriage act must remain open to the transmission of life"[8] is *morally* ambiguous. We may ask how sexual acts between infertile couples are "open to the transmission of life?"

Biological Openness to the Transmission of Life

First, magisterial teaching, following Aquinas, distinguishes between reproductive acts that are essentially (*per se*) closed to reproduction and reproductive acts that are accidentally (*per accidens*) nonreproductive.[9] Heterosexual and homosexual nonreproductive sexual acts are those that are essentially closed to reproduction. Sterile and postmenopausal sexual acts are accidentally nonreproductive and belong to the categorization reproductive acts *per accidens*. Accidentally nonreproductive sexual acts are essentially of the same type as reproductive sexual acts and thus fulfill sexual complementarity, the unitive and procreative meanings of the sexual act. Are such sexual acts, however, essentially the same type of act?

Gareth Moore notes that whether or not two acts are of the same type depends on how we classify acts according to our interest. The interest here is reproduction. Knowing the biological facts of reproduction enables us to classify certain sexual acts as either reproductive or nonreproductive acts. If science is relevant in distinguishing between such acts, it would seem that it is equally relevant in distinguishing between definitely infertile and potentially

Table 1. Types of Sexual Complementarity in Magisterial Teaching

I. Biological Complementarity

Title	Definition
Heterogenital Complementarity	The physically functioning male and female sexual organs (penis and vagina).
Reproductive Complementarity	The physically functioning male and female reproductive organs used in sexual acts to biologically reproduce.

II. Personal Complementarity

Title	Definition
Communion Complementarity	The two-in-oneness within a heterogenital complementary marital relationship that is created and sustained by truly human sexual acts.
Affective Complementarity	The integrated psycho-affective, social, relational, and spiritual elements of the human person grounded in heterogenital complementarity.
Parental Complementarity	Heterogenitally complementary parents who fulfill the second dimension of reproductive complementarity, namely, the education of children.

fertile reproductive acts. As Moore notes, "vaginal intercourse which we know to be sterile is a different type of act from vaginal intercourse which, as far as we know, might result in conception."[10]

If potentially fertile reproductive acts and permanently or temporarily sterile non-reproductive acts are essentially of a different type in terms of the "openness to the transmission of life," then we must ask what distinguishes infertile heterosexual acts from homosexual acts. The answer seems to reside in heterogenital complementarity. That is, heterogenital complementarity, not reproductive complementarity, seems to serve as an essential categorization for potentially reproductive and sterile nonreproductive heterosexual acts. If that is the case, the Magisterium's claim that homosexual acts are intrinsically disordered because they are closed to the transmission of life can be challenged. From the point of view of reproduction, nonreproductive heterosexual acts *may* have more in common with homosexual acts in terms of personal complementarity than with infertile reproductive sexual acts in terms of reproductive complementarity.

Metaphorical Openness to the Transmission of Life

Second, rather than arguing biologically for an essential type categorization of reproductive acts that are open to the transmission of life, one can argue metaphorically for this openness. James Hanigan argues for this metaphorical openness in terms of an "iconic significance of one's sexuality," whereby "one's maleness or femaleness in all its embodied reality must be taken with full seriousness."[11] Male and female sexuality are created to be spousal in that they are ordered toward interpersonal union.[12] In their genital maleness and femaleness, infertile heterosexual couples represent this openness to the transmission of life to the community in the very reality of their relationship.

A question to be posed to Hanigan, however, is this: In what way is an infertile heterosexual couple's sexuality iconically significant in a way that a homosexual couple's sexuality is not? The most obvious answer is that a homosexual couple does not have the heterogenital complementarity necessary to reproduce. Aside from this, however, it is not clear that a homosexual couple's sexuality cannot be iconically significant.

David McCarthy offers a response to Hanigan's "iconic significance" argument. He argues theologically for a "nuptial hermeneutics of same-sex unions"[13] by thoroughly integrating homosexual orientation into a theology of the body. McCarthy provides a definition of homosexual orientation, which, aside from heterogenital complementarity, is consistent with the Magisterium's understanding of heterosexual orientation. "Gay men and lesbians are persons who encounter the other (and thus discover themselves) in relation to persons of the same sex. This same-sex orientation is a given of their coming to be, that is, *the nuptial meaning of human life emerges* for a gay man in relation to other men and a woman when face to face with other women."[14] In a steadfast interpersonal union, then, homosexual couples give their bodies to one another and are "theologically communicative," that is, they are witnesses to the community of God's "constancy and steadfast fidelity."[15] In their witness, homosexual and heterosexual couples have "iconic significance" in their sexuality through embodied interpersonal union. Heterogenital complementarity is not a determining factor. Rather, two genitally embodied persons, heterosexual or homosexual, in permanent interpersonal union, who reflect God's constant love and steadfast fidelity are the determining factor.[16]

To summarize: if "openness to the transmission of life" is interpreted biologically or in Hanigan's metaphorical sense, then heterogenital complementarity seems to be the essential difference that distinguishes heterosexual and homosexual sexual acts. If it is interpreted in McCarthy's metaphorical sense, integrating orientation complementarity into a nuptial hermeneutics, both homosexual and heterosexual couples can exhibit "iconic significance" in their embodied interpersonal unions and sexual acts, thus rendering both homosexual and heterosexual sexual acts potentially truly human.

Personal Complementarity: Communion, Affective, and Parental

The Congregation for the Doctrine of the Faith (CDF) also refers to sexuality on the "personal level — where nature and spirit are united." We name this *personal complementarity,* which can be divided into several subcategories.[17] First, there is *communion complementarity* in the marital relationship, "a communion of persons is realized involving the use of the sexual faculty."[18] The male and female genitals contribute to the realization of a communion of persons in marriage expressed in truly human sexual acts. Without heterogenital complementarity, communion complementarity is not possible, a point implied by the CDF's statement on the immorality of homosexual acts. They "close the sexual act to the gift of life. They do not proceed from a genuine affective and sexual complementarity."[19]

Second, there is *affective complementarity*[20] that is central to magisterial teaching because it intrinsically links biological and personal complementarity. The CDF does not clarify here what it means by affective complementarity. The Congregation for Catholic Education (CCE), however, teaches that "in the Christian anthropological perspective, affective-sex education must consider the totality of the person and insist therefore on the integration of the biological, psycho-affective, social, and spiritual elements."[21] Since affective-sex education seeks to integrate these elements, affective complementarity must similarly integrate these elements in a truly human sexual act. Magisterial teaching strictly divides the affective elements according to gender; only when they are brought together in marriage and sexual acts is the human couple complete.[22]

The important point to note in the Magisterium's explanation of affective complementarity is the following: given the Magisterium's teaching on the immorality of homosexual acts, it is clear it regards heterogenital complementarity as a *sine qua non* for personal complementarity in truly human sexual acts. Without heterogenital complementarity, the other elements of affective complementarity cannot be realized.

While affective complementarity integrates the biological and personal elements in a truly human sexual act, we believe the Magisterium's account relies primarily on heterogenital complementarity; entails an incomplete, distorted vision of gender where masculine and feminine elements are ontologically divided;[23] and neglects experiential dimensions of human sexuality.[24]

Third, the CDF refers to *parental complementarity*. It argues against same-sex unions based on the claim that, "as experience has shown, the absence of sexual complementarity in these unions creates obstacles in the normal development of children who would be placed in the care of such persons.... Allowing children to be adopted by persons living in such unions would actually mean doing violence to these children."[25] The CDF, however, provides no scientific evidence, here or elsewhere, to substantiate its claim that homosexual union is an obstacle to the normal development of children. There is, however, abundant evidence to the contrary.

While acknowledging that research on gay and lesbian parents is still evolving, especially with respect to gay fathers, Charlotte Patterson summarizes the evidence available from twenty years of studies:

> There is no evidence to suggest that lesbians and gay men are unfit to be parents or that psychosocial (including sexual) development among children of gay men or lesbians is compromised in any respect relative to that among offspring of heterosexual parents. *Not a single study* has found children of gay or lesbian parents to be disadvantaged in any significant respect relative to children of heterosexual parents.[26]

Though there is an intrinsic relationship between heterogenital and personal complementarity, for the Magisterium, male and female genitals and their "natural" functioning are the point of departure for personal complementarity in truly human sexual acts. An important question for the theological understanding of truly human sexual acts is whether or not there can be such acts without heterogenital complementarity. We approach this question via what we call *sexual orientation complementarity*.

Sexual Orientation Complementarity and the Truly Human Sexual Act: A Reconstructed Complementarity

To be truly human, a sexual act must be integrated with the whole self. The CCE asserts that sexuality "is a fundamental component of personality, one of its modes of being, of manifestation, of communicating with others, of feeling, of expressing, and of living human love. Therefore it is an integral part of the development of the personality and of its educative process."[27] The CCE goes on to cite the CDF's *Persona humana* and its teaching that it is "from sex that the human person receives the characteristics which, on the biological, psychological, and spiritual levels, make that person a man or a woman, and thereby *largely condition his or her progress toward maturity and insertion into society.*"[28] If this is true, and we believe that it is true, then the question naturally arises about the nature and meaning of what is called sexual orientation. To define "truly human" sexual acts, we must first understand sexual orientation.

The origins and meaning of "sexual orientation" are complex. Sexual orientation is produced by a mix of genetic, hormonal, psychological, and social "loading."[29] We define sexual orientation as a "psychosexual attraction (erotic, emotional, and affective) toward particular individual *persons*"[30] of the opposite or same sex. Sexual orientation is an intrinsic dimension of the sexual human person and therefore is an intrinsic dimension of sexual anthropology. Homosexual men or women are attracted to people of the same sex psycho-affectively, socially, relationally, spiritually, and sexually; heterosexual men or women are attracted to people of the opposite sex psycho-affectively, socially, relationally, spiritually, and sexually. *Orientation complementarity* is an intrinsic dimension of a truly human sexual act in that when this attraction is expressed in sexual acts, such acts must respect and reflect one's sexual orientation, be it homosexual or heterosexual, and do so in a just and loving manner.[31]

The Magisterium teaches that a homosexual orientation "is objectively disordered," and homosexual acts that flow from the orientation are intrinsically disordered.[32] While the Magisterium consistently condemns homosexual acts on the grounds that they violate heterogenital and reproductive complementarity, it does not explain why they also violate personal complementarity other than to assert that homosexual acts "do not proceed from a genuine affective and sexual complementarity."[33] This statement, however, begs the question whether or not such acts can ever be truly human on the level of personal complementarity. Though the Magisterium has not confronted this question, monogamous, loving, committed, homosexual couples have confronted it experientially and testify that they do experience personal complementarity in and through their homosexual acts, a claim amply supported by scientific research.[34]

With experiential accounts backed by scientific evidence, we propose sexual orientation complementarity as an essential dimension of the sexual human person and a complement to the Magisterium's types of complementarities. As a complement, sexual orientation complementarity invites us to reconstruct the Magisterium's definitions of affective complementarity and genital complementarity. First, orientation complementarity cannot espouse the Magisterium's heterogenital point of departure for affective complementarity. As we have seen, for the Magisterium the point of departure for affective complementarity is an ontological unity between the biological (heterogenital) and the personal that can find completion only in heterosexual marriage and conjugal acts. The definition of affective complementarity is the "unity of the two" where the masculine and feminine affective elements (biological, psycho-affective, social, and spiritual), which for forming a couple are incomplete,[35] find completion in heterogenitally complementary sexual acts. In our model, the point of departure for affective complementarity is not the genital but the sexual human person of either a homosexual or heterosexual orientation. The definition of affective complementarity in truly human sexual acts is the "unity of the two" where the affective elements (biological, psycho-affective, social, and spiritual) complement one another.[36] In the case of persons with a homosexual orientation, these acts will be genitally male-male or female-female; in the case of persons with a heterosexual orientation, these acts will be genitally male-female.[37]

Orientation complementarity also requires us to redefine heterogenital complementarity in relation to affective complementarity. Severing the male-female ontological complementarity of the affective elements includes the genitals. No longer is heterogenital complementarity the foundational, *sine qua non* for personal complementarity. Genital complementarity, indeed, can be determined only in light of orientation complementarity. In a truly human sexual act, the genitals are at the service of personal complementarity, and they may be male-male, female-female, or male-female, depending on whether the individual person's orientation is homosexual or heterosexual. Our principle of sexual orientation complementarity embraces the entirety and complexity of the human person, and reconstructs genital complementarity to be in dialogue with, and totally at the service of, personal and orientation complementarity. The genitals may be said to be complementary when they are used in a truly human sexual act that realizes the psycho-affective, social, and spiritual elements of affective complementarity.

As we have noted, the relationship between biological and personal complementarity is both/and. Truly human sexual acts require human genitals. In couples of heterosexual and homosexual orientation, personal complementarity is embodied, manifested, nurtured, and strengthened through the use of their genitals. Orientation complementarity integrates genital complementarity into personal complementarity.

From the foregoing, we suggest that the needed complementarity for a truly human sexual act is *holistic complementarity* (see Table 2) — an integrated orientation, personal, and genital complementarity — that unites people bodily, affectively, spiritually, and personally in light of a person's sexual orientation. Though they cannot exhibit heterogenital complementarity, homosexual individuals can exhibit holistic complementarity. When we shift the foundation for a truly human sexual act from heterogenital complementarity to holistic complementarity, the principle for what constitutes a truly human sexual act can be formulated as follows.

Table 2. Holistic Complementarity

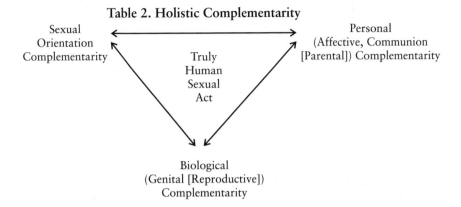

A truly human sexual act is in accord with a person's sexual orientation that facilitates a deeper appreciation, integration, and sharing of a person's embodied self with another embodied self. This personalist interpretation of complementarity allows us to expand the definition of a "truly human" sexual act to apply to both heterosexuals and homosexuals.

Notes

1. For a fuller exposition of these two terms, see Todd A. Salzman and Michael G. Lawler, "New Natural Law Theory and Foundational Sexual Ethical Principles: A Critique and a Proposal," *Heythrop Journal* 47, no. 2 (2006): 182–205; and idem, "*Quaestio Disputata*. Catholic Sexual Ethics: Complementarity and the Truly Human," *Theological Studies* 67, no. 3 (2006): 625–52.

2. Vatican II's *Gaudium et spes* declared that the sexual intercourse in and through which spouses symbolize their mutual gift to one another is to be *humano modo*, "in a manner which is [*truly*] *human*." Unfortunately, the Council offered no definition of what it meant by "truly human" and, when the phrase was introduced in the revised Code of Canon Law in 1983, it was again added without definition. The term "complementarity" was introduced in Pope John Paul II's *Familiaris consortio* (hereafter, referred to as *FC*) (no. 19, the pope speaks of a "natural complementarity") and is posited as a foundational sexual ethical principle in numerous subsequent magisterial documents, including the Congregation for the Doctrine of the Faith's "Considerations Regarding Proposals to Give Legal Recognition to Unions between Homosexual Persons," *Acta Apostolicae Sedis* 96 (2004): 41–49. Hereafter, *CRP*, this document attempts to clarify the meaning of truly human sexual acts in terms of sexual complementarity (nos. 3, 7).

3. CDF, *CRP*, no. 7.

4. Ibid.; John Paul II, *FC*, no. 11.

5. CDF, *CRP*, no. 3.

6. Ibid.

7. Pope Paul VI, *Humanae vitae*, no. 10; see also Pope Pius XII, "The Apostolate of the Midwife," in *The Major Addresses of Pope Pius XII*, vol. 1, *Selected*

Addresses, ed. Vincent A. Yzermans (St. Paul, Minn.: North Central Publishing, 1961), 169.

8. Paul VI, *Humanae vitae,* no. 11.

9. Aquinas, *Summa contra gentiles* 3, chapter 122.

10. Gareth Moore, *The Body in Context: Sex and Catholicism,* Contemporary Christian Insights (New York: Continuum, 2001), 162.

11. James P. Hanigan, "Unitive and Procreative Meaning: The Inseparable Link," in *Sexual Diversity and Catholicism: Toward the Development of Moral Theology,* ed. Patricia Beattie Jung with Joseph Andrew Coray (Collegeville, Minn.: Liturgical Press, 2001), 33.

12. Ibid., 35. Hanigan notes that male sexuality is "paternal in its ordination to the maternal, to the female, and to the raising up of new life." Similarly, female sexuality is "maternal in its ordination to the paternal, the male, and to the birthing and nurturing of new life."

13. David Matzko McCarthy, "The Relationship of Bodies: A Nuptial Hermeneutics of Same-sex Unions," in *Theology and Sexuality: Classic and Contemporary Readings,* ed. Eugene F. Rogers, Jr. (Oxford: Blackwell, 2002), 212.

14. Ibid., 212–13; emphasis added.

15. Ibid., 213.

16. We will address "orientation complementarity" in more detail below.

17. Due to the lack of space, we do not explore parental complementarity in this shortened version of the essay, though we will treat it in the expanded version.

18. CDF, *CRP,* no. 3.

19. Ibid., no. 4; *Catechism of the Catholic Church* (Vatican City: Libreria Editrice Vaticana, 2000; Washington, D.C.: United States Catholic Conference of Bishops), no. 2357.

20. This is also referred to as "natural" complementarity, in Paul II, "Letter to Women," *Origins* 25 (1995), no. 7, or "ontological" complementarity, in John Paul II, *Familiaris consortio,* in *The Post-Synodal Apostolic Exhortations of John Paul II,* ed. J. Michael Miller (Huntington, Ind.: Our Sunday Visitor, 1998), no. 19.

21. Congregation for Catholic Education (hereafter CCE), *Educational Guidance in Human Love: Outlines for Sex Education* (hereafter *EGHL*) (Rome: Typis Polyglottis Vaticanis, 1983), no. 35.

22. John Paul II, "Letter to Women," no. 7; idem, *FC,* no. 19.

23. See Moore, *Body in Context,* 121–27; Cristina L. H. Traina, "Papal Ideals, Marital Realities: One View from the Ground," in *Sexual Diversity and Catholicism,* ed. Patricia Beattie Jung and Joseph Andrew Coray (Collegeville, Minn.: Michael Glazier Books, 2001), 280–82; and Elaine L. Graham, *Making the Difference: Gender, Personhood, and Theology* (Minneapolis: Fortress Press, 1996).

24. Traina, "Papal Ideals, Marital Realities," 282.

25. CDF, *CRP,* no. 7.

26. Charlotte J. Patterson, "Lesbian and Gay Parenting" (APA, 1995), para. D; *www.apa.org/pi/parent.html* (accessed May 20, 2006). Emphasis added; see also Marybeth J. Mattingly and Robert N. Bozick, "Children Raised by Same-Sex Couples: Much Ado about Nothing," paper given at the Conference of the Southern Sociological Society, 2001; Joan Laird, "Lesbian and Gay Families," in *Normal Family Processes,* ed. Froma Walsh (New York: Guilford, 1993), 316–17; and Ann Sullivan, ed., *Issues in Gay and Lesbian Adoption: Proceedings of the Fourth Annual*

Peirce-Warwick Adoption Symposium (Washington, D.C.: Child Welfare League of America, 1995), 24–28.

27. CCE, *EGHL*, no. 4.

28. CDF, *Persona humana: Declaration on Certain Questions concerning Sexual Ethics*, no. 1; *www.vatican.va/roman_curia/congregations/cfaith/documents/rc_con _cfaith_doc_19751229_persona-humana_en.html* (accessed May 24, 2006). Emphasis added.

29. This terminology has been borrowed from John E. Perito, *Contemporary Catholic Sexuality: What Is Taught and What Is Practiced* (New York: Crossroad, 2003), 96.

30. Robert Nugent, "Sexual Orientation in Vatican Thinking," in *The Vatican and Homosexuality: Reactions to the "Letter to the Bishops of the Catholic Church on the Pastoral Care of Homosexual Persons,"* ed. Jeannine Gramick and Pat Furey (New York: Crossroad, 1988), 55.

31. See Todd A. Salzman and Michael G. Lawler, "New Natural Law Theory and Foundational Sexual Ethical Principles: A Critique and a Proposal," *Heythrop Journal* 47, no. 2 (2006): 199–200; and Margaret Farley, *Just Love: A Framework for Christian Sexual Ethics* (New York: Continuum International, 2006), 200–206.

32. CDF, "Vatican List of Catechism Changes," *Origins* 27 (1997): 257.

33. Ibid.

34. Lawrence A. Kurdek, "Differences between Partners from Heterosexual, Gay, and Lesbian Cohabiting Couples," *Journal of Marriage and Family* 68 (May 2006): 509–28; idem, "What Do We Know about Gay and Lesbian Couples?" *Current Directions in Psychological Science* 14 (2005): 251–54; idem, "Lesbian and Gay Couples," in *Lesbian, Gay and Bisexual Identities over the Lifespan,* ed. Anthony R. D'Augelli and Charlotte J. Patterson (New York: Oxford University Press, 1995), 243–61; idem, "Are Gay and Lesbian Cohabiting Couples *Really* Different from Heterosexual Married Couples?" *Journal of Marriage and Family* 66 (2004): 880–900; Ritch C. Savin-Williams and Kristin G. Esterberg, "Lesbian, Gay, and Bisexual Families," in *Handbook of Family Diversity,* ed. David H. Demo, Katherine R. Allen, and Mark A. Fine (New York: Oxford University Press, 2000), 207–12; and Philip Blumstein and Pepper Schwartz, *American Couples: Money, Work, Sex* (New York: Morrow, 1983).

35. Edward Collins Vacek, "Feminism and the Vatican," *Theological Studies* 66 (2005): 173–74, referring to John Paul II, "Authentic Concept of Conjugal Love," *Origins* 28 (1999): 655.

36. Though it is beyond the scope of this essay, as in the Magisterium's model, *how* these elements complement one another in a "truly human sexual act," heterosexual or homosexual, needs to be more fully developed.

37. While we recognize the reality of bisexual persons, space does not allow us to address this orientation in detail.

27

The Use of Sociological Studies to Confirm or Critique Roman Catholic Sexual Ethics

MICHAEL J. HARTWIG

In 1992, Pope John Paul II apologized for the way that Galileo had been treated by the Roman Catholic Church in the seventeenth century. Quoting Augustine, he stated that if there seems to be a contradiction between scripture and the discoveries of "clear and certain reasoning," the interpreter of scripture "does not understand it correctly."[1] This approach to the relationship between reason and scripture is grounded in the long history of a *catholic* approach to Christian authority. From the missionary work of St. Paul and his dispute with Peter and James (where Paul rejects a sectarian approach to moral norms) to early Christological councils, particularly the Council of Chalcedon in 451 (where Jesus is said to be fully human and fully divine), human nature and human reason have been considered integral to the authority of Christian beliefs and teaching.

Galileo utilized new scientific methods and instruments to substantiate his claims. Pope John Paul II suggested that church officials in the seventeenth century were unable to or unwilling to "all at once overcome habits of thought and to devise a way of teaching" about the profound changes in the worldview implied in the discoveries of Copernicus and Galileo.[2]

In contrast, official Roman Catholic statements about a number of sexual moral issues today reinforce claims by appealing to the findings of human sciences. This has been particularly evident in reference to claims about the immorality of gay and lesbian relationships and gay and lesbian parenting. The official magisterial statements are intended to refute cultural trends that see little difference between the moral quality of gay and lesbian relationships and those of heterosexuals. To the extent that the official claims purport to be grounded in natural moral law and confirmed by human sciences, they are considered relevant for all civil communities and cultures. The backing of the natural sciences adds legitimacy to the claims and universalizes them. An example of this use of the sciences includes the following statement from the *Letter to the Bishops of the Catholic Church on the Pastoral Care of Homosexual Persons*: "Naturally, an exhaustive treatment of this complex issue cannot be attempted here, but we will focus our reflection within the distinctive context of the Catholic moral perspective. It is a perspective which finds support in the more secure findings of the natural sciences, which have their own legitimate and proper methodology and field of inquiry."[3]

I propose to ask what kind of evidence exists to confirm or critique these claims. More specifically, what would constitute the kind of clear and certain reason that theologians in the seventeenth century should have embraced in the Galileo case and that church officials today are at risk of missing about the psychological health of gay and lesbian relationships, about their contribution to the common good, and about the goods, graces, and virtues they realize in their relationships and in the parenting of their children? What contemporary instruments invite us to consider a new way of thinking about the universe of human sexuality, covenantal marriage, and parenting? What are the telescopes of the twenty-first century that allow us to critique habits of thinking about what counts as graceful sexuality?

Official Roman Catholic arguments about homosexuality take three forms: social justice arguments (concern about the good of society), deontological arguments (concern about moral purposefulness of sexual acts), and virtue arguments (concern about character and the achievement of human excellence). While the human sciences can address all three types of arguments, the virtue arguments may be the most interesting to consider in the light of psychological and sociological studies. In the 1986 *Letter,* for example, the connection is made between homosexual activity and unhappiness. "As in every moral disorder, homosexual activity prevents one's own fulfillment and happiness by acting contrary to the creative wisdom of God. The Church, in rejecting erroneous opinions regarding homosexuality, does not limit but rather defends personal freedom and dignity realistically and authentically understood."[4] To the extent that this and other statements are framed in terms of happiness, love, personal fulfillment, and the human development of children, it is fitting to explore what evidence exists for confirming or critiquing virtue arguments.

There is growing interest in addressing sexual moral issues from the perspective of virtue theory. James F. Keenan's work in this area is foundational.[5] Eugene F. Rogers has also underscored the promising convergence of scriptural and magisterial teachings on sexual ethics with virtue language.[6] Rogers, for example, argues that Aquinas's commentary on Romans 1 seeks to underscore a harmony between natural moral law, scripture, and reason.[7] It is not surprising that Aquinas would see Romans as a place where this harmony is reinforced. In Romans, Paul lays out his vision for understanding that moral law is not arbitrary or sectarian but integral to the created order and thus knowable through right reason (Rom. 1:19–21).

There are several types of instruments used by psychologists and sociologists that are illuminating for considering the relationship between personal or relational health and certain behaviors. These include:

- Personality inventories
- Instruments that measure family health and function
- Child development instruments
- Statistical and qualitative sociological studies.

It is important to note that studies of gay men and lesbians, gay and lesbian relationships, and gay and lesbian parenting do not show that *all* gay men and lesbians are psychologically healthy or that *all* gay and lesbian families are high functioning, or that *all* children raised by gay or lesbian parents are free of psychological or developmental problems. Heterosexuals test positive for psychological problems, family problems, parenting problems, and behavior we typically regard as immoral or vicious in sexuality such as sexual infidelity, promiscuity, objectification of others, and lack of age-appropriate psycho-sexual integration. However, no one is arguing that heterosexuality is intrinsically disordered and therefore has no capacity to ground the achievement of healthy personal integration, enduring and graceful relationships, or assurance of authentic human development of children. All the studies of gay men and lesbians must show for the claims of official magisterial statements to be in question is that some gay men and lesbians, in and through their sexuality, achieve healthy personal integration, sustain high functioning families, and foster healthy and authentically human development in their children.

The two most commonly used instruments for studying psychological health are the Minnesota Multiphasic Personality Inventory-2[8] and the Sixteen Personality Factor (16PF) instrument.[9] The MMPI-2 seeks to identify underlying clinical problems in individuals. A list of these include: depression, hysteria, psychopathic deviation, masculinity/femininity (gender confusion), paranoia, psychasthenia, schizophrenia, hypomania, social introversion, demoralization, somatic complaints, low positive emotions, cynicism, antisocial behavior, ideas of persecution, dysfunctional negative emotions, aberrant experiences, hypomanic activation, familial discord, authority problems, social alienation, lack of ego-mastery, amorality, social avoidance, self-deprecation, explosive behavior, and misanthropic beliefs. The MMPI-2 is helpful in determining whether an individual possesses certain pathologies. It is one of the most commonly used tests to determine if a person or group of people manifest any pattern of psychological pathology or maladjustment.

The 16PF instrument, however, may be more interesting for measuring a range of healthy psychological indicators. The 16PF measures personality dimensions between two poles. These categories include: warmth (reserved vs. warm), reasoning (concrete vs. abstract), emotional stability (reactive vs. emotionally stable), dominance (deferential vs. dominant), liveliness (serious vs. lively), rule-consciousness (expedient vs. rule-conscious), social boldness (shy vs. socially bold), sensitivity (utilitarian vs. sensitive), vigilance (trusting vs. vigilant), abstractedness (grounded vs. abstracted), privateness (forthright vs. private), apprehension (self-assured vs. apprehensive), openness to change (traditional vs. open to change), self-reliance (group-oriented vs. self-reliant), perfectionism (tolerates disorder vs. perfectionistic), and tension (relaxed vs. tense).

As in virtue theory, health indicators in the 16PF consist in a mean between two extremes. The 16PF instrument measures a person's profile along a continuum, comparing and contrasting it with a normal range. For example in the first category, the instrument measures warmth and reserve; in the second category, abstract and concrete reasoning. In the category associated with self-reliance, the instrument measures self-reliance in relationship to group orientation. In the category associated with perfectionism, it measures perfectionistic tendencies with a toleration of disorder. The range of healthy or average responses involves a balance of the so-called "left meaning" and the "right meaning," or the extreme poles. The 16PF also measures such criteria as: self-esteem, emotional adjustment, social adjustment, emotional expressivity, emotional sensitivity, emotional control, social expressivity, social sensitivity, social control, empathy, leadership potential, creative potential, creative achievement, and dyadic adjustment.

Traditionally, interpretations of Romans 1 suggest that sexually active homosexuals are sinning and that this will be obvious by a pattern of vicious behavior in those who engage in same-gender sexual intimacy. Similarly, official statements of the Congregation for the Doctrine of the Faith, Pontifical Commission for the Family, and national episcopal conferences suggest that sexually active homosexuals are engaged in nothing more than self-indulgent behavior.[10] But there is no evidence from multiple studies conducted in the 1970s and 1980s that detects any pattern of vice or pathology in gay people as a group.[11] As a group, gay men and lesbians are indistinguishable from heterosexuals in such areas as warmth, emotional stability, right balance of dominance and deference, sensitivity, and right balance of self-reliance and group orientation. There have been few recent controlled psychological studies of gay men and lesbians because the evidence from the studies in the 1970s and 1980s was so conclusive.

Although the idea of measuring virtue with an instrument seems offensive to the subtle and personally unique ways that virtues are lived out in an individual's life, there are some interesting points of convergence between Paul's list of vices in Romans 1 and categories in the MMPI-2 and 16PF instruments. Paul refers to malice, strife, deceit, and craftiness, while the MMPI-2 refers to antisocial behavior, social alienation, and misanthropic beliefs. Paul refers to heartlessness, ruthlessness, haughtiness, and pride. The

16PF refers to lack of warmth, excess of dominance, lack of sensitivity, and extreme self-reliance.

One of the most common instruments for studying family health and function is the Family Assessment Device.[12] It measures overall health and functioning of families in the following six categories: problem solving, communication, affective involvement, affective responsiveness, roles, and behavior control. Studies continue to be conducted comparing and contrasting gay and lesbian families with heterosexual families with no evidence to date that there is any group deviation from good to high levels of functioning and health in gay and lesbian families.[13]

For measuring normal and healthy child development, a number of instruments exist. One of the more common ones used is the Child Behavior Checklist.[14] It looks for evidence of emotional disturbances, personality problems, psychosomatic disorders, self-destructive behavior, self-injurious behavior, speech and language pathology, sexuality issues (such as gender identity confusion), sleep disorders, eating disorders, disobedience, suicidal thoughts or attempts, physical problems, and substance abuse. Although it seems counterintuitive to centuries of Western heterosexual parenting habits, children who are raised by two gay fathers or two lesbian mothers show no deviation from the normal child development scales/studies so far.[15] There is no evidence of psychological disorders, gender confusion, or even deviation from the statistical norms for sexual orientation. It is interesting to note that the most prominent group in the United States that opposes gay and lesbian marriage and parenting can only cite studies of heterosexual parenting to critique gay and lesbian parenting. Their in-house director of social research, Glenn T. Stanton, co-authored a book with Bill Maier, a child and family psychologist.[16] The evidence they present are studies of heterosexual parenting that include absent fathers, absent mothers, and stepparents. The problems they cite with absent fathers/mothers in heterosexual families do not show up in studies of actual gay and lesbian parenting.

If gay men and lesbians, as a group, do not demonstrate any statistical propensity for vicious or pathological behavior, it might still be possible for the church to argue that gay men and lesbians in sexually active relationships may not be able to achieve or realize the graces, goods, excellences, or virtues associated with authentic human sexual love. For example, the 1986 *Letter* says that sex between two gay men or two lesbians is essentially selfish, self-indulgent.[17] The 2003 letter *Considerations Regarding Proposals to Give Legal Recognition to Unions between Homosexual Persons*[18] says there is no genuine affective or sexual complementarity in gay or lesbian relationships. Sociological studies, particularly qualitative ones, may be more helpful in critiquing these claims.

For example, more than seven thousand gay and lesbian couples were married in the Commonwealth of Massachusetts between May 2004 and June 2006. Many profiles of these couples have been presented in the media.

Many have been in long-term relationships of ten, fifteen, and twenty plus years. Published narratives of their relationships underscore the commitment, mutuality, unconditional love, and personal growth that have been part of these relationships. This contrasts with what we would expect if these relationships were nothing more than self-indulgent or included no affective complementarity. Do reasonable people reasoning reasonably believe that a twenty-year relationship between two men or between two women is built on mere sexual self-indulgence?

Between 40 and 60 percent of all gay men and lesbians are in steady relationships.[19] This contrasts with the idea that gay men and lesbians are simply sexually promiscuous. In one eighteen-month study of couples, 78 percent of lesbian couples and 84 percent of gay couples were still together, while 83 percent of cohabiting heterosexual couples and 96 percent of married heterosexual couples were still together.[20] Although in this study married heterosexual couples demonstrate greater endurance, the study was conducted in 1983. What might we find today if we were to survey the endurance of gay and lesbian couples that enjoy social support through marriage in, for example, the Commonwealth of Massachusetts?

Another two studies looking at sexual activity suggests that gay men have fewer sexual partners over a lifetime than heterosexual men. The study indicated that 69 percent of gay men had between one and four partners and 23 percent of heterosexual men had more than 19 partners. The mean average number of partners for gay men was 6, while the mean average for heterosexual men was 7.3.[21]

Admittedly, this is a sketch of instruments and studies. However, the overwhelming convergence of evidence is that gay men and lesbians, as a group, display levels of health, family functioning and strength, personal development, mutuality, commitment, and, dare we say, love, similar to heterosexuals. All of the major professional organizations in the United States have advocated the removal of any pathological labeling of gay men and lesbians and the removal of formal structural discrimination in laws about work, family, adoption, and relationships. This includes the American Psychological Association, the American Psychiatric Association, the American Sociological Association, and even the American Academy of Pediatrics. It is the professional competence of these organizations to judge the methodology and reliability of the outcomes of studies in psychology, sociology, family life, and child development.

Since the findings of these professionals do not confirm official magisterial statements about homosexuality (as the magisterial documents claim that they do), official Roman Catholic institutional bodies (CDF, pontifical commissions, bishops conferences, councils, or the papacy) cannot claim that their teachings are confirmed or supported by the natural sciences. But to insist that the teachings remain valid without support of the natural sciences would, of course, consist in a betrayal of *catholic* moral methodology that relies on human reason as part of what grounds its authority.

Official magisterial statements could be more explicit about what actual instruments or studies they believe confirm their claims. As noted earlier, the most frequently cited studies used to critique gay and lesbian families are those done on heterosexual families.[22] The evidence Stanton and Maier present to support the intrinsic deficiency of gay and lesbian relationships is a study in 1984 that predates contemporary social supports for gay and lesbian relationships.[23] It would be easy to conclude that during the 1980s, when gay men and lesbians suffered greater discrimination and lack of social support for relationships, internalized self-doubts and external pressures would render their relationships more fragile.

The official Roman Catholic argument against gay and lesbian committed sexual relationships is that they can never ground the achievement of interpersonal intimacy or love since sexual intercourse between two men or two women is intrinsically disordered. Thus, all the statistics need to show to bring into question the official position of the Roman Catholic Church on homosexuality is that some gay and lesbian relationships actually achieve the same graces as heterosexual couples do. It was interesting to note that during the International Catholic Ethics conference in Padua, participants reported different evidence for the successes and failures of committed gay and lesbian relationships in different parts of the world. A fruitful area of future study would be to compare and contrast different cultural attitudes about and support of gay and lesbian relationships on their achievement of sexual virtues and graces.

As with Galileo's telescopes in the seventeenth century, psychological and sociological studies will continue to present evidence that our sexual world is different than we had previously imagined. This evidence forces us to overcome habits of thought and begin to rethink the sexual universe. Official Roman Catholic leaders can continue to argue as they did in the seventeenth century that the earth does not turn on its own axis; that gay men and lesbians have no capacity to manifest or realize graces and virtues by integrating their sexual orientation in loving, committed, covenantal relationships. However, at some point, it becomes obvious to reasonable people that this argument cannot be sustained. The Roman Catholic approach to moral methodology, one that draws on reason to substantiate its claims, is in a position to lead in the development of new models of graceful sexuality. This will take courage and imagination as well as humility and a willingness to listen to the scientists of our age and to the gay men and lesbians who have had to overcome inherited habits of thought about sexuality and forge new models of integrity and virtue.

Notes

1. Pope John Paul II, "Lessons from the Galileo Case," *Origins* (November 12, 1992), par. 9. See also Michael J. Hartwig, "Galileo, Gene Researchers, and the Ethics of Homosexuality," *Theology and Sexuality* 1, no. 1 (1994): 106–11.

2. Ibid., par. 7.

3. Congregation for the Doctrine of the Faith, *Letter to the Bishops of the Catholic Church on the Pastoral Care of Homosexual Persons* (1986), par. 2.

4. Ibid., par. 7.

5. James F. Keenan, "Proposing Cardinal Virtues," *Theological Studies* 56, no. 4 (1995): 709–29; James F. Keenan, "Virtue and Identity," in *Creating Identity*, ed. Hermann Häring, Maureen Junker-Kenny, and Dietmar Mieth, *Concilium* 2 (London: SCM Press, 2000), 69–77.

6. Eugene F. Rogers, "Aquinas on Natural Law and the Virtues in Biblical Context: Homosexuality as a Test Case," *Journal of Religious Ethics* 27, no. 1 (1999): 29–56.

7. Ibid.

8. James N. Butcher, John R. Graham, Yossef S. Ben-Porath, Auke Tellegren, and W. Grant Dahlstrom, *Minnesota Multiphasic Personality Inventory-2* (Minneapolis: University of Minnesota Press, 1989).

9. Raymond B. Cattell, A. Karen Cattell, and Heather E. P. Cattell, *Sixteen Personality Factor,* 5th ed. (Bloomington, Minn.: Pearson Assessments, 2000).

10. Congregation for the Doctrine of the Faith, *Letter to the Bishops of the Catholic Church on the Pastoral Care of Homosexual Persons,* par. 7.

11. Jeramy Townsley, "Homosexuality Is Not a Pathology." Available online at *www.jeramyt.org/gay/gayhealth.html*. A sample of reviews listed on the site includes W. Horstman, "Homosexuality and Psychopathology," 1972; Adelman, *Archives of Sexual Behavior* 6, no. 3 (1977): 193–201; M. Freedman, *Homosexuality and Psychological Functioning* (Belmont, Calif.: Brooks/Cole Publishing, 1971); E. Ohlson, *Journal of Sex Research* 10 (1974): 308–15; D. Christie, *Psychological Reports* 59 (1986): 1279–82; J. Gonsiorek, *Psychological Adjustment and Homosexuality* (Select Press, 1977); B. Reiss, *Journal of Homosexuality* 1 (1974): 71–85.

12. Nathan B. Epstein et al., The McMaster Family Assessment Device, *Journal of Marital and Family Therapy* 9, no. 2 (1983): 171–80.

13. American Psychology Association, *Lesbian and Gay Parenting* (Washington, D.C.: American Psychology Association, 2005); Stephen Eric et al., "Gay and Lesbian Adoptive Families: An Exploratory Study of Family Functioning, Adoptive Child's Behavior, and Familial Support Networks," *Journal of Social Work* 9, no. 1 (2005): 17–32.

14. Child Behavior Checklist, Achenbach System of Empirically Based Assessment, Burlington, Vermont.

15. Kevin F. McNeill, "The Lack of Differences between Gay/Lesbian and Heterosexual Parents: A Review of the Literature," unpublished manuscript, University of California Riverside; available at kevin-mcneill@worldnet.att.net.

16. Glenn T. Stanton and Bill Maier, *Marriage on Trial: The Case against Same-Sex Marriage and Parenting* (Downers Grove, Ill.: InterVarsity Press, 2004).

17. Congregation for the Doctrine of the Faith, *Letter to the Bishops of the Catholic Church on the Pastoral Care of Homosexual Persons,* par. 7.

18. Congregation for the Doctrine of the Faith, *Considerations Regarding Proposals to Give Legal Recognition to Unions between Homosexual Persons* (June 2003), par. 4.

19. J. Harry in *Contemporary Families and Alternative Lifestyles,* ed. Eleanor Macklin and Roger Rubin (Thousand Oaks, Calif.: Sage Publications, 1983); Letitia Ann Peplau, "Value Orientations in Intimate Relationships of Gay Men," *Journal of Homosexuality* 6, no. 3 (1982): 1–19.

20. Philip Blumstein and Pepper Schwartz, *American Couples: Money, Work, Sex* (New York: William Morrow and Company, 1983).

21. Jeramy Townsley, "Analysis of J. Billy," *Family Planning Perspectives* 25 (1993): 52–60; R. Fay, *Science* 243 (1989): 338–48.

22. Stanton and Maier, *Marriage on Trial.*

23. Ibid., 65; reference to McWhirter and Mattison, *The Male Couple: How Relationships Develop* (Englewood Cliffs, N.J.: Prentice Hall, 1984).

PART SEVEN

CHALLENGES TO METHOD IN MORAL THEOLOGY

28

Contraception

Is Dialogue Possible between Proportionalism and the Ethic of Virtue?

GUSTAVO IRRAZÁBAL

The debate on contraception that began with the publication of *Humanae vitae* (*HV*) in 1968 made clear not only the growing theoretical and technical complexity of that particular topic in applied ethics, but also the deep differences affecting Catholic morality in the post-conciliar period. In the normative-ethical context, these differences were especially reflected in the confrontation between two positions, each of which claimed to represent the genuine moral tradition of the church, both of them rooted in the moral theology of the past and yet critical of it, but separated from each other by their anthropology, ethical philosophy, language, debating method, and to some degree by their concerns.

One of these "traditions," which many people call *deontology* but which often defines itself as an *ethic of virtue,* is the basis on which the Magisterium confirms the traditional Catholic position on contraception; the other, *teleology,* or *proportionalism,* aims to give a systematic foundation to a position critical of the official teaching.[1] The encyclical *Veritatis splendor* (*VS*) sought to settle the polemic definitively in favor of the first, but it may not have succeeded; proportionalism, though temporarily quieted, is still widely influential in the moral debate.

Is it necessary to think of this as an *either-or* confrontation, with one side winning over the other, or could it be seen primarily as a reciprocal stimulus enabling each side to move forward from within, based on its own premises?[2] In the following reflection, I would like to explore this possibility of dialogue on the topic of contraception where the confrontation began.

Contraception: An Unfinished Debate

The encyclical *Humanae vitae* describes as illicit "any action which either before, at the moment of, or after sexual intercourse, is specifically intended to prevent procreation — whether as an end or as a means" (no. 14b).

The principle of lesser evil cannot be applied to such acts, because "it is never lawful, even for the gravest reasons, to do evil that good may come of it — in other words, to intend directly something which of its very nature contradicts the moral order" (no. 14c).

Despite this firm statement, many local dioceses interpreted the encyclical quite freely. The French bishops declared, "Contraception can never be a good. It is always a disorder, but this disorder is not always blameworthy. Indeed there are cases in which couples face a true conflict of duties (*Gaudium et spes* no. 51).... Traditional wisdom allows them, before God, to seek the higher duty in this case."[3] Oddly, this episcopal document was inspired by the Jesuit Gustave Martelet, who also participated in drafting *Humanae vitae*. In his opinion, "In the often really complex situations that couples face, the true way of conscience may be not to choose the best, nor even the good, but simply the least evil."[4] In spite of the open contradiction between the text of the encyclical and Fr. Martelet's interpretation, he was considered a good interpreter of the encyclical by Paul VI himself.[5]

John Paul II has also firmly declared contraception to be intrinsically illicit: "To speak of 'conflicts of values or of goods,' and of the consequent need to establish a kind of 'balance' between them, choosing one and rejecting another, is not morally correct and only confuses the conscience of the couple."[6] But even such firm declarations have not been understood as a disapproval of the national bishops' interpretations.[7]

Nevertheless, the contradiction between these interpretations and the papal Magisterium is self-evident, and attempts to resolve it are disingenuous.[8] But these attempts come from the perception that certain extremes of moral experience must be resolved: on the one hand, that we can speak of intrinsically evil acts apart from their consequences; and on the other, that the consequences are relevant in discerning when an act should be defined as such. Although neglect of the former would lead to the collapse of the objective moral order, absolute denial of the latter leads to results that frankly go against common sense. For instance, antiovulants could be prescribed to cure a skin infection but not to avoid situations that are objectively far more serious for the couple and the family.[9]

"Common-sense morality," which is (rightly) invoked to support the existence of intrinsically evil acts,[10] can also be used to support the decisive moral relevance of the consequences, at least with regard to some of those acts. Indeed, common sense spontaneously rebels both against the direct killing of an innocent and against the prohibition of contraception even at risk of the gravest consequences. The Aristotelian recourse to *endoxa* (generally accepted opinion) as a starting point for ethical reflection would be incomplete unless both aspects are considered together.[11]

In light of this example, the problem we are discussing could be formulated as follows: Is it possible to reconcile these two aspects in evaluating moral acts, without sacrificing one in pursuit of the other?

The Debate over Moral Action

Proportionalist writers generally interpret the startling rigidity of the Magisterium on sexual matters as a consequence of what they consider its tendency to *naturalism* and *physicalism,* that is, attributing direct moral relevance to physiological processes or to the external physicality of the acts. That certainly has occurred de facto, especially in the area of the doctrine of *intrinsece malum,* but in my view it cannot be generally imputed to the principles on which the magisterial reasoning is based.[12]

Veritatis splendor, after citing this critique in number 47, responds with some important clarifications:

1. *Natural inclinations* are not merely material presuppositions, extrinsic to freedom, limited to physical goods, and thus unable to give anything more than a "general orientation for correct behavior" (nos. 47–48). On the contrary, they are an inseparable dimension of the moral act (n. 49), and acquire ethical relevance by their reference to the human person and his authentic fulfillment (n. 50), insofar as they tend toward certain fundamental goods whose specific moral value can be discovered by human reason (n. 48). Natural law is nothing more than that light of reason, by which man participates in the eternal law (n. 44).

2. The *object* of the moral act is not the physical externality of the act or the material reality surrounding it, as might be understood in a superficial interpretation of the doctrine of the sources of morality. On the contrary, it is "the object rationally chosen by the deliberate will," "freely chosen behavior," and the act seen "from the perspective of the acting person" (n. 78). We should take this to mean that it consists of a form — a content of meaning — "constituted by reason" (*Summa Theologiae* I-II, q.18, a.10).

3. The essential criterion for moral judgment of an action is whether or not its object is *capable of being ordered* to the good of the person, a characteristic that is grasped by reason in man's very being, in his natural inclinations, which have a spiritual dimension, indicating the "goods for the person" which are at the service of the "good of the person" as such. These are precisely the contents of the natural law (*VS* no. 79), which are traditionally called the "virtuous ends," insofar as they constitute ways of rationally ordering the will and the passions.

The difference from proportionalism, therefore, does not lie in its supposed naturalism or physicalism, but in a different conception of moral action. For proportionalism, the action is an *exterior event,*[13] indifferent in itself, which receives its moral qualities from the consequences it produces. For the ethics of virtue, in contrast, the action, quite apart from its intended effect, is not neutral because it encloses a content of meaning, a basic intentionality (traditionally known as *finis operis* or proximate end) which *already* has moral significance because of its relationship to the good of the person, according to its different virtuous ends.

Thus we can understand that certain acts are, by their very object, irreconcilable with moral good. When an act is described as intrinsically evil, it is not because of its mere physical externality but its *intentional structure,* that is, because of an observed contradiction between its rational content (object) with the orientation of will that this object entails (*finis operis*) and the order of virtue.

Contraception as Illicit in *Humanae vitae*

The foregoing considerations help us to understand why for so many Catholic moralists identified with the ethics of virtue the reasoning of *Humanae vitae* is *not naturalistic.* Neither this encyclical nor any other official teaching of the Magisterium describes the contraceptive methods — condoms, antiovulant pills, or diaphragms — as illicit. As physical objects they cannot be intrinsically evil: only human acts can be.

What *Humanae vitae* describes as illicit is *contraception,* that is, a type of moral action. And this is not because it alters the physiology of procreation but *because the moral structure of the act does not respect the integral meaning of human love.* As we know, such respect does not necessarily require that every act be fecund, but that in each act the will remains "open" to fecundity, an openness that is demonstrated when the couple decides to carry out or not carry out the conjugal act, in virtue of responsible parenthood, as an act that in itself possesses procreative virtuality. In some cases therefore, procreative responsibility is expressed in a modification of the couple's behavior: they will have relations or abstain, regulated by the virtue of conjugal chastity.

Contraception, in contrast, is a type of action that possesses a different intentional structure. When the couple chooses this means, they are not choosing "to suspend a procreative power that is such only in a material sense,"[14] but to *suppress* the procreative *meaning* of the act, making responsibility — the rational regulation appropriate to virtue — unnecessary, replacing it with a technical means, and also making unnecessary any modification of sexual behavior. Thus in contraception the will is not "open" to life, beyond the goodness of the ends by which it is ultimately motivated.

There is no trace of "naturalism" or "procreatism" here. The problem is not the artificial method (indeed its use as a therapeutic method is considered licit; see *HV* no. 15), but the authentically personalist concern with preserving the objective capacity of sexual behavior within marriage to express conjugal love, and not to falsify it by turning desire in on itself.

Intrinsically Evil Acts and the Ethical Context

Thus the Magisterium considers contraception to be an intrinsically evil act because of its intentional structure. But that presents us with a very delicate problem: what are the appropriate criteria for examining that structure?

The basic intentionality of an act can never be defined apart from a precise *ethical context* that gives it meaning.[15] This ethical context does not consist of indiscriminate attention to "all" the circumstances of the act (if it did, the object of the act could be "extended" indefinitely), but rather alludes to the evaluation of these circumstances by means of moral reason, in the light of their respective virtuous ends. Thus, for example, in order to speak correctly of a "lie," one needs not only a willfully false declaration but also a *communicative context* (a social sharing mediated by language). Such a context does not exist, for example, in the case of a false declaration made during a wartime interrogation or in the case of a deceptive answer to a murderer seeking the whereabouts of his next victim.

A contraceptive act is an act that embodies a contraceptive choice, that is, the choice of an act in preparation for free and consensual sexual relations that may foreseeably have procreative consequences, a choice made specifically for that reason.[16]

Thus, the definition of a contraceptive act is not applied to the use of contraceptive methods to prevent the possible procreative consequences of an expected rape; in such a situation the rape victim does not choose to engage in sexual relations or prevent the consequences of her own sexual behavior, but is simply defending herself against an attack on her own body and its undesirable consequences. Similarly a woman athlete participating in the Olympic Games who takes an antiovulant to avoid menstruation is not committing "contraception," because there is not an attendant intention to engage in sexual relations.

As we can see, here the circumstances are not indiscriminately included in the moral evaluation as "motives" or as a weighing of advantages and disadvantages, but as implications of a basic intentionality that is evaluated according to the virtuous ends that make up the person's well-being. With this understanding, the doctrine of intrinsically evil acts gains plausibility and can protect its moral objectivity; at the same time it entails the risk of physicalism that has followed this doctrine throughout its history.

Open Possibilities

In my view, a more nuanced and coherent magisterial doctrine on contraception can be achieved through a more detailed analysis of different ethical contexts.

The above-cited definition of the ethical context of contraception implies the couple's *common-sense possibility* of taking advantage of infertile periods. What happens when that possibility does not exist? In such a case, can one still speak of a *contraceptive choice*? We might consider the example of a married couple who for various reasons cannot use natural methods (the woman's irregularity, work schedules or other situations that limit opportunities to be together, etc.) and who also cannot responsibly bring new children into the world. In such a case, should we describe the use of a contraceptive method as a distortion of conjugal love (an intrinsically evil act) or as the only, however limited, way to express and cultivate love at this level?[17] In other words, does not the reasonably interpreted impossibility of using the natural method imply a change in the ethical context?

This discussion of ethical context is an opportunity to bring a more *hermeneutical* perspective into the ethics of virtue. An appreciation of the common-sense possibility of using natural planning leads to consideration, among other factors, of the socio-economic and cultural environment and the moral capacity of those who live within it, in order to achieve a properly nuanced understanding of the precise ethical context in which the norm should be applied. For example, in environments strongly conditioned by a lack of human and religious formation, a culture of machismo, a lack of employment and dignified living conditions, and promiscuity and uncontrolled, irresponsible procreation, the use of contraceptive methods might be a first (but only first and provisional) step toward procreative responsibility.

Other controversial cases can perhaps be clarified in the same way. Cannot the use of condoms to prevent AIDS be understood in a different context from contraception, that is, the protection of health? Does not the use of condoms *outside* marriage belong to a context alien to that of *Humanae vitae*, which refers to *conjugal* love? If so, would it be a contraceptive act generating additional disorder, or a mere *sign* of the preexisting disorder, and perhaps even an example of responsibility in the face of the possible consequences of the (illicit) act?

The Unfinished Dialogue

It would not be a realistic exercise of the mission of moral theologians to contribute to the progress of the Magisterium to encourage the illusion that sooner or later the Magisterium will change its method of argumentation to one based on other assumptions. It would be more helpful — recognizing a legitimate plurality of theological traditions within the church and the need for dialogue with all of them — to make explicit the motivating influence of these traditions on official teaching so that the teaching will move forward *from within*, achieving greater coherence and discovering the heartbeat of new possibilities in its own tradition.

The so-called "deontologism" of *Humanae vitae* (which in reality is a version of the ethics of virtue) has had the merit of adequately posing the relationship between the method used to regulate births and the full human meaning of the conjugal act. Teleologism on the other hand, with its tendency to neglect the immanent consequences of moral acts and to focus on the "state of things," considers this subject (assuming the responsible motivation of the couple) as a more technical question, one of proportionality between advantages and disadvantages.

On the other hand, the local dioceses, which in making pronouncements on the criteria for application of the encyclical have referred to the "conflict of duties" from a teleological perspective, have pointed out an obvious truth: the disproportionate consequences that a precipitous application of the pontifical doctrine can generate in certain concrete situations. This shows how teleologism, with its broad focus on the consequences of acts, tends to think less aprioristically than the ethic of virtue does about the concrete contexts in which the moral norm is applied.

In deepening the concept of "ethical context," the ethic of virtue and proportionalism could enlighten each other: the ethic of virtue would assume a new sensitivity to the conflicts of duties that stem from the complexity of concrete situations, a sensitivity characteristic of proportionality; meanwhile, proportionality would be challenged by the ethic of virtue to refine its criteria for a more clearly *moral* consideration of the values involved. This interaction would allow for progress toward an understanding of the relationship between the principles and the situation in terms of a *hermeneutic circle,* in which each pole would be seen as essential for a correct interpretation of the other.[18]

—*English translation by Margaret D. Wilde*

Notes

1. I refer to these streams of Catholic morality as "traditions" in a broad sense, simply in order to emphasize their inclusion as "figures" of moral philosophy that demand a narrative understanding as historical research processes and that are capable of entering into dialectical confrontation, even though they are intrinsically dependent on their respective contexts.

2. See Alasdair McIntyre, *After Virtue* (London: Duckworth, 1985), 276–77.

3. Quoted by Eduardo López Azpitarte, *Etica de la sexualidad y del matrimonio* (Madrid: Paulinas, 1992), 369.

4. Gustave Martelet, *La existencia humana y el amor,* quoted by Azpitarte, *Etica de la sexualidad y del matrimonio,* 378.

5. See *Acta Apostolicae Sedis* 60 (1968): 527.

6. *Documentos palabra* 92 (1987): 148.

7. See Eduardo López Azpitarte, "La moralidad de la anticoncepción, Discusiones actuales," *Proyección* 31 (1984): 199–207.

8. "If one wishes at all costs to avoid it [the evil of contraception], worse evils may occur, as we saw earlier. *That it is an intrinsically evil act does not mean that it is the most grievous and important of all*" (Azpitarte, *Etica de la sexualidad y del matrimonio,* 377); emphasis added. The author is not immediately aware that he is referring to a *morally* evil act, which is not subject to the principle of lesser evil.

9. See Azpitarte, *Etica de la sexualidad y del matrimonio,* 377.

10. See Gilberto Gutiérrez, "*Veritatis Splendor* y la etica consecuencialista contemporánea," in *Comentarios a la Veritatis Splendor,* ed. Gerardo del Pozo Abeijón (Madrid: BAC, 1994), 254.

11. Against the unilateral invocation made by Gutiérrez in "*Veritatis Splendor* y la etica consecuencialista contemporánea," 254–55.

12. The same affirmation is made by James Murtagh with regard to the preconciliar manuals in "Intrinsic Evil," (doctoral dissertation, Rome: Universidad Gregoriana, 1973), 60.

13. Louis Janssens, "Ontic Evil and Moral Evil," *Louvain Studies* 4 (1972): 120.

14. Giordano Muraro, "Procreación responsable," in *Nuevo diccionario de teología moral,* ed. Francesco Compagnoni et al. (Madrid: Paulinas, 1992), 1516.

15. See Martin Rhonheimer, *Ley natural y razón práctica* (Pamplona: EUNSA, 2000), 455–64; and idem, *La perspectiva de la moral* (Madrid: RIALP, 2000), 333–70; and idem, *Etica de la procreación* (Madrid: RIALP, 2004): 132–48. Referring to "ethical context" enables us to overcome many objections to the doctrine of *intrinsece malum,* such as an alleged reduction of the moral act to a "disembodied object" (see Marciano Vidal, *La propuesta moral de Juan Pablo II* [Madrid: PPC, 1994], 143).

16. Martin Rhonheimer, "The Truth about Condoms," *The Tablet* (October 7, 2000): 10–11; idem, "Contraception, Sexual Behavior, and Natural Law: Philosophical Foundation of the Norm of *Humanae Vitae,*" *Linacre Quarterly* 56 (1989): 20–57.

17. Gustavo Irrazábal, "El teleologismo después de la Veritatis Splendor," *Moralia* 26 (2003): 31–57.

18. An analogous method for mediation between principles and consequences has been developed in the field of bioethics in Diego Gracia, *Fondamenti di bioetica* (Milan: San Paolo, 1993), 571–602.

29

Benedict XVI's *Deus Caritas Est*

An Ethical Analysis

STEPHEN J. POPE

Pope Benedict XVI's first encyclical, *Deus caritas est* (DCE), was generally appreciated for its positive tone. The encyclical's good reception was facilitated by its uncontroversial message that love, not hatred and violence, is at the heart of Christianity. The same is true of its claim that the church is called to demonstrate the practical meaning of divine love through concrete acts, both those done by individual Christians moved by charity and those routinely provided by ecclesial social service agencies around the world. Moral theologians praised the scriptural basis of the encyclical's vision and its focus on virtue and intentions rather than on rules and prohibitions.

The encyclical's treatment of its central theological affirmation that God is love (1 John 4) is divided into two sections — a more theologically speculative part dealing with the nature of love and a more practical section focusing on the "works of charity." Both sections have certain strengths, but I would like to highlight the more interesting issue of ambiguities in the document. This essay argues that the encyclical's clarity and persuasiveness is diminished by its treatment of the relations between two pairs of key theological and moral terms — first, agape and eros, and second, love and justice. The encyclical's assumption that agape is a special type of love that can be clearly distinguished from eros, as well as from other forms of love, gives a problematic status to natural love. Moreover, the encyclical's placement of charity "above" justice tends to give an insufficient appreciation to the importance of justice in its own right and obscures its value as a necessary condition of the former. This generates an unfortunate diminution of the ethical significance of large-scale, institutional settings. The conclusion of this chapter maintains that recent events in the life of the church underscore the responsibility of giving more, rather than less, attention to the demands of justice.

Agape and Eros

The first pair of terms recalls the theological and moral debate that has been going on for the better part of a century, beginning with Nygren's magisterial work, *Agape and Eros*. Nygren's main target was what he took to be the infiltration of Greek into Christianity via Augustine's "Christianized" eros. Lofty eros, Nygren claims, persists in sinful self-seeking as much as hedonistic eros does and neither has any place in the unmerited love commanded by Jesus. True agape gives itself away and is completely unmotivated by its object's goodness or beauty. This dualist interpretation of Luther's two kingdoms was thoroughly critiqued and rejected by generations of Christian ethicists, but the typology was nevertheless retained, even by Nygren's critics. Thus, despite its inadequacies in enriching the Christian scriptures and significant streams of the Christian tradition, Nygren's position continues to influence Christian theology by providing the framework within which the discussion typically takes place. This is understandably, but lamentably, also the case with *Deus caritas est*.

Benedict certainly intends to oppose the kind of radical dualism of agape and eros advanced by Nygren, but unfortunately his encyclical actually shows the influence of the dualist paradigm it intends to critique. It is true that while Nygren sharply opposed agape and eros, Benedict, like his Catholic forebears in this debate, insists that agape and eros ultimately form a complementary and harmonious relation to the extent to which the former purifies the latter so that it serves the other and not just the self. Eros left to itself is corrupted by original sin and stands in need of grace. Benedict takes the Song of Songs to show that human love can move from being "insecure, indeterminate, and searching" to an orientation focused on "real discovery of the other, [and] moving beyond the selfish character that prevailed earlier" (*DCE* no. 6). Purified eros culminates in exclusive and permanent love expressed in marriage.

Benedict acknowledges that eros has been subjected to multiple interpretations based on quite disparate human experiences and textual traditions, and he concedes the difficulty of identifying which of these interpretations is most appropriate. Eros has been used to refer to sexual attraction to another person, to "falling in love," to yearning for psycho-sexual union with another person, etc. *Deus caritas est* speaks of eros in at least five ways: (1) as paradigmatically the love between a man and a woman (no. 3); (2) as a desire for happiness developed by the Greeks into religious intoxication (no. 5); (3) as "worldly" love, in contrast to the kind of love that is "grounded in and shaped by faith" (no. 7); (4) as "ascending" love, as opposed to the "descending" love (no. 7); and (5) as "receiving" from others, rather than as "giving" to others (no. 7). The encyclical treats these traits as more or less interchangeable.

One level of difficulty emerges with the question of whether self-gift is the natural outcome of the development of eros or made possible only by the influence of grace. Eros is described as desire that is naturally oriented to moral development: it starts out seeking the good in a self-centered way but gradually moves to caring for the other for his or her own sake: "Even if eros is at first mainly covetous and ascending ... [over time it] increasingly seeks the happiness of the other, is concerned more and more with the beloved, bestows and wants to 'be there for' the other" (*DCE* no. 7). Yet an ambiguity is introduced when it is said that as eros matures, an element of agape "enters into this love, for otherwise eros is impoverished and even loses its own nature" (*DCE* no. 7). The ambiguity here centers on whether agape corrects the defects of eros due to original or personal sin, or provides a new capacity for giving that is actually foreign to eros as such.

Benedict obviously does not want to say with Nygren that nature is replaced by grace, or agape by eros, but his use of the agape-eros duality makes this less than clear. Nygren regarded agape as a distinct "type" of love and certainly not as the grace-inspired perfection of all human love, whatever its object and whatever its mode of operation (ascending or descending, etc.). If agape is the perfection and elevation of natural love, then one would think that it is manifested in ascending as well as in descending love.

Benedict holds that because we are body and soul, and in need of receiving as well as giving, we should not dismiss eros as trivial any more than we should exalt it to divine status. Since "giving" and "receiving" are both essential aspects of natural love, Benedict's description of agape as "descending" love and of eros as "ascending love," and his categorization of eros as "worldly love" in contrast to love "grounded in and shaped by faith," obscures the natural moral capacity of human love, healed by grace.

According to Nygren, natural love in search of happiness ascends to God for the sake of the self, whereas divine love descends to others without concern for the self. Benedict, on the other hand, maintains that as natural love ascends to God it naturally grows in its capacity to give itself away and care for others. The former's account of natural love as inherently sinful leads him to call for its obliteration, whereas the Catholic position distinguishes between our created capacity for love, our sinful disorientation as fallen creatures, and the healing effect of grace on our nature. Benedict's distance from Nygren would have been made clearer if his treatment of love had incorporated the Thomistic distinction between integral nature, fallen nature, and healed nature.

If grace transforms all human love and does not issue only in purely self-sacrificial altruism, then love cannot appropriately be divided into "types" like agape and eros. Through grace, human love moves toward mutuality, friendship, and communion; it embraces self-love as well as brotherly and sisterly love; it encourages the believer to mystical contemplation as well as corporal and spiritual works of mercy; it is expressed in both the fellowship of the Lord's Supper as well as in the cross.

Justice and Love

The second ambiguity of this encyclical lies in its treatment of the relation between love and justice. Benedict cites the standard passage on giving to Caesar (Matt. 22:21) to emphasize the different responsibilities of church and state. The church works for the practical well-being of those who suffer, but it does not have the responsibility to administer justice in society because its mission is not political. Yet the claim that "a just society must be the achievement of politics, not the church," need not imply quietism or irresponsible otherworldliness. Not remaining on the "sidelines," the church must promote justice in society through using its pedagogical, moral, and pastoral resources. The church has a responsibility to form consciences and to train citizens in virtue (*DCE* no. 28), to promote reasoned debate in the public square, and to insist that political communities respect natural law, the common good, and human dignity. These roles explain how the church can be committed to giving public support to certain legislative proposals but not require Catholic support for particular candidates or political parties.

The ordained in particular should normally rise above partisan politics and be available to all believers rather than only those with whom they share particular political convictions.

One difficult aspect of this division of labor concerns Benedict's way of relating love and justice. Whereas the state is responsible to provide justice for members of the political community, he argues, the church is a "community of love" whose actions manifest the inner life of Trinitarian love. Opposed to Marxist claims that the poor need justice, not charity, Benedict argues that the poor need both: justice from the state and charity from the church. Love addresses more significantly the deepest needs of the person, which is often ignored by state-run bureaucratic services.

The assumption that the church's central moral concern ought to be charity rather than justice is troubling for two reasons — one external to the church and one internal. First, charity for the needy requires us to work for their rights and to address the causes of their suffering and therefore to struggle for justice in a collective, concerted way. Unfortunately, the church has at times either stood on the "sidelines" or even actively supported the oppressors. Indeed, the appeal to charity has been used to justify inaction or even complicity in oppression.

Martin Luther King Jr.'s famous "Letter from Birmingham City Jail" was written in response to critical clergymen who wanted King not to "stir up trouble" in an already divided city. Observing the church's acceptance of segregation in his own day, King complained of white churches that "stand on the sideline and merely mouth pious irrelevancies and sanctimonious trivialities." King's words apply not only to the past: "Far from being disturbed by the presence of the church, the power structure of the average community is consoled by the church's silent and often vocal sanction of things as they are."

Benedict's encyclical does not meet King's insistence that Christian love issue in concrete commitments to social justice that address the underlying structural causes of the suffering of the poor and not only their immediate needs. This might result from the fact that the pope thinks of human suffering as primarily the result of unmet material and spiritual needs — the kinds addressed in the Beatitudes and the corporal and spiritual works of mercy — rather than as resulting from pervasive and systematic human injustice. This assumption runs the risk of reinforcing complacency and what Judith Shklar called "passive injustice."

The encyclical's inattentiveness to structural injustice reflects the fact that it does not consider poverty from the point of view of those who are oppressed but rather from a transcendent vantage point "above" their struggles and historical location. But as John Paul II has written, the preferential option for the poor requires us to stand *with* the poor and oppressed and not just to offer them assistance — a stance that gives a sharp sense of urgency to one's sense of the need to work for the transformation of the social order. Benedict is concerned that the personnel who work within the church's charitable organizations "not be inspired by ideologies aimed at improving the world, but should rather be guided by the faith which works through love" (*DCE* no. 33). Yet faith can work through a form of love that promotes progress not as an ideology but as a way of addressing the plight of the poor. Instead of looking with suspicion on all appeals to social progress, the encyclical might have distinguished ideologically distorted views of social progress from those that are compatible with the gospel.

The pope insists that, "we contribute to a better world only by personally doing good now, with full commitment and wherever we have the opportunity, independently of partisan strategies and programs" (*DCE* no. 31). But it can also be the case that at times we contribute to a better world by promoting justice via partisan strategies that concretely advance the rights of the poor, for example, particular laws concerning the right to unionize, laws regulating factory emissions, etc. This would seem especially the case in those social contexts in which the church wields significant degrees of economic, social, and even political power. Assignment of justice to the state and charity to the church can obscure the church's de facto possession of power and the potential it has to effectively promote justice or to be an obstacle to it.

The encyclical's high praise for the superiority of charity can also create the impression that the church transcends justice and so need not be focused on it. Yet the concrete practice of the church, from local to the universal contexts, is different than the lofty theology with which it is sometimes described. Benedict, for example, proposes that the transparent character of Catholic organizations and "their faithfulness to the duty of witnessing to love" can inspire greater virtue in the administration of civil agencies (*DCE* no. 30). The last four years in the United States, however, calls into question the validity of this generalization. A report of the Office of the Attorney General of the Commonwealth of Massachusetts issued on July 23, 2003, concluded that six decades of sexual abuse of minors by clergy members was "due to an institutional acceptance of abuse and a massive and pervasive failure of leadership." Officers of the archdiocese made decisions, the form of which were repeated in many other locations in the country and elsewhere, to allow abusive priests to continue in active ministry even though their presence constituted a serious threat to the well-being of highly vulnerable children and juveniles. In one settlement agreed to in September 2003, the archdiocese of Boston agreed to pay $85 million to more than five hundred victims; overall the archdiocese has paid about $110 million to plaintiffs.

To their credit, the U.S. bishops adopted a child protection policy in 2002 entitled the "Charter for the Protection of Children and Young People," which includes a requirement for permanent removal from ministry of any ordained person guilty of sexual abuse of a minor. The crimes of sexual abuse constituted a serious violation of justice that included issues of accountability, the duty to report crimes to the proper authorities, concern for the well-being of those over whom one has professional responsibility, and the protection of innocent people from sexual abusers — and, in some cases, even serial predators. The church's concern with mercy for the clergy and love for its own public image allowed it to obscure the suffering of victims and ignore what, in retrospect, were some obvious imperatives of justice.

It should also be noted that the initiative for justice came not from the institutional leaders of the church but from civil authorities, politicians and lawyers, lay activists like Voice of the Faithful, advocacy groups, the media, and other kinds of popular pressure. Another cry for justice came from some accused priests who complained that the church had unfairly deprived them of their good names and ministerial status and allowed guilt by accusation to replace due process. What Reinhold Niebuhr observed of secular politics is in this case also true of ecclesiastical authorities: those holding positions of power do not voluntarily renounce their privileges and protections. Appeals to charity ring hollow when institutions ignore or evade basic standards of legal and moral justice. The hierarchy in Boston, to note one particularly egregious case, failed miserably in its exercise of justice, and few observers accepted its attempt to exempt itself from meeting its legal obligations to the victims of clerical sexual abuse.

This criticism in no way denigrates the charitable work of the church, but it does make it hard to resist the implication that the church should try to do more but at least *never do less* than justice demands. Heartfelt concern for directly encountered victims — Benedict's central image of charity — is made real by just acts, including the policy changes brought about by the

U.S. bishops themselves. The whole episode underscores the fact that love and charity are not only limited in their moral scope but also have to be directed and corrected by justice.

The unmet claims of justice also underscore our collective Catholic need to keep alive John Paul II's sense of repentance for the failures of the church to live up to its own ideals and even elementary moral norms. This includes not only the church's failures in the crises of sexual abuse in various parts of the world, but also its grievous moral failures in places like Argentina during the "Dirty War" and Rwanda during the genocide of 1994.

Conclusion

Deus caritas est offers a strong message regarding the centrality of charity to the Christian life and underscores both its theological grounding and its practical ecclesial significance. The strength of the encyclical lies in its vision of agape informing both the human desire for happiness and love and the human commitment to justice. Yet its message could have been argued more effectively had the pope developed more careful distinctions. While seeking to support the unifying power of love, it unfortunately can be mistakenly interpreted to separate agape from both eros and justice.

The overarching vision of *Deus caritas est* can be promoted by understanding that grace perfects and elevates all forms of human love and inspires the exercise of justice in both interpersonal and more broadly social domains. Justice without love can be heartless, but love without justice can be radically irresponsible.

30

Tolerance, Pluralism, and Religious Truth

JOHAN DE TAVERNIER

The tension between tolerance, pluralism, and religious truth is a major theme in interreligious dialogue. Fundamentalist tendencies in many world religions seem to confirm the viewpoint that the stronger religious identity is, the more difficult it is to escape from the intolerance of truth and to reconcile it with a positive appreciation of a pluralistic culture. Modern secularized cultures, founded in the human rights tradition, accept the pluralistic assumption in principle. In such societies, tolerance is an important pillar.

There are two risks when speaking about tolerance: the danger of banality and the risk of confusion — when different meanings are mixed up. Considering the first risk, it is interesting to add a third notion to the pair of meanings "tolerant/intolerant": the intolerable, meaning what people consider unbearable, something that really will not pass. By discovering what offended people consider intolerable, we come more easily to the core of tolerance. In addition, we pay attention to the person who regards something as unbearable. Is it the tolerant person who discovers the limits of his or her tolerance or is it the intolerant who labels everything that does not match his or her convictions as intolerable? It makes a difference, because the content of the intolerable is ambiguous from the beginning.

Paul Ricoeur on Tolerance

The term "tolerance" involves a number of ambiguities. In this respect, Paul Ricoeur refers to what the French dictionary *Le Petit Robert* defines as tolerance.[1] The first meaning is "tolerating something, not forbidding or requiring it, even if one has the possibility, freedom that results from this abstinence." It particularly concerns abstinence, but who must abstain and who must not? How can we make the transition from abstinence to freedom, which is the result of it, and what do we mean by freedom?

The second meaning of the word "tolerance," which strangely enough renders the first meaning of the word "intolerance," is the following: "an attitude that consists in admitting by the other another way of thinking and a different way of acting than the one a person has adopted himself." The first meaning probably focuses on institutions, while the second meaning looks at individual behavior. We thus move from abstinence (not forbidding or demanding something, although we are capable of doing it) to the allowing of other opinions, other attitudes. Nevertheless, who is meant by "the other": the fellow citizen, the fellow believer, the person who adheres to another belief, the stranger, another nation, another religious community? In what circumstances does one switch from abstinence to the admission of differences?

In the definition of "intolerance," the individual attitude takes precedence over public rules: "tendency of not supporting, of condemning that which is disappointing in the opinions or in the attitude of the other." It is only in the second place that intolerance is defined as the negative of tolerance in the first meaning of the word (at the institutional level): "disposition hostile to ecclesiastical or civil tolerance."

The notions of tolerant/intolerant can be applied on three levels: the institutional level (state-church relationships), the cultural level (opinions, thoughts), and the religious and theological level (the question of truth).

Tolerance on the Institutional Level

In the Middle Ages, the belief in Christendom was the first matter of importance in the Christian concept of unity. The French formula *une foi, une loi, un roi*[2] typifies the premodern era. During the Reformation, the religious matter became a political affair. The religious peace treaty of Augsburg in 1555 officially recognized the new religious pluralism. The peace regulations were based upon the principle that later would be called *cuius regio, illius religio* — namely, whoever makes the decisions within a territory also decides the religion of its inhabitants. Unlike in the old days, the sovereignty of the monarch within his territory was the most important thing, and his "freedom of religion" determined his subjects' religion. In that way religion was, for decades, a determining factor in the legitimization of the monarch's absolutism.[3]

Until the French Revolution (with its *déclaration des droits de l'homme et du citoyen*) church and state in Europe were distinguished but not separated. They supported each other. Political leaders asked the ecclesiastical leaders to consecrate them, and in exchange ecclesiastical leaders were authorized to judge something as schismatic or heretical. At both religious and theological levels it is clear that, until the Enlightenment in western Europe, Protestants as well as Catholics were convinced that there was no place for other religions in the political area where they held influence.[4] Due to the Enlightenment philosophers, the situation changed; they presented the right to freedom of religion as one of the cornerstones of individual free rights. At that point, it became conceivable that different religious beliefs could exist side by side.

What is the explanation for this evolution? How did one come to a positive evaluation of abstinence, in other words, allowing the admission of different opinions and attitudes?

At the institutional level, there is a twofold explanation for the initially negative meaning of abstinence or restraint attached to tolerance: first, the loss of the ecclesiastical consecration power in favor of secular politics and, second, the loss of secular sanctions of what the church labeled heretical. Both are consequences of the gradual realization of the idea of a secular constitutional state or lay state. It can be said that until now the term "lay" is a striking illustration of the confusion between the institutional level, where tolerance is considered nothing more than a curtailment, and the cultural level, where tolerance is an expression of a polemical relationship between the agnostic lay culture and a religious culture. The curtailment at the institutional level results in formal rights (such as freedom of opinion, freedom of association, freedom of worship, freedom of the press, freedom of religious education, and so on). Freedom of conscience and freedom of opinion correlate at this level. If one cannot express one's conscience, then it is repressed. The legislator's function is to prevent a situation in which one person's liberty of opinion obstructs another's liberty of opinion.

Moreover, what does intolerable mean at this level? It is certainly not the opinion of the intolerant person for whom everything deviating from his or her belief and practice is intolerable (*la différence comme telle*). At the institutional level, the confusion of justice and truth (or pretensions of the truth) is intolerable.

Justice is also about the conditions to limit the disadvantages of the most neglected (second principle of John Rawls). Individuals who practice their formal liberties belong to communities, such as associations, cultural organizations, and churches. Those communities have interests and social importance. Some are bigger than others; some have more or less power and moral authority than others. It is a very important task for the constitutional state to minimize the damage done to minority groups. State protection against power-based discrimination or obstruction is not enough. The state is expected to compensate for inequalities resulting from the differences in social importance.

The state must see itself as the arbitrator between the competing claims and not as a tribunal of the truth. Ricoeur calls that *la suprême ascèse du pouvoir* (the highest asceticism of power).[5] A confessional, non-secularized, Marxist or Stalinist state cannot do this ("not forbidding or requiring even if one has the possibility"). It is well understood that, at a philosophical level, a strictly neutral form of government raises better possibilities for the flourishing of an attitude of tolerance among different social groups.[6] It is also clear, however, that a fully neutral state is not possible, because even the democratic constitutional state was established not on anything tangible, but rather in a culture of which it is the expression as well as the protector.

In general, the democratic constitutional state is thought to tolerate everything, unless it runs the risk of liquidating itself. Non-democratic parties that can come into power in a democratic way are a great dilemma in this respect. A democratic constitutional state can be expected to have a rate of tolerance sufficiently high to admit extreme political thoughts that could threaten the current form of government. Could things, however, reach the stage that the democratic form of government itself is threatened? Many deem that impossible. The conclusion is that a democratic constitutional state must be tolerant with respect to the intolerant, but not at all costs. Here (and only here), Mispelblom Beyer's statement that *"tolerance is the non-tolerance of intolerance"* is applicable.[7] But tolerance, being the core of democracy, remains primordial. That means that all peaceful and democratic means on hand can be mobilized to react against what cannot be tolerated, for the sake of what is worth protecting. Here it becomes clear that tolerance is not the same thing as indifference.

Tolerance on the Cultural Level

The coming into existence of the constitutional state supposes a thorough change in mentality and culture. The development of a lay culture under the pressure of Enlightenment philosophy appears to be the basis for that mutation. The idea of tolerance has its roots in this evolution. The lay culture indeed is the result of an anti-Catholic and anti-Protestant ambition, which presents itself as critical thinking vis-à-vis *dogmatic* thinking. The Enlightenment's emancipation is directed first against many forms of clerical patronizing of the institutional area and the individual thinking, acting, and conscience of people. When people at that time talked for the first time about tolerance, they meant something polemical. They wanted to shake off the supposed intolerance inherent in the power of the Roman Catholic and Protestant churches. It is, therefore, not surprising that one often became intolerant in the name of the advocated tolerance (as in the French Revolution).

Ricoeur thinks that this delicate balance between two kinds of intolerance (theistically and atheistically inspired) has gradually developed into a delicate positive tolerance. We can call it the recognition of the right of the opponent, dissident, or the person with other beliefs to exist. That recognition will lead to a cultural conviviality of "those who believe in heaven" and "those who refuse to believe." In contrast with premodern culture, belief becomes an option. This explains why, initially, religious leaders were very reluctant with regard to that new thought. Therefore, being tolerant implies sacrifices at a cultural level. It is not easy to accept the rights of dissidents or people having other beliefs that radically contest my positions and threaten to reduce my deepest (religious) convictions to a simple opinion. It is easier to implement tolerance at the institutional level than at the cultural level. In each of us, in each philosophy of life, there is something principally intolerant. In that sense, we do not easily admit that "they" do not think as we do, that "they" have the same right to profess their conviction and to defend it publicly as we enjoy. Ricoeur describes that as the violence of conviction, or rather the violence *in* conviction. Tolerance asks us to limit that violence on the assumption that the other is completely free in his or her conviction and that he or she asks for respect. We have to accept people and permit their practices and opinions even when we strongly disagree with them.[8] Monique Canto-Sperber defines tolerance in the same sense: "Tolerance consists in abstaining from intervening in the actions and opinions of other persons when these opinions or actions appear disagreeable, frankly unpleasant, or morally reprehensible to us."[9]

What is intolerable at this level? We cannot confuse the intolerable with the object of the intolerance, that is, violence in and of our conviction. We should link the intolerable with what each individual and each community experiences as unethical "indignant" behavior and therefore undeserving of respect (for example, intolerance, acts of pedophilia, slavery, extreme inequality).[10] Respect is the power of tolerance at the cultural level. Of course, there is not always consensus, partly due to the fact that the intolerable and the tolerable are highly contextual and historical.[11] Many dilemmas are not solved. For instance, do writers or film producers in Western societies who publicly make fun of traditional Christian or Islamic images deserve our respect because they are expressing freedom of thought through creative expression? In many Muslim communities, this would be completely unthinkable.[12]

Tolerance on Religious and Theological Levels

Is there is a theological justification for tolerance? For a long time clerical dogmatism has taken for granted the violence of conviction as fear of relativism or indifferentism. Not so long ago, however, as a consequence of cultural and institutional changes, an evolution took place from the practice of conviction by aggression to an emphasis on the peacefulness of testimony. The effect of political secularization and the acceptance of pluralism in the cultural sphere is that the churches in the West have to express their message in a completely different way, that is, based purely on the power of testimony.

The path to human liberty and the right to be different was prepared by important figures like Nicolaus Cusanus, perhaps the most original thinker of the fifteenth century.[13] His starting point is the deficiency of all knowledge. Concerning religion, he says that the highest being carries the wise recognition of ignorance. The historical religions are variable hypotheses that must be ameliorated constantly and can make no claim on exclusive or absolute validity. He sees the different conceptions of God as projections or speculations of the thinking mind. Therefore, he holds a comprehensive tolerance, combined with an intense interest in any opinion or philosophy. In his work we can find the inner mystical willingness to a universalistic way of thinking that on principle respects any opinion and worldview on philosophical grounds.

During the transition from the fifteenth to the sixteenth century, Erasmus of Rotterdam set himself up as a passionate opponent of all witch-hunting. His humanism is characterized by rational persuasion and spiritual appeal. Erasmus opposes the fanaticism that would impose its own beliefs on all people and divide the human community into believers and heretics, adherents and opponents. The Christian God wants multiplicity.

An equally ardent humanist was Sebastian Castellio. Initially, Castellio was a follower of Calvin, but in 1554 he rebelled against the burning of Servetus and, under the pseudonym Bellius, lodged an objection against the killing of heretics. One should stand up for one's own truth with words and persuasion, not with the sword.

Cusanus, Erasmus, and Castellio form the leading edge of those who stood against the fanatic absolutism of authoritarian orthodoxy on the basis of rationally and ethically founded convictions. Neither the Reformation nor the Counter-Reformation followed them.

Initially Martin Luther advocated a very tolerant position. At first he was convinced that secular power should not be involved in the relationship between God and the individual soul, as people cannot be brought to faith by force. In 1529 however, out of political necessity, the death penalty was imposed on heretics (a proposal of Melanchthon). It is hard, says Luther, to see someone killed, but it would be worse to tolerate true doctrine oppressed and governmental authority under attack.

While Erasmian humanism dreamed of a united humanity both tolerant and peaceful, the Counter-Reformation tried to eradicate everything harmful to Mother Church. During the second half of the sixteenth century, the advocates of tolerant thought were engaged in a fierce struggle. In France, the chancellor Michel de l'Hôpital held the opinion that people should adopt the Christian faith through good example rather than through violence. He pleaded for a reunified Christianity. His efforts took shape in the Edict of Nantes, which granted Protestants in France freedom of conscience and worship. France, however, was not yet ripe for such a tolerant mentality. The Roman Catholic reaction led in 1685 to the abolition of that edict and to the persecution of French Protestants.

The tide turned again with Bayle, Leibniz, and consequently Voltaire, who rejected the use of force in matters of faith on different grounds. Force produces hypocrisy and conflicts with the Gospel. In 1764 Voltaire's *Traîté sur la tolérance* against clerical and royal absolutism was published, seventy-five years after the incorporation of religious freedom into the Bill of Rights in England in 1689 under the influence of John Locke. In his *Epistula de Tolerantia* (*A Letter Concerning Toleration*), Locke presents a most convincing argument against religious persecution,[14] although he declared paradoxically that those who do not believe in God should not be tolerated. Unlike Locke, Voltaire includes atheists in his demand for toleration. Tolerance asks us to admit even views to which we are opposed.[15]

In the nineteenth century, Europe reached an important stage in the struggle for tolerance. In many countries, laws guaranteed liberty of conscience, religion, and culture, following the example of the United States and France. Germany granted total freedom of religious expression in 1848. By the end of the nineteenth century states like Spain and Austria allowed freedom of worship as well.

Notwithstanding former abuses, the conviction grew that the Christian message itself demands tolerance. Those entrusted with spreading the Christian faith realized that it was contradictory to use psychological or physical pressure for that cause. Numerous arguments from faith could be used to support this stance, for instance, the way in which God appeared in this world as weak and defenseless, putting to shame the strong. Christ's word was often biting, but he never imposed it on those who listened to him. Jesus' humanness shows us that God is a God for human beings, and that God does not fight for truth with power and violence, but rather convinces people through an affectionate praxis of caring proximity.

Tolerance and Truth

Christians are not the owners of the truth, but rather servants in the love of truth. Viewed this way, belief can scarcely lead to a fanatic defense of their own convictions. But is it possible for Jewish, Christian, or Islamic believers not to think on an exclusive basis, since their claims on truth and happiness always imply arrogance or a feeling of superiority?

In the course of history, monotheistic religions (the religions of the book) have had more difficulties with forms of intolerance than polytheistic religions. The reason for that greater tolerance may be found in the lesser claims on truth in polytheistic religions. Monotheistic or revealed religions have a precisely formulated knowledge of revelation. For most Christians, for instance, that orthodox knowledge was laid down in a binding confession that is preached as a sacrosanct truth. Thus, the claim to truth is stronger, as well as the risk of intolerance. In spite of that risk, I would like to draw attention to the fact that the more defined profile of monotheistic religions has also had a very positive effect. For different reasons, the degrees of humanizing and human development have progressed more in regions where monotheistic religions are part of the cultural heritage.

The question we ask here is the following: Is tolerance possible for Jews, Christians, and Muslims? In this respect, France Quéré argues:

> If there is a domain where difference is always arousing irritation, it is the domain of religion. The religious category is different from the others in relating to a zone that does not suffer separation. Transcendence governs it, unique in its principle: either God exists or God does not exist. Either God is revealing himself in Jesus Christ, or he is not revealing himself. One cannot believe both at the same time.[16]

Quéré describes the whole paradox succinctly: all monotheistic religions pretend to hold a lease on truth, and they claim universality while disqualifying other convictions as human inventions. With this understanding, we can ask ourselves if believers are capable of being tolerant. Of course, they can allow others to have another belief, but they cannot accept in any way that another belief also holds the truth. In the best case, this weaker form of tolerance is a small honor to the person of the tolerated, but not to the tolerated subject itself. Quéré therefore concludes that behind this form of tolerance there hides an actual intolerance.[17]

In our opinion, striking illustrations of that hidden intolerance include the advancing fundamentalist tendencies in different monotheistic religions who easily consider themselves as "bastions of truth." "We'd rather die than adulterate our belief," they say, based on a perfect and immediate knowledge of God's will or on obedience to divine texts or religious leaders.

In fundamentalism, believing is seen as *sacrificium intellectus*. It explains the popular character of fundamentalism. Actually, the fundamentalist conception of truth is intolerant. Anything that does not fit into the fundamentalists' worldview is seen as a betrayal of that truth.

Is it possible to reconcile tolerance and truth? One of the best proposals in that respect came from Franz Böckle, a moral theologian who died in 1991.[18] He argued that such a tension is possible on the condition that we do not consider religious tolerance in the first place as a taking of a direct stand on the truth question, but that we look upon the tolerance question from an independent, free, faith-rooted relationship with our fellow human beings. One must not understand a tolerant attitude, originating from a strong conviction, as an opinion on a certain truth. When we talk about "tolerating," "justice and love" are most important, rather than "judging." The question behind a tolerant attitude is not at all whether my fellow human being, whose conviction I tolerate, is right or wrong, but rather whether one has the right not to be disturbed or hampered by the community while practicing or declaring one's own conviction. People do have that right, argues Böckle, as long as they do not violate other people's rights.[19] That does not mean we cannot assess someone's doing and thinking from our own religious point of view in the name of tolerance. It means that we cannot forbid the personal conviction of the other and that we cannot hamper the other in making his or her conviction public. Freedom of opinion is a natural basic right of a person. Even believers should realize that one who is intolerant on non-ethical grounds turns the truth into a lie.

Notes

1. Paul Ricoeur, "Tolérance, intolérance, intolérable," *Bulletin de la Société de l'Histoire du Protestantisme Français* 134 (1988): 435.
2. "One faith, one law, one king."
3. Chaim Perelman, "The Foundations and Limits of Tolerance," *Pacific Philosophy Forum* 2 (1963): 25.
4. Ghislain Waterlot, "Human Rights and the Fate of Tolerance," in *Tolerance between Intolerance and the Intolerable*, ed. Paul Ricoeur (Oxford: Berghahn Books, 1996), 54.
5. Ricoeur, "Tolérance, intolérance, intolérable," 450; Paul Ricoeur, "The Erosion of Tolerance and the Resistance of the Intolerable," in *Tolerance between Intolerance and the Intolerable*, 189; Waterlot, "Human Rights and the Fate of Tolerance," 67.
6. See Leszek Kolakowski, "Toleranz und Absolutheitsanspruche," *Christlicher Glaube in moderner Gesellschaft* 26 (Freiburg: Herder, 1981): 21–25.
7. Hendrik Jan Mispelblom Beyer, *Tolerantie en fanatisme: Een studie over verdraagzaamheid* (Arnhem: Van Loghum Slaterus, 1948), 153.
8. T. M. Scanlon, *The Difficulty of Tolerance: Essays in Political Philosophy* (Cambridge: Cambridge University Press, 2003), 187.
9. Monique Canto-Sperber, "How Far Can Tolerance Go?" in *Tolerance between Intolerance and the Intolerable*, 175.
10. Ricoeur, "The Erosion of Tolerance and the Resistance of the Intolerable," 198.
11. Hans Oberdiek, "The Intolerable," in *Tolerance between Forbearance and Acceptance*, ed. Hans Oberdiek (Lanham, Md.: Rowman & Littlefield, 2001), 63.
12. Walter Kerber, ed., "Wie tolerant ist der Islam?" *Fragen einer neuer Weltkultur* 6 (Munich: Kindt Verlag, 1991).
13. Joseph Lecler, *Histoire de la tolérance au siècle de la Réforme* (Paris: Aubier, 1955); Roland Bainton, *The Travail of Religious Liberty* (Philadelphia: Westminster Press, 1951); Jean Dumoulin, "Tolérance et intolérance dans l'histoire de l'Eglise," *La Foi et le Temps* 20 (1990): 407–24; Bernard Cottret, "Tolérance ou liberté de conscience?" *Etudes Théologiques et Religieuses* 65 (1990): 333–50; Ottfried Hoeffe, "Pluralismus/Toleranz," in *Neues Handbuch theologischer Grundbegriffe* (Band 3), ed. Peter Eicher (Munich: Kösel, 1985), 363–78, esp. 372–75. See also Beyer, *Tolerantie en fanatisme*, 47.
14. Harry M. Bracken, "Toleration Theories: Bayle vs. Locke," in *The Notion of Tolerance and Human Rights: Essays in Honour of Raymond Klibansky*, ed. Ethel Groffier and Michel Paradis (Don Mills, Ontario: Carleton University Press, 1991), 4; Canto-Sperber, "How Far Can Tolerance Go?" 179.
15. Alfred Stern, "Tolerance: An Historical Introduction," *Pacific Philosophy Forum* 2 (1963): 11–12.

16. France Quéré, "Difficile tolérance," *Revue de Théologie et de Philosophie* 121 (1989): 196; Don Cupitt, "Is Monotheism Essentially Intolerant?" in *Crisis of Moral Authority,* ed. Don Cupitt (London-Guildford: Lutterworth, 1972), 69–85.

17. France Quéré, "Difficile tolérance," 197. Quéré quotes Luther: "*Caritas est omnia tolerare, fidei nihil.*"

18. Franz Böckle, "Toleranz als ökumenisches Problem," in *Einheit in Christus 2. Toleranz als ökumenische Problem,* ed. Oscar Cullmann and Otto Karrer (Zurich: Zwingli, 1964), 56–79, esp. 57–65.

19. Josef Brinkmann, *Toleranz in der Kirche: Eine moraltheologische Unter-suchung über institutionelle Aspekte innerkirchliche Toleranz* (Paderborn: Schöningh, 1980), 7.